THE DECLINE OF THE OTTOMAN EMPIRE AND THE RISE OF THE TURKISH REPUBLIC

Edinburgh Studies on Modern Turkey

Series General Editors: **Alpaslan Özerdem**, Dean of the School for Conflict Analysis and Resolution and Professor of Peace and Conflict Studies at George Mason University, and **Ahmet Erdi Öztürk**, Lecturer in International Relations and Politics at London Metropolitan University and a Marie Sklodowska-Curie Fellow at Coventry University in the UK and GIGA in Germany.

Series Advisory Board: Ayşe Kadıoğlu (Harvard University), Hakan Yavuz (University of Utah), Samim Akgönül (University of Strasbourg), Rebecca Bryant (Utrecht University), Nukhet Ahu Sandal (Ohio University), Mehmet Gurses (Florida Atlantic University), Paul Kubicek (Oakland University), Sinem Akgül Açıkmeşe (Kadir Has University), Gareth Jenkins (Institute for Security and Development Policy), Stephen Karam (World Bank), Peter Mandaville (George Mason University).

Edinburgh Studies on Modern Turkey is an outlet for academic works that examine the domestic and international issues of the Turkish republic from its establishment in the 1920s until the present. This broadly defined frame allows the series to adopt both interdisciplinary and trans-disciplinary approaches, covering research on the country's history and culture as well as political, religious and socio-economic developments.

Published and forthcoming titles

Policing Slums in Turkey: Crime, Resistance and the Republic on the Margin
Çağlar Dölek

Islamic Theology in the Turkish Republic
Philip Dorroll

The Kurds in Erdoğan's Turkey: Balancing Identity, Resistance and Citizenship
William Gourlay

Peace Processes in Northern Ireland and Turkey: Rethinking Conflict Resolution
İ. Aytaç Kadioğlu

The Decline of the Ottoman Empire and the Rise of the Turkish Republic: Observations of an American Diplomat, 1919–1927
Hakan Özoğlu

Religion, Identity and Power: Turkey and the Balkans in the Twenty-first Century
Ahmet Erdi Öztürk

Electoral Integrity in Turkey
Emre Toros

Erdoğan: The Making of an Autocrat
M. Hakan Yavuz

edinburghuniversitypress.com/series/esmt

THE DECLINE OF THE OTTOMAN EMPIRE AND THE RISE OF THE TURKISH REPUBLIC

Observations of an American Diplomat, 1919–1927

Hakan Özoğlu

EDINBURGH
University Press

Edinburgh University Press is one of the leading university presses in the UK. We publish academic books and journals in our selected subject areas across the humanities and social sciences, combining cutting-edge scholarship with high editorial and production values to produce academic works of lasting importance. For more information visit our website: edinburghuniversitypress.com

© Hakan Özoğlu, 2021, 2023

Edinburgh University Press Ltd
The Tun – Holyrood Road
12 (2f) Jackson's Entry
Edinburgh EH8 8PJ

First published in hardback by Edinburgh University Press 2021

Typeset in 11/15 Adobe Garamond by
IDSUK (DataConnection) Ltd, and
printed and bound by CPI Group (UK) Ltd,
Croydon, CR0 4YY

A CIP record for this book is available from the British Library

ISBN 978 1 4744 8037 6 (hardback)
ISBN 978 1 4744 8038 3 (paperback)
ISBN 978 1 4744 8040 6 (webready PDF)
ISBN 978 1 4744 8039 0 (epub)

CONTENTS

1   Introduction   1

2   Bristol: An American Naval Officer and Diplomat   16

3   The Collapse of the Ottoman Empire and the Rise of
    Turkey in US Consular Reports   58

4   Bristol and Conflicts between Turks, Greeks and
    Armenians in Anatolia   105

5   Political and Human Landscapes of Turkey in
    Diplomatic Reports   151

6   Afterthoughts and Conclusions   189

Bibliography   202
Index   209

1

INTRODUCTION

'The first casualty when war comes is truth'; this phrase is attributed to a US senator, Hiram Johnson, during World War I in 1917 and reflects an undisputed reality about reporting wartime events.[1] Similar versions of the same motto have been uttered by other significant political figures in world history. During World War II, for example, Winston Churchill is believed to have said, 'In wartime, truth is so precious that she should always be protected by a bodyguard of lies.' The wartime grand narratives are always full of wilful omissions of inconvenient fragments of 'truth'. This established narrative, however imperfect it may be, is surrounded and protected by – if not a bodyguard of lies – an assigned 'sacred-space', which does not allow critical examination. The size of this sacred space, often guarded by emotion rather than reason, differs based on the fragility of the narrative. It is false to believe that this protected and imperfect narrative always originates from the victor. Victims too can create their own narrative and protect it with a sacred space around it. World War I provides a great example of my assertion as many narratives were created by both victims and victors, and protected by emotionally charged boundaries, which allowed them to survive until present.

This study, in its most general sense, aims at bringing in primary documents to help recover the lost balance of 'truth' and its alternative in the historical narrative. I am not naïve to claim that what is presented here is the sole truth, as the truth is more subjective than it is objective; however, I hope to present documents that can help the reader to construct or modify their own truth. As such, this research runs the risk of invading the sacred spaces created by all sides involved in the post-World War I narrative in the Ottoman Empire and later Turkey. As such, it is only expected that it will be subject to knee-jerk or calculated reactions.

The majority of documents presented here have not been brought into various accounts of World War I, which witnessed the collapse of the last Islamic Empire in the Middle East and the rise of many Middle Eastern states. Other than the birth of these post-World War I states, many other momentous events, such as the abolition of the Sultanate and the office of the Caliphate, took place at the end of the Great War. Human suffering due to decades-long wars paved the way for the complete breakdown of public order, which caused massacres that put their stamps also on world history.

This critical period coincides with the tenure of Rear Admiral Mark Lambert Bristol as the US High Commissioner in the Ottoman Empire and later the Turkish Republic (1919–27). Admiral Bristol, an avid note-taker, witnessed these events and reported them to Washington. What made him memorable for the historian is that Bristol went against the grain of popular diplomatic reports supporting the image of 'the terrible Turk', which dominated the Western and US public opinion. The American High Commissioner insisted on drawing a bigger picture where the villains were not just the Turks. His opposition to the prominent view that depicted the Turks as innately immoral and hence not capable of just government earned him many enemies in the US who accused him of being 'pro-Turk'. However, reflecting on this accusation, he defended himself by stating that if he did not entirely agree with one side, he was accused of being the supporter of the other side. Yet, he repeatedly and unrelentingly described himself as 'pro-American'.

As mentioned, Bristol's controversial standing on the inter-ethnic/inter-religious bloody conflicts in the Ottoman Empire earned him the accusation of 'pro-Turk', which was intended to discredit all his reporting. This was unfortunate because Bristol sent to Washington tens of thousands of pages of information on many significant subjects, whose reliability was carefully graded and commented on. He was meticulous about reporting in his 'War Diary' all events of the day, including some seemingly unimportant events such as with whom he dined and what the menu was. This line of tedious reporting makes his accounts long-winded yet very valuable for the historian, since usually details reveal many useful facts.

The admiral truly witnessed a significant transition period from the Ottoman Empire to the Republic of Turkey. His standing and insistence on cultivating good relations with the new Turkey quickly captured the attention of the Ankara government, which also hoped to re-establish cordial relations with the US. The Ankara government hoped to have a neutral Western country as an ally which was not contaminated with secret wartime treaties. For the Turkish side, it was also important that the US and the Ottoman Empire did not declare war on each other. Bristol also thought that good relations with Turkey could open up greater possibilities for American businessmen to enjoy a new emerging market, a market that should not be left entirely to other Allied Powers, particularly Great Britain. The mutual interest in re-establishing diplomatic relations between the two countries was obvious to the non-partisan eye. However, the anti-Turkish propaganda in the US Senate resulted in the rejection of the ratification of the Turkish-American Treaty of Commerce and Amity by six votes in 1927. This treaty was negotiated between Turkey and the US during the Lausanne Conference in 1923 and had to wait until 1930 for ratification.[2] Nevertheless, due to Admiral Bristol's diplomacy, the new Turkish government was very open to the American High Commissioner. Consequently, US diplomats were able to collect as complete information as possible about the internal dynamics of the new regime. Therefore, this study contains not only much valuable information about the early stage of US–Turkey relations but, perhaps more significantly, information on the internal affairs of Turkey.

At this point, it is fair to state that much of our knowledge of the Turkish Republican history does not originate from archival sources, but instead from memoirs of the political actors who were inclined to draw a picture that fits better into their political position or orientation. Therefore, the US archives offer us a fresh and valuable collection of primary sources. This is not to say, however, that information in these collections is free from errors. However, the possible misinformation is unintentional. Some information can be verified with that of other sources, and some information cannot be confirmed.

However, there does not seem to be any reason to question the reliability of most information presented in these dispatches, because in most cases motivations for such manipulation did not exist. For example, we cannot verify that in their war against the Western Powers the Kemalists received cash from Egypt, or how much. However, there should be little doubt that the US High Commission received this information from the first wife of Egyptian King Fuad I. There is no known motivation for Princess Chevekiar (see Chapter 5) to misinform, nor is there a reason for the US High Commission to manipulate the information before sending it to Washington.

In the same vein, one does not have to accept the view and analysis of Admiral Bristol on the emerging Turkish state. Yet, what is significant to the historian is not the accuracy of his understanding of the internal affairs of Turkey. It is rather the fact that an American High Commissioner interpreted the events he witnessed or heard in a particular way, which provided the reader with an alternative view. Therefore, one's disagreements with Bristol's conclusions do not diminish the value of these reports.

Admiral Mark Lambert Bristol was the last top US diplomat who dealt with the Ottoman Empire. Yet, there was a century of diplomatic history between the two governments that are located geographically far from each other.

A Brief Look at the US–Ottoman Relations until the End of World War I

The first Americans to make contact with the Ottoman Empire were New England ship captains and the merchants who started trading at Smyrna/İzmir in the 1780s. In 1799, US President John Adams decided that a treaty with the Ottoman Empire needed to be negotiated and, for that purpose, appointed William Smith of South Carolina as minister to the Sublime Porte. The mission, however, was abandoned, and after several other minor attempts, finally, in 1829, President Andrew Jackson commissioned Charles Rhind, David Offley and James Biddle to negotiate a treaty with the Ottoman government. The result was the signing of the first US treaty with an 'Oriental State' on 7 May 1830 and the opening of an American legation in the Ottoman capital in 1831 with David Porter as chargé d'affaires.[3] Porter remained in Istanbul, first as chargé d'affaires and then as Minister, until his death in 1843.[4] The second treaty, based on an earlier Turco-British one, also concerned itself mainly with commerce and navigation and afforded the US the 'most favored nation' status in commerce and the protection of American missionaries in the Ottoman Empire. It was the Protestant missionaries, rather than the traders, who made the most significant American impact on the culture of the region. During this period, missionaries realised that in order to be effective in the Middle East, they needed to know the cultures, languages, religious systems and political orders. Missionaries did not intend to work as agents of their governments, but rather saw themselves as agents of God. Regardless, they were instrumental in helping plant the seeds of American culture among the peoples in Asia Minor. To this end, they established schools, hospitals and churches, and created space for themselves. They played a significant role not only by spreading Protestantism among the non-Islamic people of the Ottoman Empire but, perhaps more importantly, because of their efforts to understand the society that they sought to influence, they also became an invaluable source for American diplomats, politicians and the public to explain the inner dynamics of the community they lived in.[5] Since the missionaries were not successful among the Muslim population of the empire, they lived among the Christian subjects of the land. Therefore, they witnessed mostly the sufferings of the non-Muslim population. Only a few reports give detailed information about the social and political dynamics of the Muslim population. They equated all Muslims, Turks, Kurds and Arabs alike to the governing elite. This significant omission, however, did not escape Admiral Mark Bristol's eyes. In his reports, he wished to balance out this omission with descriptions, sufferings, fears and hatreds of the Muslims as well.

It is fair to state that until World War I, the US interest in the Ottoman Empire was due mainly (though not entirely) to the well-being of missionaries and their activities in the region, and to trade. During World War I, diplomatic relations between the two countries slowed down until 6 April 1917 when the US declared war on Germany, the ally of the Ottoman Empire in the Great War. Two weeks later, the Ottoman Empire cut her diplomatic ties with the US. However, neither country declared war against the other. This fact, and the fact that the US was never part of secret negotiations among the Allied countries to divide the Ottoman land, contributed greatly to the deposit of goodwill towards the US among the Turks, so much so that the emerging Kemalist movement in Anatolia was in close contact via intermediaries with the representatives of the US diplomats in Istanbul.

As the next chapter describes, Admiral Bristol was a controversial figure in the post-World War I Allied diplomacy. He was bold and fearless and never shied away from stating his opinion. Although he despised the Ottoman administration, Bristol's sympathy for the emerging Turkish regime was visible. However, it would be a grave mistake to confuse this sympathy with blind approval of her policies. The admiral was a soldier first and foremost. Yet, he was also a very capable Open Door diplomat who was an ardent believer of realpolitik. His military background will be visible to the reader in the lengthy reports that he sent to Washington on many issues such as the faith of the non-Muslim minorities, the internal power struggle in the new regime, and international politics.

Notes on the Sources Used

For the purpose of this study, the main source is the document collection microfilmed and catalogued under the title of 'Records of the Department of State Relating to Internal Affairs of Turkey 1910–1929'. The collection contains a wide range of documents relating to the Ottoman Empire and, later, Turkey. Other subcategories that can be found in this collection concern Turkey in Europe, Crete, Turkey in Asia, Palestine, and Tripoli. I focused on reports filed between the years 1919 and 1927. Although Bristol sent dispatches from all the territories that were once part of the Ottoman Empire, my primary geographical concern was the area within the current boundaries of the Republic of Turkey. I examined reports that were sent to Washington by Bristol primarily but not exclusively. I also utilised the significant reports, letters and correspondence prepared by other US diplomats under Bristol, missionaries, Navy personnel, American journalists and so on.

The records in this collection, consisting of bound volumes and unbound documents, are mostly instructions to and dispatches from diplomatic and consular officials; enclosures often accompany these dispatches. It is from these enclosures that one can obtain copies of documents including handwritten letters of Sultans, of high-level Turkish government officials, and even of Mustafa Kemal, the first President of the Turkish Republic.[6] Also included are notes between the Department of State and foreign diplomatic representatives in the United States, memoranda prepared by officials of the Department, diaries and travel notes of US diplomats, and correspondence with officials of other US government departments and with private firms and persons.

For the purpose of orienting future researchers of this collection, it must be noted that the Department of State used a decimal system for its central files from 1910 to 1963. Individual documents were assembled and arranged according to the subject and were assigned file numbers. In this system, the decimal file consists of nine primary classes numbered from 0 through to 8, each covering a broad subject area. The records reproduced in the collection under examination are in Class 8, signifying 'Internal Affairs of States'. The country number assigned to Turkey is 67; thus, the documents bearing file number 867 relate to the internal affairs of Turkey. The number after the decimal point represents a specific subtopic. The researcher should be aware that the documents under one subject classification are generally in chronological order, coinciding with the document number assigned (which follows the slant mark). There are instances, however, when a document file number was not assigned until a date considerably later than the one on which the document was received.

Another group of documents consulted was 'Records of the Department of State Relating to Political Relations between the United States and Turkey, 1910–1929' (Record Group 59, microcopy number 365). This collection contains eight rolls and deals with political relations between the two countries. These records include instructions to and dispatches from diplomatic and consular officials with enclosures. In this collection, the files begin with class number 7, followed by 11, indicating US political relations with another country. Turkey's code, 67, in this collection follows these digits. Hence, 711.67 – political relations between the US and Turkey – are the beginning digits. The following digits indicate certain themes. For example, a document beginning 711.6712 refers to documents related to arbitration or negotiation of a treaty. The slant mark (/) following it indicates the number of the document on this subject. I used this collection mainly to follow Bristol's communication with the State Department in attempts to restore normal diplomatic and commercial relations with the government of Turkey.

Another collection that was utilised in this research is titled 'General Records of the American Commission to Negotiate Peace 1918–1931'.

The microcopy number of this collection is 820, and it is listed under Record Group 256. It contains reports, minutes, memoranda, publications in full, pamphlets, maps and personal records related to the period after World War I. I used the documents concerning negotiations related to the Treaty of Lausanne, and hence most documents coming from this collection begin with 867.00 in the rolls between 536 and 542.

These collections are the microfilms of original documents and only a few of them are in the published form by the US government in other official collections such as US National Archives and Records Service, the US Senate and so on. In the text, I tried to quote the documents as fully as possible so that other researchers can better see the context and use these quotations as sources.

A well-known collection of Bristol's private papers is housed in the Library of Congress and often referred to as 'The Bristol Papers'. The Library of Congress Manuscript Division (LCMD) has prepared a preliminary guide for these unbound papers in green boxes. Helen Bristol, the wife of the admiral, donated this collection to the library in 1946. The timespan of these papers is 1882–1939, but I focused mainly on the ones between 1919 and 1927 when he was in Turkey. However, I also looked at the papers after his retirement. A great majority of the papers I consulted were part of his 'War Diary', which was also available in the other collections I mentioned above. In fact, there was more context for Bristol's 'War Diary' in the archival collections mentioned above than that of the Bristol papers. In the archival sources, we also see the State Department's reaction to the information contained in Bristol's diaries.

Some of the archival documents were published in a series under the title of *Foreign Relations of the United States* (FRUS) in over 450 volumes. The series presents the official documentary historical record of major US foreign policy decisions and significant diplomatic activities. The collection is produced by the Department of State's Office of the Historian and contains documents from Presidential Libraries, Departments of State and Defense, National Security Council, Central Intelligence Agency, Agency for International Development and other foreign affairs agencies, as well as the private papers of individuals involved in formulating the US foreign policy. The collections are formed from the above-mentioned US archival sources and are based on the editors' preferences to highlight certain foreign policy formulations; they are, therefore, of limited use. However, unlike the raw material in the archives, this collection is indexed and country-based. I utilised the collection on Turkey in the volumes 1919–27.

The Oberlin College archives houses 'The King-Crane Commission Digital Collection', where one can find among others letters exchanged between Bristol and Henry Churchill King, who was a member of the 1919 Inter-Allied Commission on mandates in Turkey, on issues related to the subject of this research. I also made use of this collection. Bristol was mentioned in the unpublished private papers of several American individuals who witnessed the era, but I was not able to consult them. I was, however, able to access the published memoirs of key US officials, such as Joseph Grew, Robert Dunn, Henry Morgenthau and Robert Skinner, among others. I was also able to examine several US newspaper collections of articles on Bristol, including from the *New York Times*.

The Ottoman and Republican Archives

First, the researcher should be aware that the State Archives in Turkey changed its name from Başbakanlık to Cumhurbaşkanlığı Devlet Arşivleri, as Turkey abolished the office of the Prime Minister. There are only a few records on Bristol in the Ottoman and Turkish archives. In the Istanbul Ottoman archives, most of the documents on the period come from DH. KMS (Dahiliye Nezareti Kalemi Mahsusa), DH. ŞFR (Dahiliye Şifre Kalemi), and especially HR. İM (Hariciye Vekaleti İstanbul Murahhaslığı). We know that the Ankara government's interactions with Bristol are recorded in HR. İM and especially after 1924. However, the earliest record of Admiral Bristol comes in a 1919 DH. ŞFR document, which informs us of Bristol landing in Samsun by an American Navy ship, and later his investigative activities after the Greek occupation of İzmir (see Chapter 4). The documents on Bristol in the Ottoman archives go as late as 1927, which falls into the Republican period under HR. İM collections.

Documents on Bristol in the Turkish Republican archives housed in Ankara generally deal with issues concerning the upkeep of the American (Bristol) Hospital that Bristol himself helped build or invitations to Bristol to visit Turkey. The earliest document in this archive comes from 1922, and it continues until after Bristol's death in 1939. My main aim of researching the Turkish archives was to see if there was any record informing us about the

Turkish view of Bristol. On this issue, no detailed information exists other than a couple of documents after his death mentioning that he was friendly towards the new regime.

Other Primary Sources in Turkey

The late Dr Warren Winkler was the head surgeon of the Bristol Hospital between 1968 and 1994. In his private archives, there are thousands of pages of unorganised papers, letters, unbound copies of manuscripts and so on. He kindly made copies of them for me. Currently, portions of this collection can be found at the American Research Institute in Turkey (ARIT) library in a more organised way. This collection might be useful for researchers who wish to write the history of the Bristol Hospital. The ARIT also houses a collection on the digitalised pamphlets, journals and some other unpublished material by the Near East Relief in Turkey, which could be useful for researchers working on the US missionaries. A limited collection of similar sources is also available in the Bilkent University Library in Ankara.

My attempts to find substantial information on Bristol did not bear fruit in the Turkish Foreign Ministry archives as most of the documents mentioning Bristol are now housed in the Republican archives. In the Turkish Grand National Assembly archives, there were only a couple of references to Admiral Bristol in the context of discussions on the Greek occupation of Smyrna and the atrocities committed. Turkish Parliamentary minutes can be accessed online to follow these discussions, which are searchable.

Literature Review

Although several articles use the reports filed by Bristol in their arguments, there is very limited literature that is devoted entirely to the High Commissioner in book format. In English, there are two unpublished dissertations.

The first and most referred-to work is a dissertation by Peter Michael Buzanski, titled 'Admiral Mark L. Bristol and Turkish-American Relations, 1919–1922' (unpublished dissertation, University of California, Berkeley, 1960). The author uses the US archives and the Bristol Papers at the Library of Congress Manuscript Division. Although there are brief references to Bristol's views on the Turks, the backbone of the research was the issues revolving around the Armenian massacres.

Another doctoral work is by Dinç Yaylalıer, 'American Perceptions of Turkey, 1919–1927' (dissertation, University of Utah, 1996). The author examines a wealth of primary documents, focusing mainly on negotiations in the Paris Peace Conference in 1919 and in the Lausanne Peace Conference in 1923 and on discussions on US–Turkey relations in the US Senate. The dissertation is useful in identifying groups and individuals for and against Bristol and in analysing Bristol's role in re-establishing Turkey–US relations after World War I. In this context, Yaylalıer's work provides a solid base to İsmail Köse's book mentioned below. The current research differs from that of Yaylalıer in the themes it examines but has benefited greatly from the footnotes he provides.

A book-length study on the subject in Turkish comes from İsmail Köse, titled *Türk Amerikan İlişkilerinin Şekillenmesinde Amiral Mark L. Bristol'un Rolü, 1919–1927.*[7] Based on his dissertation, the book deals mainly with the period around the Lausanne Treaty negotiations and with Bristol's contribution to it. The primary sources used in this study come mainly from printed material and Bristol's private papers in the Library of Congress. For future researchers who wish to focus on the same subject, I can safely suggest that there is room for improvement, especially in the sources Köse used. The US National Archives has a collection of documents dealing specifically with negotiations of treaties that can enrich such a study immensely. The collection is called 'The Records of the American Commission to Negotiate Peace, 1918–1931' (Record Group 256) and contains a wealth of documents beyond Bristol's 'War Diary', which is housed in the Library of Congress. The roll 407 specifically deals with Turkey, but other rolls also contain many references that deal with issues like the Armenian Mandate, minorities, political clauses and so on.

In addition to these dissertations and a book in Turkish, there are a small number of essays published on the activities of Bristol in Turkey. I cite them in the text. This research benefited from all these sources, and it is the first manuscript in English devoted entirely to Bristol's tenure in the Ottoman Empire and Turkey. To my knowledge, there is no publication in any language that exclusively deals with themes as diverse as those in this book. I hope that this work will contribute greatly to our understanding not only of the US relations but, more importantly, of the internal affairs of Turkey.

Arrangements of Chapters

The book begins with biographical information on Mark Bristol in Chapter 2 and with events surrounding his appointment to Constantinople, first as the 'Senior United States Naval Officer Present, Turkey' and later as the US High Commissioner. In this chapter, I also make a case for the reliability of information Bristol provides to the researcher; the accusation of Bristol being a 'Pro-Turk' and hence a 'not reliable source' is discussed here. As he was a controversial figure, many Americans residing in the Ottoman lands initially took issue with Bristol's approach to the minority affairs in the collapsing empire. Accordingly, this chapter introduces the opponents and proponents of Bristol, particularly regarding his views about the non-Muslim citizens of the Ottoman Empire.

Admiral Mark Lambert Bristol was an Open Door diplomat, and as such he defended the US interests in this part of the world where Great Britain harboured boundless ambitions. Bristol was, in a sense, 'a squeaky brake' against the British domination in the area. Therefore, he also had to deal with British diplomatic pressure to remove him from his post. Chapter 2 discusses all these issues and more to set the stage for the following chapters dealing selectively with certain themes on which I thought it would be beneficial to offer an alternative view. His reports indeed draw a different picture of the time and space under examination.

Chapter 3 follows Bristol's reports concerning the collapse of the Ottoman Empire and the rise of the Turkish Republic. Here the reader will find details of Bristol's views on the collapsing Ottoman administration, on the mandate issue, on the rising nationalist uprising in Anatolia, and on his diplomacy dealing with both the royal and nationalist governments in Istanbul and Ankara, among many others. Most of the documents dealing with the abolition of the Sultanate and Caliphate will provide a very different narrative challenging the official account of these issues. In these reports, we see that Bristol was far ahead of his peers among the Allied diplomats stationed in Istanbul. He was the first one to recognise the potential for the nationalist/Kemalist movement in Ankara and advised a policy to Washington friendly towards the Kemalists.

The Lausanne negotiations are also discussed in this chapter, albeit in a condensed form. This issue is discussed in greater detail in the dissertations mentioned above. However, the chapter provides many other primary sources and reports submitted to the peace conference and Bristol's role in it. The admiral was a keen supporter of establishing formal diplomatic relations with the emerging Ankara regime. His efforts to counter the Greek and Armenian lobbying activities in the US are also discussed in this chapter. In fact, as the reader will see, the issue of Armenian and Greek minorities of Turkey spills over into almost every chapter. However, Chapter 4 specifically deals with it.

Information in Chapter 4 provides the reader with very detailed reports in which Bristol analyses the treatment of minorities in the emerging Turkish regime. These reports include, among others, conversations with the leaders of the minority groups, with American missionaries stationed in Anatolia, and with Turkish leaders. His analysis and conclusions changed in time; especially on the issue of the creation of an Armenian state, Bristol's views evolved considerably. His position and recommendation to the State Department, however, falls far from the desired outcome of the Armenian lobbyists in the US. Therefore, the State Department received many complaints about him. It is worth mentioning here that from the President down to the members of the State Department Near East division, Bristol received solid support for his activities in Istanbul. This chapter provides primary documents to demonstrate these points.

Chapter 4 also deals with the Greek minorities and their faith in the new Turkey. Soon after Bristol was appointed to the Ottoman Empire, the Greek military occupation of Smyrna/İzmir took place, which caused much bloodshed in the Aegean region. Many complaints were filed to the Paris Peace Conference in 1919 by the Turkish side accusing the Greeks of committing atrocities. In order to examine these claims, the admiral was tasked with a leading role in the Inter-Allied Commission to investigate the Greek atrocities. Bristol's earliest encounters with Greek forces and the Ottoman Greeks as their supporters came from this experience. The chapter, therefore, devotes considerable space to the work of the commission and follows the evolving attitude of the High Commissioner towards the Greeks of the Ottoman Empire.

Chapter 5 examines the human and political conditions of the Ottoman Empire and later the Republic of Turkey in the period immediately after World War I. Bristol has many reports that can fit into this category, which could be of great interest to the reader. This chapter commences by introducing documents that describe the devastated and catastrophic human conditions of the empire. It also describes the daily life struggles in Ottoman cities including Constantinople; the main aim of this section of the chapter is to demonstrate the physical conditions of several significant Ottoman cities, including the capital. The latter part of the chapter presents some significant events in the period under review seen through the eyes of Bristol and his associates. Among those, the reader can find the following: the escape of the Sultan from the empire, the abolition of the Sultanate, and later the abolition of the Caliphate. Sultan Vahdettin's letters to the US President, the Kemalist approach to the mandate issue, and the power struggle in the new republic are also discussed, based on the reports that were sent to Washington by Bristol.

The reader will notice that the Armenian issue inevitably spills over into almost every chapter. The partisan reader of the issue from all sides will be disappointed to see that I intentionally do not make any case for or against the killings of the Armenians as 'genocide'. I can only naïvely state that my purpose of doing so is to resist dragging this book into the controversial subject of massacre/genocide arguments and diminishing it to a study of a genocide test. My fear is that competing political discourses will carry the book away from its intended purpose. The reader will see that I use the terms 'genocide' and 'massacres' interchangeably only to show my respect for different interpretations. I fully respect the right of those who judge the killings as genocide. However, I also respect Bristol's attempts to show the 'other side of the coin', and the manipulation of the pain and suffering of peoples of Anatolia, be it Armenian, Kurd, Greek, Turk, Assyrians, Yazidis or others. I am keenly aware that a subject as polarising as this one cannot escape political implications; however, I hope the reader will judge the book based on its contribution to our knowledge of the period in which monumental events took place in the Middle East.

I have tried to use modern Turkish orthography for most of the words rendered in the Ottoman script. However, in direct quotations, people's and place names are spelled in several different ways. For example, the Black Sea town of Samsun was spelled in the document as Saumsun or Samsoum. I did not interfere with the direct quotations. I, however, have used Constantinople/Istanbul and Smyrna/İzmir interchangeably. In general, I have tried to use the proper names the way they appeared in historical sources of the time. Nevertheless, in some cases I have added the last names which did not exist then. Therefore, the reader will find Mustafa Kemal in the text more readily than Atatürk, of İsmet Paşa [İnönü]. All dates are given using the modern Gregorian calendar.

Notes

1. A republican senator served in the Senate from 1917 to 1945.
2. The 1930 version of the treaty was similar but in fact there were more advantages for the Turkish side.
3. Leland J. Gordon, 'Turkish-American Treaty Relations', *The American Political Science Review*, 22.3 (August 1928): 711–21.
4. For a sample of Porter's reports to Washington regarding commerce and trade see 'Message from the President of the United States, communicating, in compliance with a resolution of the Senate, copies of correspondence in relation to the commerce and navigation carried on in the Turkish dominions and Pachalick of Egypt. February 11, 1839', *US Senate, 25th Congress, 3rd Session. Public Documents Printed by Order of the Senate of the United States*, vol. 3 (Washington, DC: Blair and Rivers, 1939).
5. Cemal Yetkiner, 'After Merchants before Ambassadors: Protestant Missionaries and Early American Experience in the Ottoman Empire, 1820–1860', in Nur Bilge Criss, Selçuk Esenbel, Tony Greenwood and Louis Mazzari (eds), *American Turkish Encounters: Politics and Culture, 1830–1989* (Newcastle upon Tyne: Cambridge Scholars, 2011), p. 9.
6. Hakan Özoğlu, 'Mustafa Kemal'Atatürk'ün Amerika'ya Mektubu', *Toplumsal Tarih*, 150 (June 2006): 59–61; Özoğlu, 'Sultan Vahdettin'in ABD Başkanı Coolidge'e Gönderdiği Bir Mektup', *Toplumsal Tarih*, 142 (October 2005): 100–3.
7. (Ankara: Türk Tarih Kurumu, 2016).

2

BRISTOL: AN AMERICAN NAVAL OFFICER AND DIPLOMAT

Mark Lambert Bristol was born on 17 April 1868 in Glassboro, New Jersey. He claimed descent from Henry Bristol, who came to New Haven from England in 1656. Mark Bristol took great pride in his forefathers as farmers and claimed that the Bristol apple was named after his family. He was the son of Mark Lambert Bristol and Rachel Elizabeth (Bush) Bristol.[1] Coming from such a modest background, the young Mark completed his public-school education before winning an appointment to the Naval Academy, thanks to the nomination by Democratic Congressman Thomas F. Ferrol of New Jersey.

Naval Career Prior to his Appointment to the Middle East[2]

He graduated from the Naval Academy in 1887 and operated the *Galena* off New England. He served twice on the gunboat *Yantic*, in 1887–8 and 1890–1. In between these dates, he was commissioned ensign (1889) and served on the Coast Survey vessel *McArthur* (1888–90). After a stint on the *Monongahela* in 1890, Bristol was sent to the Far East with the gunboat *Petrel* (1891–4) as a watch and division officer. In 1894, we see Bristol on the gunboat *Alert* sailing in the eastern Pacific. His gunboat and torpedo career continued on land at Norfolk's equipment department in 1895, and he taught on the school-ship *St. Mary's* at New York (1895–6). In 1896, Mark Bristol was promoted to lieutenant (junior grade, or LTJG), joined the battleship *Texas* and fought at Guantanamo Bay. During the Spanish-American War, he participated in the battle of Santiago, Cuba, still on *Texas* (25 April to 12 August 1898).

In 1899, he was appointed to the Washington Navy Yard as a lieutenant and briefly served on the battleship *Massachusetts* (BB-2) in 1901. Prior to his appointment as an aide to the commander-in-chief of the North Atlantic Fleet, Admiral Francis J. Higginson, between 1901 and 1903, Bristol served for a short time aboard the *Kearsarge* (BB-5). In 1904, Bristol was head of the Bureau of Ordnance's torpedo branch, responsible for the production of torpedoes, mines and fire-control appliances for the Navy. In 1905, he served as fleet gunnery officer for the European Squadron on the *Brooklyn* (ACR-3). The same year, Lieutenant Commander Mark Bristol became an aide and ordnance officer to the North Atlantic Fleet commander, Admiral R. D. Evans, on the flagship *Maine* (BB-10), in which capacity Bristol engaged in ordnance experimentation and the design of gun sites. In 1907, he transferred to the *Connecticut* (BB-18) as the executive officer for the global cruise of the Great White Fleet. The same year, Bristol married Helen Beverly Moore Thomas, who was from a prominent family from Atlanta, Georgia.[3]

Until 1911, he inspected ordnance (weapons) at the Newport torpedo station. Later, he returned to the Far East and was given his first ship, the *Monterey* (BM-6), and then the *Albany* (CL-23), which won him several gunnery awards. Clark Reynolds suggests that 'it was during his patrols off revolution-torn China that [Bristol] first displaced his keen diplomatic tact by handling well a delicate situation at Swatow'.[4] After being promoted to the rank of captain on 1 July 1913, he was appointed as Director of Naval Aeronautics and developed an expertise in aircraft. This experience earned him a seat on the National Advisory Committee on Aeronautics in 1915; he also served as commander of the air station in Pensacola, where he began a school in free ballooning and acquired the first blimp for the Navy. In 1916 Bristol took command of the experimental aviation station-ship cruiser the *North Carolina* (ACR-12).[5] This cruiser carried troops to Europe during World War I. After briefly working at the Naval War College in Newport, Rhode Island, Captain Bristol took command of the *Oklahoma* (BB-37) in the Atlantic Fleet in 1918. The same year, he was promoted to the rank of rear admiral, under which rank he became commander of the US naval base in Plymouth, England.

Bristol in Constantinople

Bristol's appointment to Constantinople[6] came as a result of a chain of events at the end of World War I. We know that the diplomatic relations between the US and the Ottoman Empire were severed by the initiative of the latter on 20 April 1917 – thirteen days after the US entry into the war. The American Embassy in Constantinople announced the Ottoman government's decision of cutting diplomatic relations as follows: 'The Imperial Government has today informed the Embassy that as the Government of the United States has declared itself to be in a state of war with Germany, the Ottoman Government's ally, it finds it necessary to rupture its diplomatic relations with the United States today. American interests have been confided to the Swedish minister.'[7] It is important to note here that the two countries did not declare war on each other; this fact becomes very significant in the future relations of Turkey and the USA. Henry Beers suggests that 'the considerable investment of Americans in missionary, education, philanthropic, and commercial enterprises in Turkey apparently influenced the decision of the United States Government in this connection'.[8] Consequently, the US Embassy in Istanbul was transferred to the Swedish Legation, and in Washington, the Turkish Embassy was handed over to the Spanish Embassy. After this date, the US kept the USS *Scorpion*[9] in Turkish waters and used it to protect American interests. During this time, the *Scorpion* assumed duties as a flagship and dispatch vessel, continuing, at the same time, her station-ship status. On 6 December 1918, Lieutenant Herbert S. Babbitt, the commanding officer of the USS *Scorpion*, requested from Garrett Droppers, the US Minister to Greece, that a diplomatic envoy or representative familiar with Turkey be sent to Istanbul to take charge of American interests from the Swedish Legation. At the same time, Ottoman, English and Swedish authorities agreed to have an American diplomatic representative to Istanbul. The US State Department was informed of this request by the British Embassy in Washington. When the State Department received a note from the President of the American-operated Robert College to the effect that the Swedish Legation handling American interests had also taken charge of German interests, the State Department became entirely convinced of the necessity of some form of representation in Istanbul. Records show that even before this, on 30 November 1918, the State Department had already ordered

Lewis J. Heck, the former Secretary of the American Embassy in Istanbul, to return to his post with the title of Commissioner. In early January 1919, Heck was instructed to reopen the embassy and to act only as a political observer. At the same time, the Swedish Legation continued to handle all official contacts with Turkey, while the State Department asked the Navy to select a stationship to be kept in Istanbul. Soon thereafter, it further requested that a naval officer of flag rank be sent to Istanbul. The decision to send Bristol to Istanbul was made between 27 and 30 December 1918. On 8 January 1919, Bristol received orders to proceed to Istanbul as the 'Senior United States Naval Officer Present, Turkey'. Admiral William S. Sims, Commander of the US Naval Forces Operating in European Waters, sent the following order to Bristol:

1. Proceed to Constantinople, Turkey, via Paris, France.
2. On arrival [at] Paris, France, report to Admiral Benson for any final instructions or information which that officer may give you, and furnish Force Commander [a] copy of any such instructions as Admiral Benson may give you.
3. After a conference with Admiral Benson in Paris, you will stop at such other places en route to Constantinople as may, in your judgment, be desirable or necessary for the purpose of obtaining information which may be of assistance to you in the execution of your future duties as Senior US Naval Officer Present, Turkey.[10]

In Paris, Bristol met with several US officials assembled there for the peace talks, including Admiral Benson, Secretary of State Robert Lansing, Herbert Hoover of the Food Administration, Edward N. Hurley of the US Shipping Board, and President Woodrow Wilson. After consulting with them, Bristol went to Constantinople with only the most general and vague instructions. Clearly, his superiors did not know what to anticipate in Turkey. The Ottoman Empire had fought with the Central Powers against the Allies and lost. However, she had broken relations with the United States only because the latter declared war on Germany. The US never declared war on the Ottoman Empire and was never a party to any secret agreements, which stipulated the terms of dismantling the Ottoman Empire and portioning her among themselves. Yet, due to the fact that all borders of the Ottoman Empire were now in dispute, it was unclear as to the exact boundaries of the area under Bristol's control.

The western border of the area that was given to Bristol ended at the 21st meridian, which included all of Greece except Corfu. The eastern border included the area east of the 21st meridian in the Mediterranean and also comprised that territory known as the Near East.[11] This area was indeed vague, but Bristol considered it to be the entire pre-war Ottoman Empire. There was no objection. In fact, soon the US consuls at İzmir (Smyrna), Baghdad, Beirut, Jerusalem, Damascus, Aleppo and Samsun were put under Bristol's supervision.[12]

On 28 January 1919, Bristol arrived in Istanbul, not happy with his title 'Senior United States Naval Officer Present, Turkey'; he believed that this title was also ambiguous and requested that he be given the title of 'High Commissioner' to match the British representation in Turkey. Bristol must have seen the advantageous aspect of the vagueness in the instructions for his duty; after all, it allowed him to shape it to his liking. However, it was the vagueness of his official title that bothered him. He thought of it as 'unimposing' compared to the title 'High Commissioner' that his colleagues from other Allied representations were adorned with. Bristol lobbied for it to be changed to 'High Commissioner' through his wife. He wrote to her that in order to do good in Constantinople, he 'should be able to meet the foreign commissioners on an equal footing . . . [and] be recognized by Turkey and countries that have commissioners [in Turkey] as fully empowered to represent [the US] government . . . It is rank, and position [that the Allies] recognize . . . If we do not have the rank and position, we are handicapped from the beginning . . . The rank and position are not for personal vanity; they are our credentials just as much as a diploma.'[13]

Bristol also requested a small fleet, considering that a show of some authority would be necessary to back his words. Initially, on 28 January 1919, Bristol hoisted his flag on board the *Scorpion*. During the first part of 1919, the US Naval detachments under Bristol's command consisted of the *Scorpion*, the *Noma* and the *Nahma*, all converted yachts. They were assisted by four subchasers: 82, 128, 129 and 215. The *Nahma* and *Noma* were soon sold off, and four new destroyers were given to the admiral's care. In time, as the significance of the region became more visible to Washington, the number of ships increased. We know that in 1921 the USS *St. Louis* (C-20) was part of Admiral Bristol's taskforce at Constantinople.[14]

These ships were kept moving by Bristol around the ports between the Eastern Mediterranean and the Black Sea, providing communication between the significant port cities around Asia Minor and Constantinople. Between 1919 and 1920, the foremost task handled by the US Navy in Turkey was to facilitate the activities of the Near East Relief, or the NER,[15] and render assistance to American missionaries by providing transportation and protection. The Managing Director of the NER in Constantinople was Major Davis G. Arnold. The US Congress approved a hundred million dollars on 24 February 1919 'for the relief of non-enemy countries of Europe but not excluding the Armenians, Syrians, Greeks and other Christian and Jewish population of Asia Minor'.[16] The American Red Cross already had a branch in Constantinople, which became one of the headquarters for southern Europe in 1920. Hundreds of foreign humanitarian and missionary workers were dispatched to the area to handle one of the greatest humanitarian crises of human history.[17] It is important to state that these American workers, along with his captains of ships, were major sources for Bristol's intelligence-collecting effort.

Admiral Bristol was successful in expanding his naval power and in convincing the State Department to grant him the title 'High Commissioner'. After many deliberations in Washington, on 12 August 1919 he became the High Commissioner with the mandate to 'safeguard and assist [American interests] wherever and whenever possible'.[18] The Ottoman archives furnish us with a curious report indicating that Bristol was asked to refrain from using the title 'High Commissioner' but instead should use 'US representative' (*mümessil*). A letter dated 15 October 1923 to the Ministry of Foreign Affairs by an unknown writer states the following:

> I informed Admiral Bristol of the necessity of not using the title High Commissioner from now on. It is understood from his statement that he would not object to being referred to as a commissar/representative (*mümessil*), and he would ask his government to authorize him to change his title.[19]

It is possible that a request came from the Ankara government's representative in Istanbul. By 1923 the imperial government in Istanbul had ceased to exist. By the cataloguing of the letter (HR. İM or the Foreign Ministry, Istanbul delegation), we can deduce that this request indeed originated from the nationalist government in Ankara. Therefore, one can speculate that the reason for such a request was to separate the US representation from that of the other Allies. The title 'High Commissioner' would be reminding people of military occupation. Clearly, Bristol did not wish to contradict the nationalists' wish; however, one can reasonably be suspicious of his attempt to ask his own government to change his title yet one more time to 'US representative' in Turkey.

The US archives have several other documents showing the power struggle among the Allied High Commissioners in Constantinople. A letter sent from Bristol to the Secretary of State vividly describes the competition among the foreign representation in Turkey. Bristol reports:

> The Allied High Commissioners, as the senior representatives of their governments, claim that they are the ultimate authority in the matters affecting the Constantinople district and which are involved in the carrying out of the Armistice. On the other hand, General Harrington, who formerly commanded the British troops of occupation under a recent decision of the Supreme Council, has been put in supreme command of the Allied forces in this area, maintains a position that he is at the head of the military force which is carrying out the Armistice, he is under obligation to act as the situation demands to protect the safety of Constantinople and of the troops of occupation, and that this duty cannot be controlled by the High Commissioners . . . [This statement caused controversy among High Commissioners and led me] to the consideration of the status of the American High Commissioner and my own position as High Commissioner. *There is no doubt that my appointment as High Commissioner by President Wilson aroused certain jealousy on the part of the Allied High Commissioners, who desire to give the outside world the impression that they occupy a position somewhat superior to that of the other representatives in Constantinople.*[20]

The rest of the letter describes the Allied and other foreign representations in Constantinople and the power struggle among them. Bristol informs Washington that he would not make an issue of the arrogant British attitude. What Bristol was hinting at was his discomfort at seeing the British High Commissioner outranking him in the diplomatic corps in Turkey. In ordinary circumstances, Bristol should have outranked all others in Constantinople due to his seniority. However, Great Britain was keen on taking the lead on the occupation in Constantinople. Such competition for power could be seen as indicative of relations between the Allied Powers; Bristol was certainly not immune to this form of diplomatic envy, if not outright jealousy. The Allied capitols were careful to keep a lid on these competitions on the ground. For example, on 18 October 1921, Robert Bliss of the State Department responded to Bristol's letter, stating that 'your attitude . . . in not making an issue of this matter is approved, it being understood that neither American interests nor your effectiveness, as American representative, have suffered'.[21] A letter from the Department of State, Division of Near Eastern Affairs, to Robert Bliss confirmed that Admiral Bristol obviously 'accepted his position of being outranked by the other Allied High Commissioners. I do not think there is anything to be done about it now, as to suddenly insist on being the ranking commissioner would make trouble and cause unnecessary feeling and distrust on the part of the others.'[22]

This communication indicates that there was fierce competition among the Allies for the spoils of World War I in the Ottoman Empire. This competition is reflected in the relations between the representatives of these Allied Powers. As Bristol indicated in his letter, a title was not simply a title but a certificate or a diploma to perform certain tasks. The weight of the title 'High Commissioner' was significant for Bristol, not in his dealings with the Turks but in his dealings with other High Commissioners. Mark Bristol was skilful enough to carve a diplomatic space for himself in which he could protect the US interests and deal with his other colleagues in the diplomatic corps on an equal basis.

Secondary sources also point out a low-level power struggle between Admiral Bristol and the already existing US diplomatic mission in Constantinople. In order to establish supremacy over the State Department officers in Constantinople, Bristol successfully played the Navy Department against the State Department.[23] As soon as Bristol obtained the title 'High Commissioner', he took residence in the American Embassy in Constantinople. When Bristol arrived, the State Department's political officer, Lewis Heck, had already asked for and been granted a leave of absence for health reasons. Peter Buzanski points out the brief power struggle between Heck – who had been in his post as US commissioner in Constantinople since 1909 – and the newcomer Bristol.[24] In a letter to his wife, Bristol showed his frustration: 'The State Department [has] a young man of no experience [in Constantinople] except he has been a student interpreter and can speak Turkish as our commissioner, whereas the British commissioner is an admiral designated as "High Commissioner" for the British government.'[25] Heck, who was ill at the time, was no match for the seasoned Bristol. After Heck's departure, Bristol assumed the duties of taking care of the relations so far as the Mudros Armistice terms and all military and naval affairs were concerned. In addition, he considered himself responsible for establishing proper relations with the government in Turkey and also with the diplomats of all other countries in Turkey.[26] Interestingly, the *New York Times* announced Bristol's appointment as High Commissioner on 29 August 1919 and confirmed that 'Mr. Ravndal, who retains his title of Commissioner and Consul General, will continue in charge of commercial and similar matters in Constantinople. In political matters, he will be under the direction of the High Commissioner.'[27]

We know that after Heck left Constantinople, the State Department did not immediately bestow the title 'High Commissioner' upon Bristol. Between May and August 1919, it seems that the State Department and the Navy were as confused as Bristol. For example, on an inspection trip, Admiral Bristol received a letter designating him as 'Chief Political Officer of the United States in Constantinople'.[28] In a letter to his wife, Bristol wrote that 'Chief Political Officer' was another name for 'High Commissioner'.[29] The confusion arose from the fact that in May 1919, the State Department appointed the former American Consul General to the Ottoman Empire, Gabriel Bie Ravndal, as 'Commissioner', and Bristol was stripped of his title 'Chief Political Officer'.[30] As stated above, the confusion was resolved in August with the appointment of Bristol as 'High Commissioner' and Ravndal as his subordinate.

From August 1919 onwards, Mark Bristol, in addition to being the High Commissioner, held the following titles in Constantinople: Senior United States Naval Officer in Turkish Waters, representative of the United States Shipping Board in the Near East, Chairman of the Constantinople Chapter of the American Red Cross, General Assistant of the Near East Committee, and General Director of all United States Consular Offices in Turkey.[31] It is also important to note that Bristol served as one of the

American delegates to the Lausanne Conference between 23 November 1922 and 5 February 1923.[32]

It should be noted that Mark Bristol created two separate administrative structures, one for the Navy Department and the other for the Department of State. Each administrative structure was capable of functioning independently with its own staff. Bristol's diplomatic staff included several secretaries, a commercial attaché, a military attaché and a counsellor.[33] According to Buzanski, the main reason for this was Bristol's concern that one of his appointments could at any time be eliminated.[34] In such a case, Bristol wanted his other organisation to carry on independently. Robert Bachman suggests that these two administrative structures complemented each other. 'In this way', concludes Bachman, 'it was arranged that whenever the time came for the Navy to withdraw, the Embassy files would be left complete.'[35] It is not hard to see that Bristol wished to remain relevant in case he lost one of his primary appointments.

Regardless, these files were filled with information with great detail as he created a large intelligence-collecting apparatus. For example, Bristol instructed every destroyer captain under his command to act as an intelligence officer and to keep a daily diary for the intelligence section stationed in the American Embassy building in Istanbul. Therefore, he had access to a large volume of intelligence reports, military or otherwise. Furthermore, Bristol asked a number of people that he trusted to provide reports about the information they gathered in Turkey. Those who reported to Bristol included businessmen, missionaries, relief workers and journalists. Bristol forwarded these reports to Washington by including his own views about the reliability of them.

What is of great value to the historian is the fact that Bristol himself was an avid note-taker, so much so that his reports were sometimes regarded as too long. A former aide, Howland Shaw, commented on this by saying 'if something could be said in seven lines, the Admiral would take seven pages'. Yet, this form of very detailed reporting, which sometimes included the menu of a particular dinner or the length of a particular meeting to the minute, was as helpful to Washington as it is to the historian. Although not trained as a diplomat or intelligence officer, Bristol was careful in grading material regarding the reliability of the information he sent to Washington. However, undoubtedly unintentional mistakes did occur. Peter Buzanski states that since Bristol was not a trained diplomat, he made serious errors of judgement in terms of intelligence collecting.[36] Buzanski, for example, shows a US archival document, 867.00/1243, which is a letter from Bristol to the Secretary of State. Buzanski states, 'On one occasion Bristol reported that British General Townshend was on his way to Turkey with Rauf Bey [Orbay], then a prisoner at Malta, to confer with Mustafa Kemal. Upon receiving this telegram, Secretary of State Bainbridge Colby wired back: For your information, General Townshend arrived in New York April 16.'[37] Buzanski shows this report as an example of the unintentional misinformation Bristol sent to Washington. Yet Buzanski either did not read Bristol's report himself or manipulated it. The above-mentioned letter to the Secretary of State by Bristol, in fact, starts with a statement: 'unconfirmed but plausible report here from nationalist sources says that . . .' Clearly, Bristol was grading the information based on its reliability. Indeed, such careful consideration for the reliability of the information he gathered and relayed to Washington is very typical of many of his reports. If there was a doubt in his mind, he included this in his reports. This certainly does not mean that his judgement and intelligence reports were free of any mistakes. However, they were certainly unintentional and minimal, considering the fact that Bristol loved to write a report for every minuscule detail he encountered in Turkey.

Another criticism of Bristol's reports comes from the fact that he appointed Robert S. Dunn as his Chief Intelligence Officer. Based on a report in the US archives (867.00/1495), Buzanski discredits many reports sent by Dunn that were not in line with the overwhelming accounts that depicted the Turks as uncivilised killers. Buzanski states, 'The value of the intelligence unit was further diminished by the presence on the staff of the Admiral's handpicked Chief Intelligence officer, one Lieutenant Robert S[teed] Dunn . . . For three years, the purple prose of Lieutenant Dunn is evident in countless intelligence reports, which were the result more of barroom gossip than of serious intelligence gathering.'[38] Buzanski bases his conclusion not on counter-evidence but on the statements made in an inner-office memorandum by Harry G. Dwight to Warren Robbins (both members of the State Department's Near Eastern Affairs division). This memorandum blames Dunn for writing 'too yellow journalistic' reports.

Ironically, the same report relies on gossip that 'Admiral [Bristol's] intelligence officer [Dunn] has turned Turk, being known in Islam as Mehmet Ali Bey'.[39] Here again, we see an attempt at a character assassination to discredit reports filed by Dunn.[40] Richard Hovannisian, a well-respected Armenian scholar, labelled Dunn as an 'Armenophobe who had been a Buddhist monk in India and later converted to Islam assuming the name Mehmet Ali Bey'.[41] Neither piece of information was true. Dunn never set foot in India, nor did he convert to Buddhism or Islam. He was an agnostic.[42]

Needless to say, Mark Lambert Bristol was a controversial figure as he was never diplomatic in putting forth his views. This characteristic earned him both opponents and supporters. Let us very briefly look at these groups who supported and wished to discredit the High Commissioner.

Opponents of Bristol

Opponents of Bristol can be listed as proselytising missionaries, some members of the Near East Relief (NER) organisation, influential American historians, politicians, diplomats, and Armenian and Greek lobbies in the US.[43] An overwhelming majority of the American press did also not share Bristol's views. The American public was also firm in its stand against the Turks as they heard about the atrocities committed on the Armenians by the Young Turk administration.

There were deep roots of American missionaries in the Middle East. As early as 1810, the Congregationalist Church of New England had formed the American Board of Commissioners for Foreign Missions (ABCFM), the first organised missionary society in the US, and began sending evangelists to the region. The missionaries in the Ottoman Empire held a variety of perceptions about the Turks, depending on their geographical location in Turkey. Some scholars suggest that the missionaries who established their mission within the predominantly Turkish areas were more neutral, whereas those who lived among the Armenians were particularly anti-Turk.[44] There was no doubt that missionaries were more successful in converting Armenians in general than either Muslims or Jews. It is, therefore, understandable that their sympathy sided with the Armenian case if they lived with them. They, of course, witnessed their sufferings first-hand. Yet, they were oblivious to the sufferings of the other side as they were not in contact with the Muslims, only with the government officials.[45] In the eyes of these missionaries, many of whom were long-time residents of the empire, the rising nationalist movement in Turkey under the leadership of Mustafa Kemal was another manifestation of the CUP regime, which brutally massacred the Armenians. Their vision of the nationalists was coloured by the events of 1915, and their mistrust of any Turkish administration ruling over the Christians was very visible. Many, however, went further, calling for the outright destruction of the Turk from the scene of history.

The Near East Relief was another organisation active in the Ottoman Empire whose members held varying opinions of the American High Commissioner. The American Committee for Armenian and Syrian Relief (ACASR) was formed in 1915 at the behest of the American Ambassador in the Ottoman Empire, Henry Morgenthau, in response to the deportations, massacres and atrocities committed against Armenians, Assyrians and Greeks across Anatolia during World War I. In conjunction with Ambassador Morgenthau, philanthropic businessman Cleveland H. Dodge and Protestant missionary James L. Barton jointly created the ACASR to provide emergency humanitarian aid to suffering minority populations in the Ottoman Empire. The US Congress chartered the organisation in 1919 and renamed it the Near East Relief (the group briefly operated under the title 'The American Committee for Near East Relief' from 1918 to 1919). The Committee successfully mobilised the American public toward unprecedented grassroots support of humanitarian efforts in the Near East and embarked on an ambitious nationwide campaign from 1915 to 1930. As will be seen in Chapter 4, Bristol had many disagreements with some of the NER members who exaggerated or completely lied, so he claimed, about the situation on the ground in their speeches in local churches in the US. Some of these relief workers were heavily involved in fundraising activities in the US churches and had reasons to be partisan about the realities as reported to Bristol. The nationalists expelled many of those who actively pursued pro-Armenian and Greek policies in Anatolia. Angered by these deportations, these relief workers, when returned to the US, contributed greatly to the anti-Turkish campaign with their personal stories in the press and church meetings. For example, the *New York Times* published the story of Dr Ruth Parmlee, who had worked for the NER in Turkey since its inception and was deported by the Ankara government, stating that 'the followers of Mustapha Kemal were corrupt from the lowest to the highest . . . She attributed the action of the Kemalists [expelling her] to a disinclination to have outsiders remain too long in their midst', hence they were viewed as xenophobic.[46]

Another group of Bristol opponents came from among the ranks of diplomats, politicians and historians. Henry Morgenthau, who was the Ambassador of the US in Constantinople during the Armenian massacres of 1915, had a great distaste for the Turks. He was never shy in pointing out the events of 1915 in demonising the Turks. His reports to the State Department during his tenure give historians much-needed details about the killings of the Armenians. However, he was not in Turkey during the nationalist regime, and he continued to paint the Turks as bloodthirsty savages who were 'psychologically primitive to answer the British landing at Gallipoli by murdering hundreds of helpless British'.[47] He also gave many interviews to the American press regarding the events that took place in Anatolia after his tenure in Constantinople. For example, *The Literary Digest* published an article titled 'The Butchery of Christians in Asia Minor', in which Morgenthau claimed that Turks killed and tortured many Christians after the recapture of Smyrna (İzmir).[48] Bristol, who was then the High Commissioner in Constantinople and was very much involved in the activities surrounding the recapture and the burning of Smyrna, drew entirely different conclusions on the subject (see Chapter 4). It is important to note here, however, that despite the significance of the events in the Near East, it appears that the two American diplomats did not directly come into contact with each other to discuss the issue. I have not found any evidence that they met or addressed each other in person. This seems rather odd.[49]

Supporters of Bristol

Despite strong and widespread opposition to Bristol's views and actions in Turkey, there is a sizeable group of respected people who were also based in Turkey and had long interacted with the locals. This group included businessmen, travellers, professors and ranking military personnel who were anxious for the normalisation of relations with a new Turkey. They agreed with Bristol on the grounds that their business activities in Turkey were greatly harmed by the war, and the speedy establishment of political stability was the only due course that should be taken. Such normalisation of relations with Turkey was as good for business as it was for the protection of the Christian minorities. Among the most prominent members of this group were Caleb Frank Gates, the president of the Robert College; Mary Mills Patrick, the president of Constantinople Women's College; James L. Barton of the NER; and Annie T. Allen, an American missionary and a representative of the NER.[50] This group shared Bristol's enthusiasm in establishing relations with the nationalist Turks and supported his position with their letters to Washington and statements in the press.

Among this group, Barton and Allen were two of the Americans who experienced the sufferings of the Armenians. Allen was born in Harput among the Armenians as a child of a missionary family and spoke perfect Turkish. Barton had a personal concern for Armenians because of his years with them in Harput. At the conclusion of World War I, Barton was in favour of the creation of an independent Armenia and pressured the US Department of State to assist in the creation of such a state. When the Turkish nationalists emerged and established the new regime and government, however, Barton joined the Bristol camp and came to the conclusion that an independent Armenia in Anatolia was an illusion. Barton was completely on the same page as Bristol in the view that the rights of minorities could only be protected within the framework of the Turkish Republic. To achieve this end, America had to come to terms with nationalist Turkey.

It must be stated that supporters of Bristol were in the minority and only had hearings within the State Department's Near East division. Even the American president, Woodrow Wilson, was not in sympathy with the Turks, to say the least. The Armenian and the Greek lobbies in the US were very strong, and the lobbyists and partisan scholarship even now do not hesitate to paint Bristol with the scarlet letter 'pro-Turk'. These accusations of being a Turkish sympathiser were levelled against Admiral Bristol throughout his tenure in Turkey. The label 'pro-Turk' was used to discredit his reports that shed a very different light on affairs on the ground.

Was Bristol Pro-Turk?

There has been much written about Admiral Bristol's 'pro-Turk' position, especially in relation to the Armenian and Greek minorities of the Ottoman

Empire. There is little doubt that Bristol sympathised with the nationalist Turks from time to time, but especially when he noticed misinformation, manipulation or gross exaggeration about the vicious nature of the 'Turkish race', as he called it. Bristol tried to be as neutral as possible about the good and bad traits of the 'Turkish race'. For example, in a report, he stated, 'The Turk has some individual traits of character that are so far superior to those of the other races that one is led to sympathize with the Turk, though you never forget the bad traits of his character that are illustrated by the acts committed against the subject races.'[51] Consistent with his time, Bristol tended to essentialise characteristics of ethnic/religious groups in the Middle East. Yet, he never elevated the Turk to the level of Western people.

Heath Lowry, a scholar of Turkish Studies from Princeton, was among the first to question the appropriateness of the label 'pro-Turk' for Bristol:

> The common interpretation of Bristol as 'anti-Greek,' 'anti-Armenian,' and 'pro-Turkish,' which finds all too frequent expression in the works of Armenian scholars, can hardly be sustained by anyone who studies his 'Papers.' Bristol held no brief for any of the peoples of the Middle East. His attitude *vis-a-vis* the indigenous inhabitants of the region may best be summed up via a series of comments 'typical' of those scattered throughout his voluminous private correspondence.[52]

Bristol summarised his attitude towards the peoples of Anatolia in a letter of 18 May 1919: 'I have often said to you, these races in the Near East are all very much the same, and if you put them all in a bag and shake them up you would not know which one would come out first.'[53]

Heath Lowry, who pointed out many quotations in 'American Observers in Anatolia ca. 1920: The Bristol Papers', is himself known as a 'pro-Turk' scholar by some of his peers. Therefore, one can question his intentions in disputing the 'pro-Turk' label for Bristol. Yet, Lowry's conclusion on this labelling of Bristol is shared by other scholars, including Peter Buzanski, who cannot be categorised in the same political/intellectual group as Lowry. In his dissertation on Bristol, Buzanski also concluded that 'Not to be pro-Armenian meant not that one was neutral but anti-Armenian; not to be pro-Allied was to be pro-Turk. Mark Bristol had to do nothing but to be neutral in order to be regarded as unneutral and pro-Turk in the eyes of such people.'[54]

Although more politically oriented scholars' publications try to diminish Bristol's credibility, independent scholars can readily attest to the honesty of Bristol in reporting his observations to Washington. Bristol biographer Buzanski suggests that 'it was impossible to be neutral about Bristol. One either agreed with him and backed his policies, or one disagreed with him and classified him with the "terrible Turk."'[55] Yet, in his mind, Bristol was giving voice to 'the other side of the story', the one that did not have any representation in the United States. In the aftermath of World War I, the political atmosphere in the US was unquestionably anti-Turk but also decidedly uninformed about the Turk. For example, a young Turkish woman, Selma Ekrem, narrated her experience on a trip to the US:

> Here in America, lived a legend made of blood and thunder. The Terrible Turk ruled the minds of the Americans. A huge person with fierce black eyes and bushy eyebrows, carrying daggers covered with blood. I did not fit into the legend of the Terrible Turk, and so I was not one. In fact, many people were disappointed to meet a real true Turk who turns out to be fair, meek, and not very unlike an American.[56]

It was this form of public opinion in the US against which Bristol was operating. Anti-Turkish bias was also visible in the political establishment of America. A recorded conversation between the admiral and Senator William H. King (a Democrat from Utah who represented Utah in the US Senate from 1917 to 1941) is telling. Senator King, confirming his own biases against the Turks, put forward the claim that many people in the US think he is a pro-Turk. Describing this meeting, Bristol notes his response to King in his diary dated 13 July 1925:

> I told [King] I was quite aware of this idea of a good many people, but this opinion I believe came from the fact that *in this part of the world if you maintained a strictly neutral attitude without being 'pro' any of these races or nationalities, these latter immediately believed you were not only not in sympathy with their cases but were even 'anti' to the cause of each. There was only one thing I tried to be, and that was pro-American* and strictly impartial as regards every other nationality and race.[57]

One should point out that Bristol's statement still holds true, a century later. In all political matters, the champions of political positions do not leave any grey area for independent thinking. If you are not fully in line with the political stand of a group, you are accused of being 'anti' its political stand and hence the enemy. However, the role of the historian should involve approaching all data with equal scepticism. We know that Admiral Bristol tried to do just that. Clearly, he was more critical of the reports by the Greek and Armenian lobbies spreading in the US simply because, he believed, they were the ones who had access to American public opinion and the means to manipulate it. Because of his bold criticism of what he deemed 'misinformation regarding race-relations' circulating in the US, Bristol almost always found himself on the defensive for his position towards inter-religious relations in Anatolia.

For example, in discussion with Bishop J. H. Darlington in Constantinople, Bristol repeated, 'There is nothing pro-Turk about me, but if you do not advocate an independent Armenia, the Armenian propagandists state I am favorable to the Turks or pro-Turk.'[58] The Department of State, Division of Near Eastern Affairs, was bombarded with letters from Christian lobbying groups accusing Bristol of being pro-Turk, not fully sympathising with the aspirations of the Christian minority and being more interested in pressing US business than US philanthropic interests in the Near East. In a memorandum to the Secretary of State, Allen Dulles[59] states that he received many letters advancing the above-mentioned accusations against Admiral Bristol; however, states Dulles,

[I]n addition to the strong support of all [of] our business interests in Constantinople, [Bristol] enjoys the confidence of many of the missionary and relief workers in the field, especially those who have adapted themselves to the existing situation rather than to a conception of the situation based on pre-war experience.

It is true that Admiral Bristol is not always as tactful as he might be. He has been outspoken in his belief that the various races of the Near East are very much alike, and that it is not just to tell half the story by mentioning only Turkish outrages without any reference to atrocities which have been committed by Greeks and Armenians or errors of the policy of great powers which have thrown the Near East into a turmoil and aroused the national and religious feelings of Moslem against Christian . . . In my opinion, he deserves the Department's continued support, even though we may expect further criticism against him from the same sources.[60]

This memorandum clearly indicates that the State Department was fully aware of the discrediting activities of some lobbies in the US and that Bristol's neutral stand was appreciated and relied on. Accordingly, Admiral Mark Lambert Bristol continued to send reports that were prepared by himself and his staff to Washington. In them, he did not shy away from criticising the Turks and documenting the atrocities committed by the Turkish side.

More reasonable criticism of Bristol came from his favouritism in keeping American business interests above the plight of Christian minorities – mainly the Armenians and the Greeks. Bristol was indeed an Open Door diplomat; however, American trade vs minority interests was not a zero-sum game for him. His point was solid: antagonising the Turks would do much more harm to the Christian well-being. Bristol judged that protecting human rights in Turkey depended heavily upon being fair to all sides and not provoking one side that had the potential to harm the others.

Yet, even at the present time, Bristol is treated unfairly, for he went against the grain in political discourse. This smudging campaign against Bristol goes so far as stating that his attitude towards charity organisations, also helping Muslim communities, is a sign of his pro-Turk tendencies. For example, we know that during his tenure in Turkey, Bristol was instrumental in the erection of a hospital first in Çarşıkapı, then in Nişantaşı, Istanbul. This hospital, known for many years as the Bristol Hospital,[61] continued to serve the population of Istanbul for decades without any regard for race, nationality or religion. However, originally there were debates over whether or not it should serve only Americans or Christians. In a board meeting on this subject, Bristol brought up the issue of funding for the hospital, which could only last one more year. To the board, he explained:

> We should come to a decision 1) as to whether the hospital should be run simply by and for the American Community, 2) as a hospital for the American community and the Christian Community, and 3) as a hospital for the American community and as a public utility for the benefit of everyone in Constantinople. I expressed the private opinion that of these three methods the last, that is, to operate the hospital as a truly public utility, was the most desirable method and at the same time was the one that would probably meet with the greatest success . . .
>
> Armenians have come to the hospital and demanded attention and free treatment, stating that the American Hospital was there to take care of

the poor Armenians. The Greek doctor had made arrangements for Greek patients to be received in rooms at much-reduced rates. [However,] I have been informed that the Turkish patients attending the clinic had been told to go elsewhere because they had their own hospitals to take care of them. Mr. Blackett stated that when questions arose to Turkish patients remaining in the hospital, [with] only a recommendation made by the Turkish physician, the Armenian physician ruled against it and in every case, the recommendations of the Armenian doctor had been taken, and the Turkish patients had been sent away from the hospital. It had come to my attention from reliable sources that the Turkish Medical Fraternity were not in sympathy with the hospital because they stated that it was run for the benefit of the Christians alone . . .

[In the end, everybody agreed that] the hospital would take into consideration anything except that which pertains to the care and treatment of the patients of the hospital, without any regard to religion, politics, or anything else of that kind.[62]

From this report, we learn that the medical staff of the hospital included Greek, Armenian and Turkish as well as American doctors trying to further the interests of their communities. Bristol's effort to step in to make the hospital free from inter-ethnic, inter-religious rivalries is much appreciated. Bristol, on many other occasions, suggested that charity organisations should serve all needy regardless of their background. Interestingly, this blind policy of the hospital and other Christian charity organisations in Turkey has become a source for criticism and is taken as proof of Bristol's pro-Turk tendencies. For example, in an essay in the newer version of the book *Ambassador Morgenthau's Story*,[63] his grandson Henry Morgenthau III claims, 'Unabashedly pro-Turk, [Bristol] encouraged American relief agencies to extend Christian charity to needy Turks as well as to their oppressed Christian minorities.' Morgenthau III further supports his view by first admitting that Bristol warned the Turks to be tolerant towards the Christian minorities, 'yet, he [Bristol] made it clear to the Turks exactly where he stood personally'.[64] The author quotes Bristol, saying, 'Armenians are a race like the Jews; they have little or no national spirit and have poor moral character.'[65] However, he entirely omits the similar statements Bristol made for all the groups in the Ottoman Empire, including the Turks. By selectively quoting Bristol's statement, Henry Morgenthau III attempts to support his claim that Bristol was pro-Turk, and hence not credible. Yet, there is no record of Henry Morgenthau, the grandfather, who was very active in criticising the Turks, criticising Bristol, despite the fact that he was aware of the anti-Bristol campaign in the US.

Bristol: An Open Door Diplomat

One of the most significant reasons for the labelling of Bristol as pro-Turk was the fact that he was an ardent supporter of the Open Door Policy advocated by Woodrow Wilson, and wished to apply it in Turkey. Let us briefly look at this foreign policy issue.

It can be argued that the Open Door Policy of the US stands as one of the most important foreign policy statements ever issued by the US State Department. Initiated in the late nineteenth and early twentieth centuries, it came as a response to European commercial competition in China. In response to being isolated in the Chinese commercial markets, the US promoted a system of trade which would allow open access to all countries equally. On 6 September 1899, Secretary of State John Hay issued an 'Open Door Note' and dispatched it to the major European powers which were competing in China. It proposed that Chinese markets would be open to all countries on an equal basis, keeping any one power from total control of the country. In a sense, this policy gave an opening for the US to jump into the game of commercial competition in the international arena.

President Woodrow Wilson later adopted this policy during World War I, especially after the Bolshevik Revolution in 1917, when the US entered the Great War. Wilson laid down several guidelines for the United States' foreign policy, which can be delineated as anti-imperialism, self-determination, some form of collective security, world order and an Open Door trade policy. As the world headed towards polarisation, Wilson aimed at establishing a permanent world order based on liberal capitalist internationalism, which would be safe from both the threat of imperialism and the danger of the socialist revolution. The American president was an ardent believer that the liberal values of the US would soon dominate world politics, which would lead the United States to the establishment of an international system of political order where commerce would be practised freely.

In contrast to the socialist theories of Lenin, Wilson believed that the international capitalist system did not have to follow the footsteps of the militant imperialism of the past. It could establish a programme of trade and economic development of the backward areas of the globe, through which the US could spread its prosperity to these countries. However, in order to do so, the United States needed access to the world markets to sell its products.[66]

Irked by the British and French opportunism in the region, Bristol regarded Wilson's Open Door Policy as a great tool to counter European monopoly in the Ottoman Empire. He declared that United States foreign policy in the Middle East follow the guidelines of the principles of the Open Door. This would benefit the US as well as the Turkish interests. According to Thomas A. Bryson,

> Admiral Sims' order regarding American interests and Point Three of Wilson's Fourteen Points, calling for the 'removal of all economic barriers and the establishment of an equality of trade conditions,' provided Bristol with the necessary instructions relevant to that portion of his mission dealing with American economic interests. Between 1920 and 1923, Bristol asserted on at least six occasions that American foreign policy in the Near East was based in part on the principle of the Open Door and that he was working diligently for its implementation. As will be shown, the Admiral applied this principle not only to the Allies who were then seeking to gain control of Turkey and her former empire but also to the Turks and to the American missionaries and businessmen as well.[67]

Bryson is correct when he states that Bristol was trying to achieve a six-fold aim by upholding the principles of the Open Door Policy:

> first enhance American goodwill in Turkey; second, create a climate in that country conducive to economic expansion; third, neutralize Allied efforts to monopolize commerce with Turkey; fourth, create an American infrastructure that would facilitate economic penetration; fifth, fashion an integrated American economic system that would result in increased economic benefits; and sixth, encourage American business concerns to compete aggressively for new markets in the Middle East.[68]

It is important to note that in Bristol's mind the Open Door also meant that missionaries and relief workers should allocate relief supplies not only to Christians but to Muslims as well, which was also not a welcomed stand for some missionaries. In other words, there was enough for the opponents of Bristol to accuse him of the betrayal of the Christian people.

Can Bristol's six-point aim be considered a betrayal to the moral obligation of protecting the minorities from the wrath of the Turks? After all, as will be discussed in Chapter 4, Bristol was accused of sacrificing the Christian minorities of the Ottoman Empire to US commercial interests. This accusation cannot be sustained in the light of Bristol's humanitarian record. As mentioned above, he was adamant in his view that the best protection of the minorities in the empire was surely not to antagonise the Turks, who could potentially inflict considerable damage to them.

Regardless, we do know that there were many attempts by Bristol's opponents from different backgrounds to remove him from his post in Constantinople, as he proved that he would not shy away from rocking the boat, especially for a group of missionaries and surely for Great Britain. They were, however, unsuccessful.

Attempts to Push Bristol out of Constantinople[69]

Because of his unique position on issues such as the Armenian and Greek conflicts with the Turks, US mandate over projected Armenia, relations with the emerging Kemalist administration and the role of the American missionaries in Turkey, Admiral Bristol made enemies from among American relief workers who were mainly missionaries and even some members of the US Department's Near East division. Externally, the British Foreign Office and the Greek government complained about Bristol's views and attitudes towards Allied politics in the Near East.

For example, we know that the first attempt to remove Bristol from Constantinople came from the Greek government. Eleftherios Venizelos, Greek Prime Minister of the period, registered his complaint with the Department of State regarding Bristol's 'anti-Greek' position in the 'Commission of Inquiry', which investigated the Greek invasion of Smyrna and the atrocities committed by both Turks and Greeks (see Chapter 4). This committee, comprising representatives from the US, France, England and Italy and headed by Admiral Bristol, held a total of forty-six meetings between 12 August and 15 October 1919. Their report concluded that Greece bore a greater responsibility for the killings of civilians than the Turkish side in Smyrna, which certainly was not innocent.[70] It was this conclusion that motivated Venizelos to charge Bristol for pro-Turk tendencies and to request his removal.[71]

Bristol replied by denying allegations that he was favouring Turks and hostile towards the Greeks. With his usual patience, the admiral explained his position one more time:

> I have endeavored to consistently maintain a neutral and just attitude towards all races and factions ... It is difficult for an American to appreciate the mentality of the natives, resident here, but it is an incontrovertible fact that the attitude of neutrality is misunderstood and construed by each faction as hostile to their particular cause.[72]

Bristol had to make many similar statements throughout his tenure to defend his position in Turkey. Warren Robbins of the US State Department's Near East division was not too pleased with Bristol and countered that it was not always the 'locals' but 'other reports, such as those from Consul Horton at Smyrna, etc., would lead one to believe that [Bristol] is pro-Turkish, if not anti-Greek'.[73] Robbins was underlining the fact that even US State Department employees were complaining about Bristol's one-sided treatment of the affairs in Constantinople. It is, however, a fact that decision-makers in the State Department were in line with Bristol and followed his suggestions in formulating policy towards Turkey.

Accusations for a 'pro' or 'anti' any group are not in short supply in dealing with controversial subjects among the scholars. Peter Buzanski has argued that 'George Horton of Smyrna was a fanatic philhellenist, and was recognized as so by Bristol and the Department of State. His wife was Greek. During the Turkish capture of Smyrna, at the end of the Greco-Turkish War, Horton suffered a breakdown, resigned from the diplomatic service, and spent the balance of his life writing anti-Turkish pro-Greek books.'[74] The reader should obviously be mindful of the subjectivity of these kinds of labelling, whether it be for Bristol (pro-Turk) or for Horton (pro-Greek).

In any case, the second opposition to Bristol as High Commissioner came from some members of the Near East Relief. Relations between Mark Bristol and the NER began cordially enough; Bristol acknowledged and praised work by the NER in Turkey, and James L. Barton, Director of the NER, reciprocated in kind.[75] Bristol cooperated with the NER on many occasions, most significant of which was the transportation needs of the members of the NER via US destroyers from one port to another. Soon, however, disagreements emerged. For example, Bristol learned that some NER speakers were disseminating 'distorted propaganda' in the US to raise funds for the NER. In order to do so, these missionaries were touring the US telling audiences of Turkish massacres of Christians taking place under his watch. These lecturing activities in churches, it must be mentioned, provided the NER with a major source of income. Admiral Bristol was adamant when he heard this, and stated:

> It is a horrible crime to deceive our people in the United States in the way they have been deceived . . . Someday our people are going to be undeceived and realize that they have constantly heard but one side of the story and that side of the story has always been distorted and inaccurately stated.[76]

Bristol was claiming that the Americans were not being told factual details of the massacres. He was also objecting to the fact that stories were intentionally told in a one-sided manner. The Greek and Armenian massacres of the Turks should also be mentioned in these speeches in order to be fair; this would reflect the accurate frame of events. Against this objection, Charles Vickrey, Secretary of the NER committee, admitted that while Greeks and Armenians were also killing Turks/Muslims, there was, in fact, a difference in the scale and number of these massacres. This response infuriated Bristol even more. The US High Commissioner responded:

> I told [Vickrey that] I had no patience with that kind of an excuse. I believe that it is just as bad to steal five cents as five dollars, and in the same way, it is just as bad to massacre hundreds as massacre thousands or even millions.[77]

The reader can judge what argument he or she subscribes to; however, the statement clearly shows Bristol's disagreement with the NER from time to time.

Another significant point was that Bristol quoted a conversation with Harold C. Jaquith in which the admiral mentioned the High Commission's several correspondences with various NER representatives. In his diary, Bristol noted that 'there were statements in writing from representatives of the NER committee that "*if they told the whole truth they would not raise money for their relief work*" [emphasis added]. Jaquith was making the same point. Bristol's reply was, "This was obtaining money under false pretenses."[78]

Admiral Bristol repeatedly protested about the one-sided reports of the NER missionaries. For example, he wired the State Department his dislike of the propaganda activities of the organisation:

> The activities and propaganda of the Near East Relief Committee, which directly continue to exaggerate the atrocities committed by the Turks while any similar acts by Christian races are not given publicity are tending to imperil the philanthropic work of Americans in the interior of Turkey as well as the lives of Christian races. It also works against our commercial interests, and at the same time, it impairs my ability to protect further general American interests here.[79]

It should be mentioned that some critics of Bristol furthered the argument that he abandoned the Christian plight for the sake of securing commercial interest.[80] As is clearly shown in this quotation, US commercial interests were only one consequence of what Bristol considered one-sided and manipulative propaganda executed by some members of the NER. Bristol never denied the gruesome atrocities committed by the Turks (or the Kurds) but pointed out that they told only one side of the story. It is a mistake to suggest that Bristol's position was due entirely to his desire to protect US commercial interests and that, in the process, he sacrificed Christians and their cause in the Near East.

Finally, William W. Peet, the treasurer of the American Board of Commissioners for Foreign Missions (ABCFM), got into a dispute with Bristol regarding the evacuation of 60,000 Armenian orphans from Turkey. Bristol was adamant, fearing that such a big move would trigger a mass exodus of Christians in panic. He noted in his diary,

> I went on to point out to Dr. Peet that even if the orphans were taken away by us, the rest of the Christian population would be stampeded in spite of everything we could say . . . that there was no danger, and therefore we are taking away the orphans. Thus it seemed to be better to sacrifice these orphans, if necessary, to establish confidence in the mass of the people.[81]

Interestingly, the Department of State agreed with Bristol on this assessment of the situation.[82] According to Buzanski, Bristol did not feel that 60,000 Armenian children would be slaughtered as he trusted in the emerging

Turkish/Kemalist government. Such trust did not exist in Dr Peet. Therefore, Peet approached James L. Barton and Charles V. Vickrey to collaborate in an attempt to remove Bristol from his post. It was Dr Barton who complained to Charles Evans Hughes, the US Secretary of State, about Mark Bristol early in 1922.[83] In addition to the Cilician Armenians, Barton accused Bristol of not doing enough to pressure the Kemalists to reinstate several expelled missionaries from Turkey.

The State Department was firm in defending the admiral against these charges. Barton was informed that the State Department fully approved Bristol's position on not evacuating the Armenians from any Turkish territory. The letter to Barton concluded with the statement that 'while granting that in questions of policy or method, there is usually room for honest differences of opinion[,] the Department would be most unwilling for your Board or for its constituents to harbor any essential doubt as to the goodwill of so indefatigable a public servant.'[84]

Upon this response, Dr Barton tried his hand one more time to remove Bristol from his post, levelling similar charges against him. In another letter to the Secretary of State, Barton insisted on Bristol's indifference to the demands of American missionaries. He further stated that the only people who agreed with Bristol's policies in Turkey were the Turks themselves, and that Bristol trusted the word of the Turks more than he did that of the Americans. In his conclusion, Barton asked that Bristol be replaced as High Commissioner in Constantinople with a professional diplomat with wide experience in the region who could cooperate with missionaries and with representatives of Great Britain.[85]

The only action taken by the State Department in connection to this letter was to request information from Bristol regarding the expulsion of missionaries from Anatolia and what measures he took to stop it. It seems that Bristol seized this opportunity to lay out his views of missionaries in Anatolia rather bluntly. In his reply to Secretary Hughes, Bristol stated that making a *pro forma* protest to the Sultan was a useless gesture. Instead, he had hoped to approach the nationalists in Ankara through a well-respected American missionary in Turkey, Annie Allen. However, the untimely death of Ms Allen prevented this from taking place. Clearly, Bristol was convinced that the nationalists in Ankara were in charge and any appeal to

Istanbul was fruitless, for the imperial government in Istanbul lacked the authority to control events on the ground.

Bristol counterattacked by suggesting that the American missionaries in Turkey were having a hard time adjusting to new political realities there. Prior to World War I, the Capitulations had given them more space to operate and protected them from the consequences of their actions. They were protected because the Ottoman central government had control of the provinces. Yet, after the conclusion of World War I, local authorities gained more power, and many Turks became unfavourably inclined towards the missionaries, categorising them clearly in the rival religious (Christian) camp. American missionaries were clearly identified with the Armenians, who wished and fought for the destruction of the Turkish state. According to Bristol, this perception by the Turks had the potential to greatly harm the future missionary, philanthropic, educational and, most significantly, commercial activities of the US in this part of the world. Here, Bristol made a significant analysis. He observed that the American missionary work contributed nothing to the solution of inter-faith violence in Anatolia. Minority races (i.e. Armenians), educated by Americans in the Ottoman Empire, were taught Christian and American principles. Although this education made them more effective intellectually compared to their fellow Muslim citizens in the empire, it made them more divorced from the Turkish environment. Predicting that the area would remain 'Turkish' in the future due to the success of the Kemalist movement in Anatolia, Bristol questioned the wisdom of missionary activities. He suggested:

> [T]he American missionary and educator if he is to continue his work in the Near East, will have to give much thoughtful consideration to the question of how to adjust the Christian races to the environment in which they at present physically find themselves. That environment is a Turkish environment, and I believe that it will continue to be a Turkish environment.[86]

This letter was written on 9 May 1922, four months before the victory of the Kemalists against Greek forces in İzmir, which is considered the seal of Turkish victory against the 'Christian/imperialist aggressors'. The foresight of Bristol is commendable, as many even in the Ottoman imperial circles doubted that such a victory could be realised. It seems that Bristol was convinced from 1921 onwards that the Kemalists/nationalists in Ankara would eventually triumph.[87]

Around this time, the US Secretary of State, Charles Evans Hughes, received another complaint about Bristol, this time from the British.[88] Sir Auckland Geddes, the British Ambassador to the United States, stated that Bristol was quite antagonistic towards England, interfering continuously with the Allied efforts to maintain order in Turkey. The British diplomat also complained that Bristol was operating under the false presumption that the Allies were misusing their authority in Constantinople to the detriment of the United States. Secretary Hughes bluntly rejected the British accusations and firmly defended Bristol. He was not shy about sharing with the British diplomat his misgivings about the Allied actions in Turkey. Hughes also asked Allen W. Dulles, a one-time Bristol aide in Turkey, to brief the British.[89] In response to this complaint, Hughes's manner towards Bristol was rather diplomatic; after complimenting him for his service in Turkey, the Secretary of State gently rebuked the admiral:

> It would be a gratification to me . . . if, without sacrificing those interests, you could bring about more cordial cooperation with our Allied colleagues . . . I desire you, therefore, on receipt of my letter to make renewed effort to establish that informal contact with your Allied colleagues, which may facilitate the settlement of questions which arise between you and the Allied missions without allowing them to reach an acute issue.[90]

Bristol was aware of the pressure Hughes was under for some time in Washington from the Allied forces as the Kemalists were advancing towards victory. Allen Dulles was in the habit of informing his former boss in Turkey of the developments in Washington; therefore, Hughes's letter to Bristol did not discomfort him greatly, as he knew that Hughes had penned the letter under pressure.[91]

According to Admiral Bristol, the US position on the dilemma of keeping the balance between the pressures of the US missionaries, of the Allied Powers and the US interests in the Near East was simple. Bristol stated it very clearly in a personal letter to Allen Dulles:

> It seems to me . . . that we need not be caught between these two fires; that is the protection of business interests on one side and Christian minorities on the other . . . If we should stand out for a strict fair play with a square deal for

everyone and insist upon the rights of the minorities in all cases being respected, we would get on the sound ground. In the same way, where a majority of the population is subjected to oppression by the military force of a minority, we should stand up for this majority without distinction of race or religion. In the same way, we should insist upon our business interests being given just consideration of the same principle of fair play for everyone concerned.[92]

In the same letter, Bristol suggested that the best remedy to release the pressure was to give the American public the fullest picture of conditions in the Near East.

The British effort was the last known attempt at the removal of Bristol from his post as the US High Commissioner in Constantinople, with one exception. We know that Britain also complained about Bristol's 'pro-Turk' stand at the Lausanne Conference in 1923.[93] After the victory of the Kemalists in Smyrna in 1922, the State Department was fully convinced of the need to establish and maintain healthy relations with the Ankara government. Admiral Mark Lambert Bristol was just the right man for the task. Bristol scholar Peter Buzanski correctly concluded that 'given the political realities of 1919–1922, the State Department recognized that Mark Bristol was a champion of American rights who was willing to fight even if he had no weapons. Therefore, Bristol was given a free hand most of the time.'[94] We know that President Calvin Coolidge insisted that Bristol remain in his current post despite anti-Turk lobbies in the US.[95]

His Superiors' View of Bristol

In the second half of 1925, Bristol visited the USA for five months. He delivered several speeches in Army and Naval Colleges, gave interviews to radio stations and newspapers, and attended dinners honouring him. A letter dated 7 November 1925 by Charles E. Hughes, Secretary of State, to E. E. Pratt, Secretary, American Chamber of Commerce at New York City, informs us that there was a dinner in honour of Admiral Bristol during this time; the Secretary of State was unable to attend it but sent a letter to the host. In his letter, Secretary Hughes wrote:

> I greatly regret that my engagements make it impossible for me to attend the dinner in honor of Admiral Bristol on Monday evening, I should like to join in this deserved tribute to one who has rendered most faithful and efficient

service to his country. I suppose that no representative of the United States in recent years has been placed in a more difficult position than that held by Admiral Bristol in the Near East. He brought to the discharge of his important duties not only ability and knowledge but a strength of character and sense of justice, which gave him rare equipment for his task. He has made all our people his debtors, and it is a pleasure to join you and others present at the dinner in doing him honor. He is an ideal public servant.[96]

Another attached letter, from the Secretary of Commerce (1921–8) and the future President of the United States (1929–33) Herbert Hoover, also praised Bristol in the following manner:

Surely we can all take genuine delight in honoring Mark Bristol. No American active in post-war reconstruction work abroad has touched a higher standard in the rendering of substantial public service. The United States had many and strikingly varied interests in Turkey – philanthropic, educational, humanitarian, and commercial. Admiral Mark Bristol has zealously guarded them with a fine balance of judgment and with scrupulous respect for the just interests of those with whom he dwelt [dealt?], which clearly earned for him the confidence of Government and people.[97]

The praising letters of the future American president Hoover and Secretary of State Hughes were indeed representative of the American administration's admiration towards Bristol. Despite much propaganda against him, coupled with intense lobbying activities to remove him from his post as High Commissioner, Admiral Mark Lambert Bristol had garnered the support and respect of his superiors. This also testifies to the fact that Bristol put American interests first, and his reports and analyses were considered accurate and fair, despite the fact that they went against the grain and public sentiment in the US at the time.

Admiral Mark Lambert Bristol did remain in Turkey as High Commissioner until 24 May 1927, when diplomatic relations between the US and Turkey were restored at the ambassadorial level. In a telegram dated 19 March 1927, Secretary of State Frank B. Kellogg informed Bristol that his position as the US High Commissioner in Constantinople was concluded. The telegram read as follows:

The President having particularly in mind your future career in the Navy, directs me to inform you that he does not feel you should be asked to remain in Turkey after June 1st next. While the loss to this Government inevitable in the termination of your present mission is keenly appreciated by the President and by myself, we realize that to prolong your stay in Turkey beyond June 1st might interfere with the plans of the Navy Department. It is my earnest desire to cooperate with the Navy Department to the fullest possible extent to the end that your services in Turkey may receive the recognition they so clearly deserve.[98]

This dismissal was not due to any lobbying activities against Bristol but resulted from the need to appoint a professional diplomat with the rank of ambassador. After the failure of the Treaty of Lausanne in the US Senate in 1927 by six votes, William Braisted points out, Bristol requested his transfer back to the Navy in the Asiatic Fleet.[99] It is noteworthy to report that the US Department of State and the Navy always considered Bristol a great asset and were grateful for his services. After his diplomatic mission was completed, Bristol resumed his Navy career.

We know the exact date and hour of Bristol's final departure from Turkey. In his 'War Diary' on 23 May 1927, Bristol notes his last day: 'This [entry] winds up my official diary, which I have written daily since I took command of the "NORTH CAROLINA" the 16th of April 1917. I will leave here tomorrow at 1:15 P.M. by the Simplon express for Paris to proceed to the United States to be relieved as United States High Commissioner in Turkey.' So Bristol left Turkey on 24 May 1927. In his last report relaying his diary to Washington, Bristol recorded his conversation with Ali Said Pasha.[100] In an entry dated 16 May 1927, when asked his final suggestions for Turkey, Bristol suggested to Ali Said Pasha to plant trees and reforest the plains: 'This could be best done by getting every citizen in the country on certain holidays to plant trees and then give exemption from taxes for those who obtained the best results in growing trees.'[101] Mark Bristol did not witness Mustafa Kemal's first visit to Istanbul on 1 June 1927. He could have described this monumental event, which marked the end of the eight years of separation between Istanbul and Mustafa Kemal, in much more detail than the next entry (867.00/1972) in the US archives prepared by his successor Joseph Grew.

On 9 September 1927, Bristol assumed command of the Asiatic Fleet with the rank of admiral.[102] Unlike in the Near East, Bristol occupied only one official appointment in China, that of the Commander in Chief of the US Asiatic Fleet, which prevented him from working to promote US business and missionary interests in China, an aspiration Bristol still maintained.

One of the rare diplomatic actions by Bristol in China was his attempt to reach a settlement of the Chinese Civil War between the Communists and the Nationalists in 1927. Although he was not a diplomat in this post as he had been in Turkey, we know that Admiral Bristol interviewed Chiang Kai-shek, the leader of the Chinese nationalists, in November 1927. Chiang began the conversation by complimenting Bristol on his service in Turkey. The admiral answered that he had worked very closely with the Turks and made many friends among them.[103] It seems that the admiral was trying to give the impression that he was capable of working closely with nationalists. Clark G. Reynolds, in his book *Famous American Admirals*, claims that Bristol was not successful in the diplomatic sphere in the two years that he was in China.[104] Needless to say, Bristol's fame in diplomacy preceded him to China, yet he did not have much chance to exhibit his diplomatic skills as he was there solely as a sailor.

Upon conclusion of his tenure in September 1929, Bristol reverted to rear admiral rank, the highest permanent rank in the US Navy at that time. His next and last appointment was to the General Board at the Navy Department, a group of selected elder senior naval officers advising the secretary on naval affairs. In the spring of 1930, Bristol became chairman of the Board's executive committee, a position close to the top of the naval establishment in Washington.[105] He retired on 1 May 1932.[106]

In his retirement, Mark Lambert Bristol was involved in many charity activities[107] related to Turkey and followed up the construction of the American Hospital in Istanbul.[108] We do not have specific information about the health of Bristol in retirement. In a letter to his nephew, John B. Bristol, dated 1 April 1939 the admiral does not give any clue as to the severity of his illness: 'I am going into the hospital on Monday to be taken under observation for several days and then to decide whether or not an operation is necessary. It is one of those cases of old age, and I will be glad to have it over with. Otherwise, we both are well, and your aunt Helen is going strong in her business as usual.'[109] We know Mark Lambert Bristol did not come out of the hospital alive; he died on 13 May 1939. Unfortunately, we do not know exactly the nature of his illness. After his death, two US ships were named USS *Bristol* in his honour, in 1941 and 1945.

The tenure of Bristol coincides with a very significant period in Middle Eastern/Islamic history, as many consequential events took place. Therefore, Bristol's reports and dispatches shed much-needed light on the dark corners of the late Ottoman and the early Turkish Republican history. The following chapters will attest to this proposition.

Notes

1. In the CIA archives, there is printed material which gives brief biographical information on Bristol; see <https://www.cia.gov/library/readingroom/document/cia-rdp80b01676r003600050014-5> (last accessed 28 September 2020). It is authored by Bern Anderson. Collection: General CIA Records, Document Number (FOIA) /ESDN (CREST): CIA-RDP80B01676R003600050014-5.
2. Unless otherwise indicated, all information about Mark Bristol's early Navy career came from Clark G. Reynolds, *Famous American Admirals* (Annapolis: First Naval Institute Press, 2002), pp. 42–3; Peter Michael Buzanski, 'Admiral Mark L. Bristol and Turkish-American Relations, 1919–1922', PhD dissertation, University of California, Berkeley, 1960, chapter 2; Henry P. Beers, 'United States Naval Detachment in Turkish Waters, 1919–24', *Military Affairs*, 7.4 (Winter 1943): 209–20; William R. Braisted, 'Mark Lambert Bristol: Naval Diplomat Extraordinary of the Battleship Age', in James C. Bradford (ed.), *Admirals of the New Steel Navy: Makers of the American Naval Tradition 1880–1930* (Annapolis: Naval Institute Press, 1990), pp. 331–73; Robert S. Parkin, *Blood on the Sea: American Destroyers Lost in World War II* (New York: Da Capo Press, 2001), p. 171; Lewis Heck, 'Rear Admiral Mark L. Bristol', *World Affairs*, 102.3 (September 1939): 158–9.
3. Buzanski gives the date as 2 November 1907; however, an unpublished essay by Walter S. Hiatt (the last name is not very legible) gives the year as 1908. See also 'The Bristol Papers', Library of Congress Manuscript Division, box 61.
4. Reynolds, p. 43.
5. In his diary, he gives the date of this event as 16 April 1917; see 867.00/1071, Bristol, 'War Diary', entry dated 9 June 1927.
6. US sources use Constantinople for Istanbul. I use both interchangeably throughout the text.
7. 763.72/3991, Secretary of the Embassy in Turkey (Tarler) to Secretary of State, Constantinople, 20 April 1917.

8. Beers, p. 209.

9. The converted yacht *Scorpion* served as the flagship vessel for Bristol. When it retired in 1927 after returning to the US, it was believed to have 'the longest tour of foreign service of any vessel in the US Navy to date. It began in October 1908, when she was first ordered to the Mediterranean'; *New York Times*, 29 March 1927, p. 3. For more information, see 'Famous Old Scorpion at Last Hauls Down Flag and Retires', *New York Times*, 6 November 1927, p. 9.

10. 'Bristol Papers', box 64, folder January 1919–September 1928. Buzanski mistakenly gives the date as 6 January; see Buzanski, p. 26.

11. Buzanski, p. 26. The reader should be warned that the term 'Near East' was a geographical expression without clear boundaries then as it is now.

12. Beers, p. 214.

13. 'Bristol Papers', box 13, folder 'Family Papers', Mark Bristol to Helen Moore Bristol, 5–6 January 1919; also cited in Buzanski, p. 28. Bristol's handwriting is very hard to read; therefore, for his handwritten letters to his wife I rely on Buzanski's transcription.

14. *Hearings. The United States Congress House. Committee on Appropriations: Naval Appropriation Bill, 1922, Sixty-Six Congress, Third Session* (Washington, DC: Government Printing Office, 1921), p. 16. Here are all US vessels in Turkish waters as of 1921: *Scorpion, St. Louis, Brooks, Fox, Humphreys, Overton, Sturtevant, Williamson, Kane*, C-96 and C-338; see 867.00/1443. Some other reports give a slightly different list of ships. Probably, some vessels temporarily came and left Turkish waters; cf. 867.00/1449.

15. Near East Relief was originally organised in the United States in 1915 as a response to US Ambassador to Istanbul Henry Morgenthau's request to render humanitarian assistance to Armenians and Assyrians, and was originally known as 'The American Committee for Syrian and Armenian Relief'. Its history can be read in <http://www.neareast.org/who-we-are> (last accessed 29 September 2020). For an example of its activities see US Congress, *Near East Relief: Report of the Near East Relief for the Year Ending December 31, 1923* (Washington, DC: Government Printing Office, 1924).

16. Beers, p. 212.

17. For example, by the end of 1923 the NER alone employed 166 American personnel in the Middle East. The largest task of the NER was the orphans. As of 1 December 1923, there were 60,092 orphans registered with the NER, which also evacuated 16,788 orphans to Greece and 5,312 of them to Syria. Many of these orphans came from Harput, Kayseri, Sivas and Merzifon and they were

transported to their destinations by means of donkeys, camels and carts; see *Report of the Near East Relief, 1923*, pp. 9, 18, 19. For a collection of reports, see also <https://archives.saltresearch.org/handle/123456789/43> (last accessed 28 September 2020).

18. Buzanski, p. 39. A British document confirmed his new title in a report on 30 August 1919; see National Archives of Great Britain, CAB/24/87.

19. Letter to the Minister of Foreign Affairs; the signature is not legible. President's Ottoman Archive (POA) HR. İM. 21/222. Unless otherwise indicated, all translations are mine.

20. 867.01/78, from Bristol to Secretary of State, 12 September 1921; emphasis added.

21. 867.01/78, from Robert Bliss to Bristol, 18 October 1921.

22. 867.01/77. At the bottom there are two initials, WDR/LVD. I assume these are the initials of the authors of this letter. The letter is dated 5 October 1921.

23. Buzanski, p. 31.

24. Ibid. p. 32.

25. 'Bristol Papers', box 13, folder 'Family Papers', Mark Bristol to Helen Moore Bristol, 5–6 January 1919; see Buzanski, p. 28.

26. As mentioned above, the vagueness of Bristol's appointment afforded him the opportunity to assume these duties; however, the obvious challenge, as far as his relations with the Turkish government were concerned, was that soon there emerged the alternative Ankara government to the imperial Istanbul one. This book will show how Bristol observed and graded the Ankara government and promoted it in establishing good relations with Ankara.

27. See also *United States Naval Institute Proceedings* 45.7 (July 1919): 1816.

28. Admiral W. S. Benson to Admiral Bristol, 7 May 1919, as cited in Buzanski, p. 36.

29. Admiral Bristol to Helen Bristol, 12 May 1919, as cited in Buzanski, p. 36.

30. Buzanski, p. 37.

31. Robert Bachman, 'The American Navy and the Turks', *Outlook*, 132 (September–December 1922): 288–9.

32. Editorial, 'Rear Admiral Mark L. Bristol: The President of American Peace Society', *World Affairs*, 101.2 (June 1938): 66.

33. Beers, p. 214.

34. Buzanski, p. 40.

35. Bachman, p. 289. This was also the view of Beers, p. 214.

36. Buzanski, p. 41.

37. Ibid. p. 49, n. 68.

38. Ibid. p. 41.

39. 867.00/1495, 'Memorandum for Mr. Robbins', 4 October 1921. Coming from a different intellectual and political background, Heath W. Lowry of Princeton University published an article that responds to character assassinations of Robert Dunn in Richard Hovannisian's work *The Republic of Armenia: From Versailles to London*, vol. 2 (Los Angeles and London: University of California Press, 1982). Lowry criticises Hovannisian for relying on Buzanski's statement to discredit Dunn's reports; see 'Richard G. Hovannisian on Lieutenant Robert Steed Dunn', *The Journal of Ottoman Studies*, 5 (1986): 209–52. Papers of Robert Dunn were housed in the Dartmouth College Library in containers; see <http://ead.dartmouth.edu/html/stem42.html> (last accessed 28 September 2020).

40. The same is true for the reports sent by US Ambassador Henry Morgenthau accusing Turks of massacring Armenians. Morgenthau was labelled as pro-Armenian or Turcophobe. This is equally problematic.

41. Hovannisian, p. 353, n. 109.

42. Dunn, himself, denied such rumours in his memoir: 'Moslem I could not be . . . For three years in Turkey I stuck to my agnostic guns, treated every race or belief alike'; *World Alive: A Personal Story* (New York: Crown Publisher, 1956), pp. 313–14.

43. Dinç Yaylalıer, 'American Perceptions of Turkey, 1919–1927', PhD dissertation, University of Utah, 1996, p. 8. Buzanski also defines the opponents and proponents of Bristol along similar lines: 'missionaries, relief workers, Armenians, Greeks took one approach; while businessmen, Turks, American residents in Turkey not associated either with relief or missionary societies held opposing views [on Bristol].' See Buzanski, p. 99.

44. Yaylalıer, p. 9.

45. Seçil Akgün, 'The Turkish Image in the Reports of American Missionaries', *The Turkish Studies Association Bulletin*, 13 (September 1989): 97.

46. 'Anatolia Deportee Here; Dr. Ruth Parmlee, Ousted by Kemalists, Says They Are All Corrupt', *New York Times*, 17 June 1922, p. 5.

47. Henry Morgenthau, *All in a Life-Time* (New York: Doubleday and Page, 1922), pp. 236, 275.

48. 'The Butchery of Christians in Asia Minor', *The Literary Digest*, 23 September 1922, pp. 34–5.

49. I have been unable to find any lead concerning the interaction of the two diplomats. If such a lead exists, I hope the future generation of scholars will be able to locate it.

50. She was a very significant figure in Bristol's relations with the nationalists in Ankara and was very forthcoming in challenging the misinformation spread in the US. Ms Allen died in 1922 and ABCFM, the Bursa station, issued a statement praising her service to the missions. This information is significant because she was also labelled as pro-Turk for her stance against misinformation. See <http://www.dlir.org/archive/orc-exhibit/items/show/collection/12/id/16655> (last accessed 28 September 2020).

51. 'Bristol Papers', box 16, 25 May 1919.

52. Heath Lowry, 'American Observers in Anatolia ca. 1920: The Bristol Papers', in Justin McCarthy et al., *Armenians in the Ottoman Empire and Modern Turkey (1912–1926)* (Istanbul: Bosphorus University, 1984), pp. 42–58; p. 42. See also 'Robert Dunn Papers', <http://ead.dartmouth.edu/html/stem42.html> (last accessed 28 September 2020); Selma Ekrem, *Unveiled: The Autobiography of a Turkish Girl* (New York, 1942); Roger R. Trask, 'The "Terrible Turk" and Turkish-American Relations in the Interwar Period', *The Historian*, 33 (1970): 40–53.

53. This well-known quotation is from a document in box 31 of 'The Bristol Papers', a letter dated 18 May 1919 from Bristol to Sims; see also Levon Marashlian, 'The Armenian Question from Sevres to Lausanne: Economics and Morality in American and British Policies, 1920–1923', PhD dissertation, UCLA, 1992, p. 108; Braisted, p. 344.

54. Buzanski, p. 174.

55. Ibid. p. 21.

56. Selma Ekrem was the granddaughter of Namık Kemal, the Young Ottoman playwright whose dramatic pleas to reform the empire prompted Sultan Abdulhamid II to exile him. See *Unveiled: The Autobiography of a Turkish Girl*, p. 302. The book was originally published in 1930 by Ives Washburn and the latest edition by First Gorgias Press (2005) is a facsimile reprint of the 1930 edition. See also Trask, 'The "Terrible Turk"' (Trask's reference can be found on pages 43 and 44); Thomas A. Bryson, 'Admiral Mark L. Bristol, an Open-Door Diplomat in Turkey', *International Journal of Middle East Studies*, 5.4 (1974): 450–67; George Horton, *The Blight of Asia* (Indianapolis: Bobbs-Merrill Company, 1926).

57. 867.00/1884, from Bristol to Secretary of State, 17 July 1925, 'War Diary'; emphasis added.

58. 'Bristol Papers', box 2, 'War Diary' dated 24 June 1920.

59. At the time, Allen Dulles was working for the Department of State; later he became the Director of the CIA.

60. 867.4016/596, 'Memorandum for the Secretary', 15 June 1922.
61. The same hospital is now known as the American Hospital. This hospital was originally established in Çarşıkapı, Istanbul, under the leadership of Bristol. After expanding and moving to Teşvikiye, in 1939 the hospital finally moved to its current location in Nişantaşı. In the Prime Minister's Republican archives, there is a document indicating that Bristol and his wife were invited to the opening ceremony. For the invitation to the ceremony, see 30-10-298-268-804-11; for a letter by Luther Fowle informing Prime Minister Refik Saydam of the death of Bristol and hence the fact only his wife would attend, see 30-01-5-22-9. The letter informs us that Bristol died in Johns Hopkins Hospital on 13 May 1939, but the hospital reopened on 14 October 1939.
62. 867.00/1802, Bristol to Secretary of State, dated 19 June 1924.
63. See Epilogue, 'The Rest of the Story', in *Ambassador Morgenthau's Story* (Detroit: Wayne State University Press, 2003), p. 303.
64. Ibid.
65. Ibid.
66. See Yaylalıer, pp. 20–3.
67. Bryson, p. 452.
68. Ibid. p. 453.
69. I made extensive use of Buzanski, chapter 6 to write this section. Unless otherwise indicated, I rely on his direct quotations for some US archival documents that I failed to locate. However, I have included the folder number for readers in case they have better luck locating them.
70. See Buzanski, chapter 4.
71. The US Secretary of State's letter on 29 June 1920 to Bristol about this complaint can be seen in 123.B773/18a, as cited in Buzanski, p. 206, n. 124.
72. Bristol to Secretary of State, 10 July 1920, 123.B773/19, as cited in Buzanski, p. 206, n. 125.
73. Memorandum attached to Bristol to Secretary of State, 10 July 1920, 123. B773/19, as cited in Buzanski, p. 206, n. 126.
74. Buzanski, p. 176. See also Horton.
75. Buzanski, p. 176.
76. Bristol to Edward C. Moore, 3 May 1920, 'Bristol Papers', as cited in Buzanski, p. 207, n. 132.
77. Bristol's 'War Diary' entry of 25 July 1921, 'Bristol Papers'. See also Buzanski, p. 178.
78. Buzanski, p. 207, n. 134; see also 'War Diary' entry of 24 June 1921, 'Bristol Papers'.

79. Bristol to Secretary of State, 22 June 1921, 860.J4016/76, as cited in Buzanski, p. 178.

80. See for example the argument by Levon Marashlian in his PhD dissertation (p. 95). Some authors went so far as to call Bristol a bigot 'whose chief motivation was to make the new Turkey a happy hunting ground for American business'; see the book review by James B. Gidney of Joseph L. Grabill, *Protestant Diplomacy and the Near East: Missionary Influence on American Policy, 1810–1927* (Minneapolis: University of Minnesota Press, 1971), in *The American Historical Review*, 77.3 (June 1972): 831–2. Gidney makes similar smearing labels for Bristol without presenting any argument in his several book reviews for other books which regard Bristol as 'even-handed'.

81. Bristol, 'War Diary' entry of 22 November 1921, 'Bristol Papers', as cited in Buzanski, p. 181.

82. 367.116/808, Secretary of State to James L. Barton, 18 February 1922, as cited in Buzanski, p. 181.

83. 123.B773/31, George R. Montgomery to Secretary of State, 6 January 1922; Buzanski, pp. 182–3.

84. 367.116/808, Secretary of State to James L. Barton, 18 February 1922, as cited in Buzanski, p. 183.

85. 367.116/815, James L. Barton to Secretary of State, 27 March 1922, as cited in Buzanski, p. 185. The ABCFM archives contain a letter indicating Barton's effort to lobby against Bristol's position in Constantinople as High Commissioner; see Barton to G. Montgomery, 19 December 1921, ABC 3.2, vol. 358, p. 543 (Haughton Library, Harvard University), as cited in Robert L. Daniel, *American Philanthropy in the Near East, 1820–1960* (Athens, OH: Ohio University Press, 1970), p. 166, n. 53.

86. 367.116/820, Bristol to Secretary of State, 9 May 1922, as cited in Buzanski, pp. 186–7.

87. Buzanski, p. 179.

88. Buzanski states that this complaint was registered by Sir Auckland Geddes, the British Ambassador to the US; however, there is not a reference for this claim. See Buzanski, pp. 188, 209, n. 160. We know that Lord Curzon was suspicious of the activities of Bristol; see *Documents on British Foreign Policy, 1919–1939* (London: Her Majesty's Stationery Office, 1972), p. 413, n. 3.

89. Dulles later became the head of the CIA (1953–61). However, in the 1920s, after his service in Turkey under Bristol, he was the chief of the Near East division in the Department of State.

90. 124.676/39a, Secretary of State to Bristol, 4 May 1922, as cited in Buzanski, p. 189. Buzanski (p. 209, n. 161) states that the essence of this letter was cabled to Constantinople on 5 May 1922, and the document in the US archives was numbered 124.676/39b.

91. We know that there was competition among the Allied High Commissioners in Constantinople to assume the leadership of the diplomatic corps in the city. Bristol vividly described it in his letter to the Secretary of State dated 12 September 1921, numbered 867.01/78.

92. Bristol to Allen W. Dulles, 24 May 1922, in 'Bristol Papers', as cited in Buzanski, p. 191.

93. We have a reference for this claim in the US National Archives. The complaint was registered by Robert Craigie, file number 133.B773 in Record Group 84 (Records of the Foreign Service Posts of the Department of State). This is cited in Braisted, p. 347.

94. Buzanski, p. 198.

95. 123.B773/97, Frank B. Kellogg (Secretary of State) to Secretary of the Navy (Curtis B. Wilbur), 4 May 1925, as cited in Braisted, p. 371, n. 76.

96. 867.00/1914; the letter was attached to the report sent to Washington dated 2 February 1926.

97. 867.00/1914; ibid.

98. 123.B773/147c, Secretary of State to High Commissioner in Turkey (Bristol), 19 March 1927.

99. Braisted, p. 348; telegram from StaNav (Bristol) to BuNav, 27 March 1927, Record Group 45, Naval Records Collection, WT File.

100. Bristol is very likely referring to Ali Sait Akbaytogan, who was one of the top generals in the republican regime.

101. 867.00/1971; Sheldon Crosby attached Bristol's last instalment of the 'War Diary' to a report and sent it to the Secretary of State on 9 June 1927.

102. Bristol received letters from the White House and the Secretary of the Navy confirming his appointment on 20 June 1927 and 28 June 1927 respectively, 'Bristol Papers', box 64.

103. Bernard D. Cole, *Gunboats and Marines: The United States Navy in China, 1925–1928* (Newark: University of Delaware Press, 1983), p. 145.

104. Reynolds, pp. 42–3.

105. Braisted has a rather informative section on this portion of Bristol's career in his article; see pp. 357–67.

106. Heck, pp. 158–9.

107. Among these, the most notable was the American Friends of Turkey. See Rıfat Bali, *The Saga of a Friendship: Asa Kent Jennings and the American Friends of Turkey* (Istanbul: Libra, 2010).
108. The Admiral Bristol Hospital in Istanbul also had a nursing school attached to it.
109. Mark Bristol to John Bristol, 'Bristol Papers', box 13, 1 April 1939.

3

THE COLLAPSE OF THE OTTOMAN EMPIRE
AND THE RISE OF TURKEY IN
US CONSULAR REPORTS

When Bristol arrived in Turkey, the US enjoyed a benevolent reputation. The fact that the US was not part of the Allies, which declared war on Turkey, participated in the secret wartime treaties and competed in positioning themselves to benefit most from the death of 'the Sick man of Europe', contributed greatly to the deposit of goodwill towards America in Turkey. According to Thomas A. Bryson, 'Bristol was careful to avoid pursuing any policy that would mar the American image in Turkey.'[1]

We do know that one of the main reasons for Bristol's appointment as a naval officer was to increase the naval presence in Turkish waters in case there was a need for a show of power to protect US interests, that is, missionaries and tradesmen, and to check other competing European powers for influence.[2] Bristol's initial appointment was as 'Senior United States Naval Officer Present, Turkey'. In this capacity, he was not able to send many reports to the State Department dealing specifically with political affairs in Turkey. Therefore, we see that the majority of reports describing the situation in the empire were sent by either Lewis Heck or Bie Ravndal, US commissioners in Istanbul. However, from the second half of 1919 onwards, we see that many of the diplomatic reports sent to Washington bear Bristol's signature as the sole author.

The reader should keep in mind that the year 1919 was critical for the future of the Ottoman Empire, which was waiting for the signing of a peace treaty with the victorious Allied Powers. When Bristol arrived, the empire was fighting for her survival, and the nationalist movement which culminated in the emergence of the Turkish Republic had not commenced as yet. As soon as Bristol arrived at Constantinople, he witnessed secret alliances, competing interests and speculations about the future of the Ottoman Empire among the Allies. Bristol learned, evaluated, judged and reported all these events to Washington. He never shied away from sharing his evaluations, conclusions and suggestions with the State Department. These US diplomatic reports in the period under review contain much information on how the US mission in Turkey perceived the collapsing Ottoman Empire and later its disposition towards the emerging Ankara government. The fate of the empire was the most pressing concern for the American government, and Bristol's earliest reports reveal his initial conclusions for its political future. This chapter will follow the evolution of Bristol's views on the Ottoman Empire and later the Turkish Republic.

Bristol dispatched many reports to his superiors detailing his views on the possible future of the Ottoman Empire at the Paris Peace Conference. In the capacity of Senior Naval Officer Present, Turkey, Bristol also shared his opinions with his superiors at the Navy's European Command. We know that Bristol reported to the Departments of State and the Navy. After arriving at the Ottoman Empire in the capacity of a naval officer, Bristol sent out his earliest observations to his superiors in the Department of the Navy. His initial comments regarded the division of the empire:

> Examination of the voluminous mass of documentary evidence in interviews with residents of various parts of Turkey and consideration of all political and religious viewpoints together with first-hand information personally gathered have compelled me to accept two definite conclusions. First, no Turkish government at present be permitted to exercise authority anywhere in Europe or Asia. Second, the region comprising the Turkish Empire both in Europe and Asia should not be divided into independent states at the present time.
>
> History of centuries, evidence of present chaotic conditions throughout Turkey, the recent stupid, barbarous, and unspeakable treatment of subjugated races all prove the soundness of the first conclusion. The various races of the Turkish Empire live hopelessly intermingled. The fact that they thus live in spite of race and religious differences proves conclusively [that] they are interdependent . . . Practically, any division of the territory into independent states, which

can be made at the present time, would place a minority of population inflamed by race hatred to the utmost degree in control of a majority . . . If the [Paris] Peace Conference is going to announce a division of Turkey, it is firmly believed that the complete armed occupation of Turkey should be accomplished before such announcement is made in order to prevent bloodshed and disorder.

The self-evident fact is that financing Turkey as a whole, likewise developing a complete system of railroads, telegraph lines, inland waterways, and harbor facilities and preventing commercial barriers by frontier lines must be the best plan.[3]

This report was prepared only two months after Bristol's arrival at Constantinople and showed a good grasp of the current situation on the ground. His disdain of the Ottoman administration is visible. 'If the Turkish [read Ottoman] rule is established again', stated Bristol, 'it will be the crime of this century. I suggest that if the United States is a party to such a decision, we are also a party to this crime. Also, if we remain silent and do not raise our voice against it, we will be a party to this crime.'[4]

Bristol clearly was bitter about the corrupt Ottoman administration, but he was equally resentful about the international politics revolving around the dying empire and its multi-ethnic, multi-religious citizens. We do know that around this time, Britain was forcing the US to take the Armenian mandate in the empire, and this issue was at the forefront of diplomatic exchanges. Bristol seems very well informed about the dynamics of multi-religious groups in the empire. He fiercely opposed the idea of the US accepting an Armenian mandate (see Chapter 4), instead favouring a US mandate on the entire Ottoman Empire. In his mind, if one outside power dictated decisions for the entire empire, it eliminated internal ethnic/religious competition aligning with a foreign power. Otherwise, rival groups within the empire would surely fight proxy wars. This prediction surely proved the admiral correct later in the Near East in relation to British and French mandates in Palestine and Syria.

It must be said from the outset that the US High Commissioner did not have much respect for the British policy towards the Ottoman Empire and the Near East. In a letter to the US Secretary of State, Bristol pressed the fact that the US was not showing much interest in this part of the world, and Great Britain would secure this area for her own economic interest:

I have gained the impression from the Department's dispatches and from the press of the United States that there is not a great deal of interest in the affairs of the Near East . . . However, I feel that the problems to be solved in the Near East are of much interest to the United States . . . If we do not now take an interest in this peace treaty and protect American rights, we will find, in the near future, that American trade will be shut out of this part of the world . . . I must call attention to the evident imperialistic tendencies of Great Britain, [which] is receiving large territories under the guise of mandatory for these territories . . . It is inconceivable that anyone who thinks of the past history of England is taking these territories under her protection in accordance with the principles of the League of Nations . . . It seems to me that the mass of people in the United States should have their eyes open to this expansion of the British Empire.[5]

The admiral was very open in his criticism of the British aims in the region. When discussing the mandate issue with the British general Richard Webb, Bristol pointed out that if the US accepted the mandate, it should be for the whole of the Ottoman Empire at the 1914 borders. Webb retorted by asking if these borders would include Mesopotamia and Palestine. Bristol responded, 'Yes.' Webb, in return, stated that English people would never yield Mesopotamia, which they had conquered in wars against the Ottomans. Upon hearing this, Bristol responded: 'You could never make the United States understand this because they had entered this war upon the principle that it was not a war of conquest, also that [British claims] for Mesopotamia would be considered by the United States simply a desire to monopolize the oil fields of Mesopotamia and South Kurdistan.'[6] Bristol was indeed very suspicious of the intentions of Great Britain and her allies. Of course, Great Britain was not satisfied with Bristol's non-conformist position and, as mentioned in Chapter 2, was happy to label him readily as 'pro-Turk' and hence a sympathiser of the 'enemy'.[7]

Soon after Bristol arrived in the Ottoman Empire, he witnessed many foreign intrigues. Bristol thought secret plots and agreements to be dishonest and distasteful. As an example of British conspiracies, one lesser-known plot dealing with the internal affairs of the empire can be mentioned. A US document numbered 867.00/972, and dated 28 October 1919, relays an intercepted intelligence to both the State Department and the US Navy. Bristol reports that the British officials contacted Sultan Vahdettin, the last Sultan of the empire, for his blessing of a plot to stop the nationalist movement led by Mustafa Kemal and his friends. Bristol sent the following brief note: 'Received conclusive evidence associated closely with the British officials carrying an intrigue [to] overthrow Turkish new Nationalist movement to extent bribery *cause disturbances* [original emphasis] and giving pretext [to] allied interference with result secret treaty with Sultan to be placed before Peace Conference . . . There are rumors not approved on account of the Sultan.'[8]

The grammar of the text indicates that the report was probably a telegram. Bristol grades this intelligence as reliable and reports that Vahdettin did not give such consent. The plot did not take place, but this report indicates that one of the first things that Bristol witnessed in Constantinople was how Great Britain was behaving to bypass the limits of being fair. Therefore, it is not surprising that Bristol watched every move of the British in Istanbul with suspicion.

Bristol's analysis of the British intentions for the peace treaty to be signed after World War I was spot on:

> [Bristol stated that England, at the Lausanne Peace Conference], is doing everything in her power to provide a peace that will give her the lion's share of the spoils of Turkey and leave the other people to shift for themselves. Such a peace is not based on humanity. It is needless to blind oneself to the fact that England is working for simply imperialism and commercial advantage . . . There is no doubt that the oilfields of Mesopotamia and Kurdistan are some of the richest in the world. There is no doubt that she is taking steps to monopolize these oil fields against all comers. If she is able to carry out her plans, with control of oil fields of Java, Borneo, Burma and her large interest in America, both North, and South America, England will control the oil supply of the world, and in a few years, America will have to ask England for oil . . . Now, it is time for America and England to come to an understanding. It is absolutely essential for the future peace of the world that this understanding is brought about. There can be no understanding between England and the United States until such time as England is willing to admit that the United States is no longer a provincial [power] and, likewise, admits America as equal in all respects.[9]

Throughout 1920, Bristol sent many similar reports to the State Department, warning them about the British policies in Turkey. In another report on 23 November 1920, Bristol repeated his claim against the British designs:

It would seem that England's policy here in the Near East has been one of opportunism, by taking up with one scheme after another as any scheme appears to have some chance of success. It remains to be seen if she finally picks a winning horse. Based on the principle of 'Right will always prevail,' and the fact that the policy that England is pursuing in this part of the world is not right, I believe that England will fail in the end to monopolize political control of this part of the world and commercial domination.[10]

Needless to say, Bristol predicted England's failure to dominate Turkey. British authorities were aware of Bristol's view of them and were always suspicious of Bristol's influence on the developments in the region, especially during the Lausanne Conference in 1922–3. A short anecdote should explain this point. Joseph Grew, US Minister to Switzerland, one of the US delegates in Lausanne and later the first US Ambassador to Turkey (1927–32), wrote the following in his memoirs. Lord Curzon, during the Lausanne Conference, 'is fearful of Bristol's influence on a delicate situation. In his English way, he said, "You have a—er-er an Admiral Bristol joining you I believe." [Richard] Child replied: Lord Curzon, we not only have *an* Admiral Bristol joining us; we have *the* Admiral Bristol joining us.'[11]

As for his views on France, Bristol states that after seeing how they operate in Constantinople, his admiration for the French nation was very much impaired. 'I am beginning to fear', stated Bristol, 'that they are playing politics first, last and always, and doing it are making some very bad mistakes.'[12] Bristol's suspicion of the Allied operations in Constantinople forced him not to rely on information he received from his Allied High Commissioner colleagues. He therefore relied heavily on his own intelligence network. Let us look at how Bristol viewed the collapsing Ottoman Empire and the rising nationalist/Kemalist movement in Anatolia.

Views on the Collapsing Empire

In one of the earliest reports that Bristol sent to Washington, he described the situation as the following:

Turkey [Ottoman Empire] is politically, financially, morally bankrupt; and that on account of the problematical future of the country there is an imminent danger [of] social disorder and anarchy. The situation is likely to create international complications, which would be most unfortunate just at the close of the war . . . Only adequate way to forestall on such danger is a speedy appointment of strong mandatory power with full authority to establish just and stable government and to lay foundations [of] national prosperity and independence.[13]

In his early days in Constantinople, Admiral Mark Bristol educated himself with reports prepared by embassy staff on the Ottoman Empire. Before he relayed these reports to Washington, he would grade the reliability of the information gathered. For example, a report numbered 867.00/364, prepared on 14 August 1919, described the situation in the Ottoman Empire and the possibility of the Ottoman government collapsing due to pressure from the Kemalists in Anatolia. The report is sent from Constantinople to the American Embassy in Paris by Bie Ravndal, a political officer in the embassy:

> Things Turkish seem to be reaching a crisis. All of Anatolia not occupied by the Allied troops appears in open rebellion against the government . . . The government's authority is confined to a limited sphere around Constantinople . . . The position of the Cabinet seems untenable, but if Damat Ferid Pasha resigns, he will probably be replaced by Damat Tewfick . . . Ultimately, it is not unlikely that the question of the Sultan's abdication may be raised by Mustafa Kemal's partisans in favor of the Crown Prince, who is preferred by so-called intellectuals who furnish the brains to the insurgent movement. The Allied commanders here may soon find themselves in the very difficult position of having to defend the government, which is discredited by its own people . . . Last Monday evening in a political party meeting, a few hotheads advocated the proclamation of a republic, but they were promptly arrested.[14]

Bristol was in total agreement with this assessment. There are several significant points we can extract from this letter. We do know that this report was prepared only three months after the occupation of Smyrna and the commencement of what is later known as the Turkish War of Independence with Mustafa Kemal's landing of Samsun to organise the fragmented local rebellions in Anatolia. It is also clear that the Istanbul government was quite helpless, and its authority did not extend beyond the borders of the Ottoman capital. Grand Vizier Damat Ferid Pasha's resignation was expected, and his replacement was believed to be Tevfik Pasha. These predictions proved to be correct. It is also worth noting that the report entertained the idea that

Mustafa Kemal's supporters could pressure the Sultan for the abdication of the throne. We do know that the Sultan did not abdicate but escaped from Istanbul. In a letter to the US president several years later, Vahdettin claimed that he did not escape but temporarily left his throne. Perhaps there were direct and indirect attempts by the Kemalists to pressure the Sultan to escape. In fact, two days after Sultan Vahdettin did escape Istanbul on 17 November 1922, Bristol informed Washington: 'Departure of Sultan has caused little or no excitement here. The local press treats it as an escape of an individual traitor and considers it good riddance. The attitude of the Angora Government not yet known.'[15]

Another very significant point mentioned in the report is that as early as 1919, there were unspecified groups in Constantinople to discuss the idea of a regime change to a republic. In sum, this report indicates the disarray of the Ottoman government waiting for a peace treaty. The High Commissioner believed that the Ottoman government should not remain in power, and the empire as a whole should be put under a US mandate. Before the nationalists controlled the power entirely, Bristol advocated the following policy regarding the Ottoman Empire. In a memorandum dated 25 April 1920 to C. Vaught Engert, Assistant High Commissioner in Constantinople, Admiral Mark Lambert Bristol very clearly, and in detail, describes his views on the subject:

> I have been on duty in Turkey as Senior Representative and High Commissioner since 28 January 1919. The policy that I have continually advocated has been:
> a) The non-partition of the old Turkish Empire as it existed in 1914.
> b) The abolition of the old Turkish administration over this Empire.
> c) The taking of such steps that would prevent, once and for all, and forever, the re-establishment of the old Turkish Administration over this Empire or any part of this Empire, or any part of the world.
> d) That one strong power should be placed over the whole of the old Ottoman Empire to establish good government.
> e) That all the people of the old Ottoman Empire should be given universal education, and especially vocational training, and be taught one language in addition to the language that the various races speak.
> f) At some future date, when a majority of the people are able to write and read and understand what they are voting for, that they be given

self-determination as regards the formation of autonomous governments in the respective states thus formed.

g) That absolute freedom of religious worship be guaranteed and, as soon as
possible, the separation of church from state. (This latter is a very difficult
proposition, but is absolutely essential to good government in this part of
the world.)

There is no part of the Turkish Empire, except certain parts of Arabia,
where the Arab tribes occupy the country, where there is a majority of any
race in any given territory so that that territory could be set apart as a nation
of that particular race. All figures and statistics by different races are fraudu-
lent or incorrect, and their arguments, based on such statistics, are, therefore,
false.[16]

Bristol's view on many subjects related to the future of the Ottoman Empire
evolved over time; however, he always advocated the removal of the Ottoman
government from power and that it should not be established in the current
form ever again. The admiral was a very quick learner and a keen observer,
qualities that allowed him to arrive at sound conclusions on the inner dynamics
of the Middle East. There is no indication that Bristol came to Constantinople
with any prior diplomatic training, or that he possessed a strong bias that he
later struggled to change in facing the realities on the ground. On the contrary, he advocated those Americans who came to Turkey to strip their prejudices based on their exposure to the anti-Turkish propaganda prevalent among
the American public. However, he soon developed a distaste for the Ottoman
administration, which he deemed corrupt. He did not separate the Muslims
from the non-Muslim subjects of the Ottoman Empire. He regarded all of
them as possessing similar characteristic traits due to the corrupt Ottoman
system and the very low education level of the Ottoman population. Bristol
observed:

> In the old Ottoman Empire, there are about 25,000,000 people, of which
> not over 5% are literate. Of the total population, not over 5,000,000 are
> non-Moslem (it must not be forgotten that some of the Anatolian Greeks
> have become Mohammedans). Of this total of the population, all have suf-
> fered from the vile administration of law and government by the Turkish
> rule. They are all ruled by small minorities of corrupt politicians and cor-
> rupt priests. The whole is suffering from the combination of church and

state, in which the church is probably as corrupt as it was at any time in the Dark Ages. The big idea would be to take this whole country and give these 25,000,000 people the benefits of modern civilization.[17]

By church, Bristol means the religious establishment in the Ottoman Empire. As is clear, he does not separate any religion. This quotation is in line with his other evaluations of the Ottoman administration, which he deemed 'corrupt'.

As mentioned elsewhere, the year 1919 was a period of confusion on many grounds, least of which, for the US, was the understanding of the nationalist/Kemalist movement in Anatolia. It was clear that the Ottoman Empire had been very sick for a long time. Would it survive the defeat of World War I with a modified administrative structure? What was the aim of the nationalist uprising; was it to secure the empire with a different adminis-tration, or to replace it? How should the US position herself towards the new and more popular Kemalist movement? The reader should understand that in 1919 and 1920, the answers to these questions were far from certain. Bristol, a military man himself, was very closely following the rise of the nationalist movement in Anatolia.

Early American Contacts with the Nationalists

The US had certain advantages in keeping a link with the nationalists through non-governmental agents to avoid direct contact with the Kemalist movement. It is clear, however, that the nationalist uprising in Anatolia commanded close attention, and among the Allied High Commissioners, Bristol was the first to draw close and somewhat sympathetic attention to them. Therefore, it should not be a surprise that an American journalist was present at the first congress of the nationalists in Sivas (4–11 September 1919). The *Chicago Daily News* reporter Edgar Browne was first in Istanbul in the summer of 1919. We do know from his private papers that Charles Crane of the King-Crane Commis-sion had suggested he go to Sivas to observe at first hand the work of the Nation-alist Congress and to dispatch any resolutions of that body to Paris, where the Peace Conference was then in session. Crane indicated that American officials would be eager to have unbiased information about the extent of the power of the Kemalists.[18] Browne met many nationalists, including Refet [Bele] and Rauf [Orbay], and recorded their views of the current situation and the nationalist aims. On 25 August 1919, Browne telegrammed Crane that the people of Anatolia and the military were against the Istanbul government, not necessarily the Sultan himself, and he heard the word 'revolution' in many conversations. He also observed that unless the Greek occupation lifted in Smyrna, the nationalists were ready to fight to the death. Browne also informed Crane: 'Everyone showed utmost friendliness for the United States and American assistance in the form of a mandate will be most acceptable.'[19]

The US mandate of Armenia occupied most of the 1919 and 1920 diplomatic correspondence. As it is known, Woodrow Wilson sent two commissions, the King-Crane and Harbord, to the Ottoman territories to collect information. Since there are ample publications on this subject,[20] I will very briefly restate that Bristol was against the US mandate in Armenia; he supported the mandate for as long as it comprised the entire Ottoman land in the 1914 borders. The following statement should suffice to summarise his points:

> the old Ottoman Empire should not be partitioned, but should be united under one mandatory and . . . the Turkish rule should be abolished for all races . . . [Bristol pointed out that] If the Peace Conference is going to announce a division of Turkey, it is firmly believed that complete armed occupation of Turkey should be accomplished before such an announcement is made in order to prevent bloodshed by disorder . . . However, if it is decided to partition the country, I urge that military forces occupy Turkey so to protect the minority.[21]

As early as 1920, Admiral Bristol was convinced that the nationalists in Anatolia would be a force to be reckoned with. He advised the State Department that Kemalists were 'as near a nationalist movement as anything could be in Turkey and that this movement must be considered seriously'.[22] His curiosity is reflected in the reports he sent to Washington. He wished to learn as much as possible about the intent and strength of the movement. He immediately got acquainted with the power struggle between the nationalists in Anatolia and the Istanbul government. Although his distaste of the Istanbul government was very visible in his earlier reports, the High Commissioner remained neutral in his dealings with the royal government in Istanbul and the nationalists in Ankara. He continued to be friendly but non-committal to both groups at the beginning of his tenure. Nevertheless, soon after, probably partly because of his military background and partly because of his distaste for the corrupt Ottoman administration, Bristol sympathised with the nationalist leaders. Buzanski is correct when he states: 'Bristol was in a better position to assess and evaluate the successes and failures of the revolutionary organization [the nationalists], while the Allies, definitely committed to the Sultan's government, tended to underestimate Kemal and his followers.'[23] To achieve his aim, Bristol collected as much information as possible on the nationalists through his resources, among whom an American missionary, Annie Allen, was quite significant. She was born in Harput in 1868 as a child of two missionaries. After completing her college education in the US, she returned to Turkey and worked for the NER. Allen was fluent in Turkish and enjoyed a great rapport with the nationalists in Anatolia. We know that she had interviewed Mustafa Kemal during her visit to Ankara between 9 and 14 April 1920 and relayed the information to Bristol.[24] Allen was the only American residing in Ankara during the early days of the nationalist government, and accordingly, she served not only as the representative of the 'American Near East Relief in Anatolia', but also as 'an unofficial delegate of the American High Commission at Constantinople'.[25] Heath Lowry claims that Annie Allen's visit to Ankara 'marks the real beginning of a de facto American recognition of the Nationalist Movement'.[26] Although this statement seems a bit of an exaggeration, for Bristol had already been exchanging information with Ankara by other means, Allen's reports were certainly one of the most significant sources for Bristol in forming his opinion about the nationalists. Annie Allen's so-called 'shuttle diplomacy' served not only the American interests but those of the nationalists as well. For the nationalists in Ankara, this proved to be a useful backchannel to be unofficially recognised as a legitimate force by a Western Power.

Another person who functioned as a conduit for information from Mustafa Kemal to Bristol was Halide Edip (Adıvar), a well-known member of the nationalist circle in Ankara who spoke English well. Halide Edip was an alternative bridge between the admiral and the nationalists. In other words, as an intelligent woman, she was the window for the nationalists opening towards the US, which surely countered some gender-based biases against the Turks among Americans. Halide Edip was also in contact with American journalists who were in Anatolia. For example, Paul Williams of the *Chicago Tribune* exchanged much information with Halide Edip, who shared a written summary of current developments in Anatolia and asked the journalist to relay the information to the admiral, as it might be of interest to him. Such indirect contact with Bristol through American journalists seems to be one of Halide Edip's strategies.[27]

Clarence K. Streit of the *Philadelphia Public Ledger* was another American journalist active in Anatolia in 1921. During his stay, Streit came into contact with nationalists and gained an insight into the nature of the nationalist cause. He claimed that the Ankara government trusted the United States much more than it did other European powers and argued: 'The Turks not only want an Open Door maintained, but they want to trade with us especially.'[28] Streit went as far as suggesting that at least de facto recognition should be granted to the nationalists. In his manuscript, after challenging the anti-Turkish biases, Streit remarked, 'I had come to Turkey prejudiced against the Turks. I left it like so many others who have come to know the Turks by living with them, their friend and sympathizer.'[29]

The journalists coming to Anatolia were a very useful tool for Bristol to tell the other side of the story in the US, which was his main aim: educating the American public and hence American policy-makers. There are a number of American journalists who served this purpose, such as Paul Williams from the *Chicago Tribune*, who was the first American correspondent to hold an extensive interview with Mustafa Kemal in Ankara.[30]

American High Commissioner Mark Lambert Bristol was surely in a much better position to receive information about and to analyse the rising Kemalist/nationalist movement compared to his Allied counterparts. While the British officials were judging the nationalists as a small, revolutionary movement made up of outlaws, Bristol knew, thanks to the reports he received from many capable men and women in contact with the nationalists, that theirs was indeed a quite well organised and disciplined uprising. The nationalist movement, concluded Bristol in 1919, 'is the best thing that has taken place since I have been out here . . . There are some good men at the head of this movement, and the present cabinet is not bad.'[31] This opinion of the nationalists would not change during his tenure in Turkey despite the fact that Bristol would later have his share of disagreements with the Kemalists. He was right on target when he predicted that nationalists would take up guerrilla warfare and offer stiff resistance that might last for years.[32] By 1920, Bristol was fully convinced that the government in Constantinople was a puppet one, installed by the Allies, and its power could not extend beyond the city, if there. On 28 March 1920, Bristol wrote to his superior, Admiral Knapp, in the Navy that the nationalist forces represented the whole of the Turkish people and even most Muslims in this part of the world.[33]

Although Bristol was aware of the potential for the nationalists to replace the Istanbul government, he was also on good terms with the Sultan and his representatives. In 1921, we see that the Istanbul government also was attempting to reach out to the Americans. The Istanbul government was testing the waters with the American High Commissioner in terms of normalising the relations. Admiral Bristol recorded an informal meeting with a certain Blacque Bey, who came to the admiral's office to unofficially discuss the issue of sending Ottoman representation to Washington. The conversation took place on 27 January 1921 and is recorded in the admiral's 'War Diary':

> During the forenoon, I received a call from Blacque Bey. He belongs to the Turkish Diplomatic Service, in which he served for 23 years . . . He came and said, in a private and confidential manner, to inform me that the Council of State had decided to send him to the United States to represent the Turkish Government . . . It was the intention of the Council to ask the United States to allow the Turkish government to send a representative to Washington as a delegate, without any diplomatic status, to represent the Turkish government informally, and at the same time to apply for a resumption of diplomatic relations. If diplomatic relations were re-established, Blacque Bey would then become the Ambassador . . . Blacque Bey requested my ideas on this subject. I told him I could not say anything for my Government because I have no instructions on this subject. Personally, it was my opinion that any steps towards the resumption of diplomatic relations would have to come from the Turkish Government because that Government had originally broken diplomatic relations . . . I told him that personally, I thought there was a chance that the United States would consent to the arrangement proposed. At any rate, the question could be approached informally and thus avoid a direct refusal on the part of our Government.[34]

Richard Edward Blacque Bey was the son of an Ottoman diplomat, Edouard Blacque, who served as a representative in Washington for six years from 23 August 1867 to 4 August 1873, as the first Ottoman ambassador to the United States.[35] We do know that Richard Blacque Bey followed in his father's footsteps and remained in the Ottoman diplomatic corps, serving in several European capitals. However, he left Turkey after the nationalist victory in 1923 and died in the United States in 1927.[36] Clearly, the Ottoman government was using a well-known family member to create a rapprochement with the American government. However, such an attempt proved to be futile with the success of the Kemalists and the rise of the Ankara government.[37]

Another attempt to reach out to the Americans came the very next day. Bristol records another interesting conversation with a representative of the Istanbul government:

> In the forenoon, Sefa Bey, the Turkish Minister of Foreign Affairs, called with one Roth Bey [who was his translator] . . . The main subject was the question of obtaining American business interest in certain property belonging to the Sultan's Civil List [i.e. Sultan's private property]. The idea was that some American companies would take up this property and develop it under an arrangement for dividing profits, and in the end, the property would revert to the Civil List . . . I assured Sefa Bey that if he would send me a description of the property and of the proposition, I would see what I could do to get American interest to take up the proposition.[38]

No further information can be found in Bristol's diary. We do not know the details of the Sultan's property which he wished to contract out to the American companies. Nor do we know if Bristol acted upon the proposal. What is clear, however, is that the Istanbul government's attempts to further her interaction with American business and government did not materialise.

Interestingly enough, we see that the Ankara group was also trying to convince the Americans to recognise the nationalists as the sole authority for concessions and hence official recognition. In a sense, the Ankara government was competing against that of Istanbul in seeking an alliance with the United States. The nationalists came to Bristol with their own proposals for cooperation. They were as aware of the US business interests in Turkey as the Istanbul government. Therefore, any proposal they prepared, nationalists knew, must include the business interactions as it was the soft belly of the American foreign policy. Bristol recorded an interesting conversation with the representatives of the Ankara government on 28 July 1921:

In the afternoon Hussein Bey, professor at Robert College, called accompanied by Emin Bey and Suphi Bey. The two latter claim to be representatives from the Angora Government, Emin Bey has been here before . . .

They stated that they had several projects in which they desired American capital to become interested. They thought this was the proper time to negotiate before the French and the other Allies who were pressing for these concessions got in ahead of the Americans. They wanted the Americans because they felt that America has no political aspirations, whereas the European Allies have not only commercial aspirations but political aspirations also. They gave me a list of the projects they wanted to consider. There were seven, as follows: 1) railways; 2) mining; 3) forestry; 4) shipping (Black Sea trade); 5) agricultural implements; 6) banks; 7) factories. I suggested that there should be [an 8th one]-, schools. I then went on to point out that education was essential to the future development of the country. I told them that I was greatly interested in developing schools that would take up the work along broad lines of education of all the Ottoman subjects of Turkey without any regard to race or religion and to make these schools ordinary schools that would teach the simple branches and at the same time give vocational training to cover the various projects suggested by Emin Bey and Suphi Bey. They stressed a desire to meet any Americans to consider these projects and also the question of education. They thanked me for my interest in their suggestions.[39]

Until 1921, Bristol seems to deal with the Ankara government mostly indirectly through intermediaries. However, when we come to 1922, especially after the nationalist victory over the Greek forces, the American officials had little doubt that Ankara had superseded the Istanbul government and the nationalists needed to be directly communicated with. In this spirit, one of the most pressing concerns of the US administration and the anti-Turkish lobbies was the protection of the Greek population in Anatolia. In return, Ankara found an Allied Power to which the protests would be directed in the person of Admiral Mark Lambert Bristol. On 31 August 1922, Hüseyin Rauf Bey [Orbay], then the President of the Turkish Council of Ministers, registered his protest on the scorched earth policy of the withdrawing Greek army in Western Anatolia, stating, 'It is clear that the Greek Army has decided to burn the whole occupied country and exterminate systematically the whole civil population.'[40]

Bristol's response was bittersweet in tone but, regardless, in full realisation and confirmation of the nationalist authority as the new regime in Turkey. He stated:

> I take this occasion in a spirit of personal friendship and with the most disin-
> terested of motives to call your attention to the fact that the eyes of the world
> and especially of the people of the United States are turned upon the struggle,
> which is taking place at the present time in Asia Minor. I am convinced that
> this is the greatest opportunity that Turkey has had to show the world that *a*
> *new regime has been established and is successfully maintaining the highest prin-*
> *ciples of civilization and humanity*, and that the members of the Government
> at Angora are statesmen in whom not only the minorities living within the
> boundaries of Turkey, but the entire world can have confidence. I venture
> to call your attention to the fact that the present time is a crucial one in the
> history of the Nationalist Movement and of Turkey; that the public opinion
> of the world is hanging on a balance and will be swayed one way or the other
> according to the attitude of the combatants in the present struggle be they
> Greek or Turk. At the present moment, the Turkish forces, as is only natural,
> are elated at the victories recently achieved over their opponents. I trust you
> will not take it amiss, therefore, if I venture to impress upon you as earnestly
> as is within my power to do the expediency of the Turkish High Command
> taking the most energetic steps to ensure the populations of the occupied
> territories against reprisals which are often the saddest and most regrettable
> part of a war, and which, if carried out in the present instance by the Turkish
> forces would serve to antagonize the public opinion of the world, and would
> give the opponents of Turkey an opportunity of starting propaganda which
> could not fail very seriously to impair the cordial relations which we all hope
> to see established in the future between Turkey and the rest of the world, and
> which would seriously diminish the influence and prestige of the persons in
> the Angora Government who are responsible for the actions of the armed
> forces.[41]

This message to Rauf Bey is a clear indication that at a diplomatic level, the US not only recognised the Ankara government as legitimate but also confirmed the regime change. The tone of the communication reflects a veiled threat to the new government about the treatment of the Christian minorities under Ankara's control. After the 1919 occupation of Smyrna, the main theme in the diplomatic correspondence between Bristol and Washington and the Turkish governments appears to be the protection of the minorities in Turkey. The pressure on the US government to use the protection issue as a club to beat the Istanbul and later the Ankara governments comes mainly from the Christian lobbying activities in the US, and also from Great Britain to politicise the issue to gain traction against her own dealings with the Turks. Therefore, Bristol was constantly asked to share the American government's worry about the Greek and Armenian minorities of the Ottoman Empire. In 1922, when the Greek forces in Anatolia were soundly defeated and the Turks recaptured Smyrna, the worry became greater.

The following communication between Bristol and the Secretary of State, Charles Evans Hughes, represents the US government's interest in the subject. Secretary Hughes telegrammed eight questions to Bristol and asked him to reply promptly and fully.

1. Has any exodus of Christian populations of Constantinople begun?
2. Do you consider that the Christian population in Constantinople would be safe after the reoccupation of the city by the Turks?
3. What guarantees do you think could be obtained from the Turks, which would render their situation more secure?
4. What is your estimate of the number of the Christian minorities at present in the territory in Anatolia under Turkish occupation?
5. What is your estimate of the present population of eastern Thrace, exclusive of Constantinople, the proportion of Christians, and the number of persons who will leave this territory previous to re-occupation by Turkey?
6. Department has now received mail reports through you, Consul General Horton, and Vice-Consul Barnes regarding the Smyrna fire. It appears that three American citizens lost their lives, that American relief workers were robbed and threatened, that American sailors guarding the International College were attacked. What action, if any, was taken by American representatives in Smyrna to protest to Turkish authorities against such acts and to prevent their recurrence?
7. Press reports indicate that at one moment during the Smyrna fire, British naval forces warned the Turkish authorities in the city that if killings continued, the Turkish quarters would be bombarded. Is this correct, and if so, what attitude was taken by American naval forces present?

8. Was any American protest made to Turkish authorities in Smyrna against the indiscriminate killing of Armenians and apparent systematic terrorization of Greek refugees during and subsequent to? Report fully and promptly.[42]

Bristol replied four days later:

1. Impossible to estimate, number of departures from Constantinople but probably in the neighborhood of 10,000. Departures are continuing but up to this time, this cannot be characterized as a general exodus of the Christian population . . .
2. I am inclined to believe that the Christian population of Constantinople as a whole would be safe excepting for those Ottoman Greeks and Armenians considered by the Turks as traitors on account of having aided the Greeks or Allies since the armistice. At the same time, there is certainly a danger of reprisals being instituted by the Turks in case overt acts are committed by the local population, which might serve to stir up racial animosity. Undoubtedly all races would take advantage of any confusion to pay off old scores and take reprisals. See reports [by Inter-Allied Commission of Inquiry on the Greek Occupation] of recent Greek troops and civilians devastating Anatolia and committing outrages also Turkish outrages in Smyrna . . . It is also possible that a heterogeneous population of Constantinople might [result?] in looting and burning city, especially Christian races, if deciding to leave, might burn their own property to prevent its falling into the hands of the Turks. Population estimated 400,000 Turks, 150,000 other Moslems, 400,000 Greeks, 140,000 Armenians, and 100,000 Jews, Europeans, and others.
3. In my opinion, only effective guarantees would involve total exclusion of Turkish troops from the city either for occupation purposes or victory celebrations and the continued occupation by strong foreign police during the transition period. I believe the distinction should be drawn between actual guarantees and either verbal or written promises. Undoubtedly strong promises not to molest the Christian population could be secured similar to that of Refet Pasha mentioned above.
4. Estimate, making allowances for massacres during the Great War and recent exodus due to the Greek collapse gives about 1,350,000 Christians at present in Anatolia under Turkish occupation. The total population of

Anatolia about 11,000,000. This estimate, while probably more accurate than that regarding Eastern Thrace, is still unreliable.

5. Extremely difficult to estimate the population of Eastern Thrace because, since 1912, there have been successive military occupations in that district due to the Balkan wars as well as Great War with consequent migrations. Closest estimate before present exodus appears to give about 400,000 Turks, 250,000 Greeks, and 50,000 Bulgarians, Armenians, et cetera. Reliable reports received to the effect that approximately 250,000 Christians have already left Eastern Thrace since signing the Moudania Convention. This estimate includes about 40,000 refugees who have arrived from Brousa and other places [in] Anatolia.[43]

In regard to the question of the killings of American citizens of Ottoman origin, Bristol explained the incidents briefly and reported that the issue was immediately raised and increased Turkish guards promptly obtained for the American citizens of Smyrna. For Hughes's question number seven, Bristol indicated that there was no foundation to the report that Great Britain threatened the Turks against the killings of the Christians in Smyrna. As for the question regarding the killings of Armenians and Greeks in the city, Bristol stated that after the burning of Smyrna, disorders happened, and Turkish authorities were warned. As a result, 'All such representations were cordially received, and all requests for the guard on American property were promptly granted and efficiently executed; however, no determined effort was made by the Turkish military authorities to protect refugees or suppress disturbances, especially in the Armenian district.'[44]

Bristol's gradual influence on American foreign policy can be seen in public speeches made by US government officials. While until 1922 it would be hard to find any statements regarding the suffering of the Muslim population, in that year we see some references to the issue, thanks to the Bristol reports. In a speech, for example, on 30 October 1922 in Boston, the US Secretary of State made the following statement:

The Christian world has been filled with horror at the atrocities committed [in] Anatolia, especially in connection with the burning of Smyrna, rivaled only by the wholesale massacres and deportations of the Armenians in 1915.

While nothing can excuse in the slightest degree or palliate the acts of bar-baric cruelty of the Turks, no just appraisement can be made of the situation which fails to take account of the incursion of the Greek army into Anatolia, of the war there waged, and of the terrible incidents of the retreat of that army, in the burning of towns, and general devastation and cruelties. Anatolia in war has been the scene of savagery.[45]

In this entry, the savagery of the Turks was still mentioned; however, what is noteworthy is that they were also portrayed as victims. For an American politician to mention this in a speech is significant, for we know that the American public at the time had very little tolerance for the Turks. This subtle but significant change in tone in public declarations by America's top diplomat owes its emergence to the reports filed by Bristol.

Constantinople's transfer of power to the nationalist government in Ankara obviously caused great concern for the Western governments. In the diplomatic reports, this consternation was rather easy to follow. One of the fears was that Constantinople would turn into a second Smyrna, burned, looted and subject to conspiracy. The diplomatic correspondence of 1922 was dominated by this fear.

In these reports, we also see a great effort by the British diplomats to influence the American government to take military action against the national-ists. A memorandum by Secretary Hughes to British Ambassador Geddes spells out such pressure and the US refusal to comply with the request. After a lengthy meeting with Ambassador Geddes, who requested military commit-ment of the US in case needed, Secretary Hughes stated that

while our military forces [in Turkey] were small, this country [the USA] still had its great capacity for the military endeavor and could within a short time equip a force to meet any situation, and that generally, it would do more than it promised to do, but that it required the determination of the American people expressed through the Congress to accomplish these results and *the Executive at this time could not make a pledge of military cooperation in such a war*.[46]

The lack of interest in acting together with the government of Great Britain was also visible in the matter of the upcoming peace conference. Bristol was also instrumental in influencing his government to sign a separate peace treaty with Turkey. On 5 October 1922, just a month and a half before the Lausanne deliberations, Bristol suggested to his Secretary of State that 'the only other plan I can suggest is to negotiate a separate agreement with Turkey as soon as the Government at Constantinople and the Nationalists get together, and we can deal with a central authority. It will be exceedingly difficult for us to carry on these negotiations as we will be faced by Turks flushed with recent military and possibly diplomatic victory, and we will have but little means of bargaining.'[47]

Clearly, Bristol did not wish to act together with other Allied governments. It also seems that he was still considering the possibility of a rapprochement between Istanbul and Ankara. Yet, we do know that when the Lausanne Conference opened on 20 November 1922, there was no representation from the Sultan's government.

Lausanne Negotiations

The Lausanne Conference in 1922–3 was the official beginning of treaty negotiations between the US and the new regime in Turkey. This was the final confirmation of the fact that the US recognised the Ankara government over the remnants of the defunct Istanbul one. We know that the original invitation to the conference also included the Istanbul government; however, three weeks before the opening of the conference, on 1 November 1922, the Ankara government abolished the office of the Sultanate, which resulted in the last Ottoman Sultan's escape from Constantinople on the British battleship HMS *Malaya* on 17 November 1922. Therefore, during the negotiations, it was clear that there was no more government in Istanbul. This development pre-empted the British aim of dividing the Turkish side.

Bristol was always suspicious of Britain's good faith in motivation and negotiations for peace. He had long been warning the State Department that the US should cut her own umbilical cord and negotiate a separate peace deal with Turkey. This was indeed what we see in Lausanne; the American representation was trying to sign a separate treaty with Turkey to protect her own interests.

Therefore, the US diplomatic correspondence regarding Turkey in 1923 was overwhelmingly dominated by the reports and discussions of the Lausanne negotiations.[48] In the first part of the negotiations, between 20 November 1922 and 4 February 1923, American representatives, including

Bristol, who were at the conference as 'observers', expressed the views of their government upon questions affecting American interests. They asked for reassurance from Turkey regarding the protection of foreigners residing in the country and requested recognition and protection be accorded by the Turkish authorities to American missions, schools and hospitals. American representatives supported the principle of the 'Open Door' and the equality of economic opportunity and advocated freedom of navigation and passage through the Straits. They associated themselves closely with the representatives of the Allied Powers in impressing upon the Turkish government the necessity of agreeing to adequate measures for the protection of the non-Muslim minorities in Turkish territories.[49]

At the end of these negotiations, Turkey and the US signed 'the Treaty of Amity and Commerce' on 6 August 1923. The treaty caused much controversy in the US Senate with deliberations lasting until 1927, and finally it was not ratified by the US Senate. Interestingly, a similar but different treaty was signed in 1930 to normalise the relations between the two countries.[50]

We do know that Mark Bristol had his first visit to Ankara between 6 and 13 April 1924, during which he also visited the Turkish Grand National Assembly (TGNA).[51] During his visit, Bristol met several ministers and also the Prime Minister İsmet [İnönü] and discussed the future of Turkey–US relations. The admiral seemed confident with the future of the American interests in Turkey. 'I believe the relations which I have established', stated Bristol 'will in the future facilitate the protection of American interest.'[52] Secretary Hughes paid careful attention to Bristol's visit to Ankara as a new treaty with Turkey was being prepared for the Senate vote. The Secretary of State wanted to know the following information:

1. The attitude toward American interests shown by the Turkish authorities.
2. Stability of existing government and its ability and willingness to fulfill international obligations.
3. The attitude which the Turkish authorities show toward the treaty with America and the likelihood that it will be ratified by Turkey at an early date. The Department is considering submitting this treaty to the Senate soon and wishes your report so that before doing so, it may have the benefit of the observations which you made on your trip.[53]

In response, Bristol stated that no major incident had taken place to harm the American interests, except that the medical department of Constantinople College had closed, the Marash School had been denied permission to reopen, and the military transport tax had risen. Bristol saw no reason why the Turkish side would reject the new treaty but urged Washington to ratify it as soon as possible. Most significantly, he put Secretary Hughes's doubts about the stability of the new Turkey to rest by stating: 'I believe the Turkish Government is stable and can fulfill its international obligations.'[54]

As the ratification on the US side was delayed, Bristol sent a graver telegram to Washington, indicating that the Turkish side was contemplating taking more hostile action towards the US interests, and asked for instructions. 'In my opinion, the situation is graver than it has been at any time during my service as High Commissioner,'[55] he concluded. With the personal interference of Ismet Pasha, Bristol later reported that the crisis was averted. The year 1924 ended with no major event in terms of bilateral relations, but it solidified the conclusion that the new government was here to stay.

In terms of bilateral relations, 1925 was not too different from the previous year. The treaty between Turkey and the US was not brought to a vote. However, in 1926, the then Secretary of State Frank B. Kellogg informed Bristol with caution that there were not enough votes in the Senate, and Bristol should do his best to maintain the status quo with the Turkish government.[56] In response to his assessment of the new Turkish regime, Bristol sent a lengthy reply to Washington:

> The domestic situation of Turkey appears to be good, if not better, than at any time since the new regime came into power. Efforts to balance the budget and the application of new taxes disturb the financial and economic situation. The new taxes have [increased] an unusual amount of criticism, but if past experience means anything, it is likely that after the first outburst, the public will accept the new tax measures with the usual indifference. I believe the Turks have given up hope of interesting American capital in Turkey. In the interior, security and order are better than in many years. The crop outlook is as good as, if not better than, last season. Turkey's international relations appear to be improving at the present time. Turkey's negotiations with Great Britain over the Mosul question and with Greece over the exchange of populations are proceeding favorably. Although it is a grave mistake to predict future

political situations in Turkey and the Near East, my opinion is that the present and future domestic and international situations of Turkey are such that the rejection of the Lausanne Treaty or the postponement of action thereon would be a grave mistake. The many possibilities involved, as I have endeavored to point out in this telegram, seem to put grave responsibility upon all concerned for the Government of the United States to provide protection for American interests in Turkey . . . and no fervent or sentimental interests should be allowed to prevent this protection being extended without delay.[57]

Bristol's views on the new Turkish government, as can be seen above, progressively changed for the better. He, however, was astonished to see that the Turkish population was indifferent to the regime change. He pushed for the ratification of the treaty, yet his attempts were not successful in winning the vote in the Senate. However, he was successful in convincing the State Department about the urgency of establishing formal relations with Turkey. Under Secretary of State (later the US Ambassador to Turkey) Joseph Grew issued 'A Statement of the Outstanding Reasons Why the Treaty with Turkey Should Be Ratified' to the Senate.[58] In it, Grew listed seven points that were almost identical to Bristol's suggestions to the State Department. Grew countered the reasons given by 'the American Committee opposed to the Lausanne Treaty', which consisted of members of the anti-Turkish lobby politicians and others, led by Armenian lawyer and activist Vahan Cardashian and the pre-war US Ambassador to Germany James W. Gerard.[59] Cardashian, who bombarded the State Department with letters of objection to the treaty, was not portrayed in US archival documents of the time. One of Cardashian's letters was forwarded to Bristol with a note by the State Department dated 11 February 1924. It read:

My Dear Admiral Bristol: . . . The fact that we reply to any of Cardashian's letters need not indicate that we take him too seriously. We have quite a large dossier on him, which we would be glad to supplement by anything you might obtain in Constantinople for he is a troublemaker and as long as he can induce Gerard to sign his letters and endorse his pamphlets he can cause us a certain amount of trouble . . . I have been told, but not yet been able to verify it, that Cardashian was at one time legal advisor to the Turkish Consulate General at New York. I have also in the files a copy of your dispatch . . . containing a repudiation of Cardashian by Armenian

Patriarchs of Constantinople and of the head of the Protestant Armenian community in Turkey subsequent to his publication of the booklet entitled 'Wilson the Wrecker of Armenia.'[60]

Certainly, there was no love lost between the State Department and Cardashian. Allen Dulles asked the US High Commissioner to collect more information about Cardashian, possibly to discredit his lobbying attempts in the US Senate. Robert Scotten, replying from Istanbul on behalf of Bristol, admits that not much information about Cardashian was available except that he had left the Ottoman Empire in 1914 for the USA and was the Turkish Commissioner at the San Francisco Exposition in 1915. In any case, Cardashian was successful in his lobbying activities.

The State Department was in disagreement with Cardashian's position that the US had a moral obligation to the Armenians, and the signing of any treaty with Turkey meant recognising the new regime and hence betraying the Armenian cause. Joseph Grew of the State Department disagreed: 'It is impossible, except by going to war, to detach from Turkey any territory for an Armenian home and we are under no obligations, legal or moral, to do so. The Treaty of Sèvres was never ratified, and we were not even a signatory.'[61] Grew's last bullet point succinctly summarises the view of the State Department on the ratification of the treaty and on the nationalist government in Ankara. He concluded:

> Opinions regarding modern Turkey may differ, but this has nothing to do with the ratification of the Treaty. If there was no ethical impropriety in our having a formal treaty and diplomatic relations with the Governments of Abdul-Hamid and of the Young Turks, why should this impropriety be considered to exist now? Certainly, the Turkey of Mustapha Kemal Pasha is not worse than the Turkey of Abdul-Hamid and of the Young Turks. Even Mr. Morgenthau, as late as 5 April 1917, urged that diplomatic relations with Turkey [should be established].[62]

On 26 June 1926, the Under Secretary of State, Grew, sent clear instructions to Bristol on the subject of the US Senate delaying the vote for the treaty and asked him to use his personal influence on the Turkish government to extend the modus vivendi agreement. Grew authorised Bristol to use the carrot-and-stick approach to secure the American interests in Turkey. Yet, he acknowledged that the situation of the delay of the ratification was a delicate matter. 'The Department realizes fully the delicacy of this negotiation', instructed Grew, 'and therefore does not wish to impede you by giving you too precise instructions as to how to introduce this subject into your conversations at Angora.'[63] The State Department was acutely aware of the failure of the ratification of the Turkish-American Treaty for three years and was hoping that in December 1926 the issue would be resolved.

On 3 July 1926, Secretary of State Kellogg gave the good news to Bristol that the US Senate would take up the ratification issue in January 1927. Kellogg commented on Bristol's achievements in calming the Turks down: 'The Department is pleased to learn of the efforts which you have made to prepare Turkish officials for the further postponement of action on the treaty. It is confident that if there is any possibility of the modus vivendi being renewed, it will be as a result of your conversations at Angora.'[64] The modus vivendi was renewed on 20 July 1926, by an exchange of notes, for a further period of six months from this date. The ratification vote, on the other hand, had to wait until 1927.[65]

On a side note, I must share an interesting observation regarding this collection of diplomatic exchanges in 1926. In a telegram to the Secretary of State on 15 May 1926, Bristol, for the first time, uses the term 'Stamboul' next to Constantinople, which is in parenthesis. This was very rare in his writings, and I do not remember seeing it elsewhere in this collection. Bristol, however, did not continue to use the word 'Stamboul' for Constantinople. We do not know why he used it here or stopped using it later.[66]

On 18 January 1927, Secretary of State Kellogg broke the bad news to Bristol: 'The treaty failed of approval by the Senate, the vote being 50 for and 34 against [two-thirds of the majority needed]. Be prepared to proceed to Angora immediately upon receipt of complete instructions, which are being telegraphed to you separately.'[67] Damage control was again the mission of High Commissioner Admiral Mark Lambert Bristol. Kellogg asked him to do everything in his power to assure the Turkish government that the US government had done everything in its power to secure the vote, and this result should not harm the bilateral relations. The next day, Bristol telegrammed the Secretary asking for authorisation to tell the Turkish government that the US President was in favour of the treaty, and the ratification would be brought up again at a later date. Bristol also asked, 'Could the Department inform me as to the procedure for the resumption of diplomatic relations? Would a Chargé d'Affaires or an Ambassador be sent?'[68]

Kellogg responded that Bristol should tell the Turkish government of President Coolidge's commitment to the treaty, but he was non-committal about the issue of restoring full diplomatic relations. Instead, Kellogg instructed Bristol that he should share the newspaper articles published in the US supporting the ratification. Bristol responded in kind and asked his staff to relay the translation of an article published in the Turkish daily *Milliyet*. The editorial was quite optimistic:

> The American Constitution places in the hands of the President the conduct of foreign affairs. The President is absolutely responsible for foreign relations. Therefore, if he believes the entering into relations with Turkey to be absolutely necessary, he may do this even without a treaty. So extensive is the executive authority in the United States. In view of this explanation, it is necessary to await the action of the President of the United States and not to attach too much importance to the decision of the Senate.[69]

It was the practice of the new Turkish government not to establish diplomatic relations with the Allied Powers until a peace treaty was signed and ratified. In this, Turkey normalised all her diplomatic ties with the Allied countries except the US. It was the desire of both governments to do so, but since the ratification failed in the Senate, Kellogg suggested that, perhaps as opposed to a formal treaty, which was desired but very likely to be delayed again, an exchange of notes could be sufficient to re-establish formal diplomatic ties at the level of ambassador. The consent to this move came from the Turkish Foreign Minister Tewfick Rauschdy Bey [Tevfik Rüştü]. After several edits, the text of the exchange of notes was signed on 17 February 1927 in Ankara.[70] During this time, Bristol was in Ankara negotiating the terms of the new 'exchange of notes' that allowed the exchange of ambassador.[71]

With the agreement signed, the State Department was preparing itself for the appointment of a career diplomat in Turkey. On 19 March 1927, Bristol received a telegram from the Secretary of State:

> The President having particularly in mind your future career in the Navy, directs me to inform you that he does not feel you should be asked to remain in Turkey after June 1st next. While the loss to this Government inevitable in

the termination of your present mission is keenly appreciated by the President and by myself, we realize that to prolong your stay in Turkey beyond June 1st might interfere with the plans of the Navy Department. It is my earnest desire to cooperate with the Navy Department to the fullest possible extent to the end that your services in Turkey may receive the recognition they so clearly deserve . . . It is understood that the Secretary of the Navy will issue you appropriate orders as Commander of the Naval Detachment in the Eastern Mediterranean.[72]

Secretary Kellogg instructed Bristol to present Joseph Grew's name to Ankara as the new US Ambassador in Turkey and to inquire about the Turkish government's approval. Bristol replied to Kellogg, confirming that Ankara had no objection. Ambassador Grew presented his letter of credence to the President of Turkey on 12 October 1927.

Until Bristol's departure from Turkey on 24 May 1927, he observed many events in the country. The most significant of these was the collapse of the 600-year-old empire and the emergence of the Turkish Republic under the leadership of Mustafa Kemal Atatürk, who modernised the country with a strong hand. The section below follows Bristol's evolving approach towards the Kemalists' regime.

Bristol's Views of the New Turkish Regime

On 29 October 1923, the new Turkish regime was declared a republic, and Mustafa Kemal became the first president of it. Admiral Bristol was openly in favour of the declaration of the republican regime in Turkey and of the initiation of Mustafa Kemal's reforms to modernise the country. Curious about the new developments, the State Department paid careful attention to the formation of the new Turkey. At this juncture in history, one of the most frequently asked questions put to the High Commissioner concerned the despotic tendency of the new Turkish president for radical political and social changes. Many in the US were curious about the functioning of democracy under Mustafa Kemal. We see Bristol's views on democracy *à la Turca* in an entry in his diary. In it, he notes a conversation with Senator William H. King, a Democrat from Utah, and an ardent opponent of the Turks. In 1920, Senator King was visiting Turkey and hoping to learn Bristol's – and also by and large the State Department's – views on the new Kemalist regime. Bristol recalls his response to King's question regarding the nature of democracy in the new Turkey:

> As to the general character of the present regime in Turkey, I told the Senator bluntly that, in my opinion, [the regime] was not a democracy and that it was hardly reasonable to expect that it should be a democracy. I said that an *enlightened dictatorship was the best that could be hoped for in Turkey for some years to come.* The Senator questioned me regarding Moustapha Kemal Pasha. I said that the President was unquestionably a man of great force and fully capable of holding the present regime together.[73]

For Bristol, social and political change for the better in Turkey could only be accomplished through a strong leader who was powerful enough to stand against the reactionaries and still hold the country together. Bristol's observations on Turkish public opinion are rather telling and insightful in understanding the attitude of the Turkish public who were weary of conflict. His views can also be extrapolated to other periods in Turkish history. For example, another report sent to the Secretary of State by Bristol deals with the closure of the new regime's first oppositional party, the Progressive Republican Party, in 1924 and includes significant observations regarding the political climate of Turkey and the politicisation of the Turks. The letter informs Washington that

> The suppression of the Progressive Party . . . has aroused little interest and, except for various official or semi-official commentaries, has received no attention in the press. Whether the Government's policy of not permitting any sort of opposition will prove successful in the long run is debatable, but the immediate success of this policy is not to be questioned. *The average Turk does not care for politics and has almost superstitious respect for what those in power think and do.* He may mildly disagree with some act of the Government, but it is an affair of a day or so, to be forgotten completely after an incredibly short time. There is nothing cumulative in this process, and the idea of the last straw which breaks the camel's back cannot, therefore, be applied to Turkish politics. As long as the taxes are reasonably low, the average Turk is quite content to let the Government do what it wants.[74]

This observation is rather telling in that it gives us clues about why Bristol thought of an enlightened dictatorship as being highly suitable for the new regime. Since political consciousness did not exist in Turkey, and Turkish people only respected those in power, it would be better for US interests that an enlight-ened despot who was friendly to US interests and who could hold the country together retain power. It might seem odd, yet understandable, that the closing of the first opposition party did not trigger any upheaval in 1924. However, the reader should remember that the abolition of the Sultanate in 1922 and the regime change in 1923 did also not meet with visible reaction.

Despite this background, there exist documents indicating that some-times even Bristol was critical of the lack of democracy in Turkey in 1925. For example, in reference to several political moves by Mustafa Kemal to purge political opposition, Admiral Bristol assesses that

> Angora is rapidly modeling itself on the Tcheka.[75] Its aim is seemingly to remove all political opposition; its methods are to convict on the basis of a settled policy and not on the evidence presented; its victims, in addition to nonconsequential citizens, are men of influence and standing. It has tried editors not only for the offensive use of a word but for a state of mind. It has succeeded in so terrorizing the press, that its most flagrant lapses from equity have not even been criticized; it has so terrorized the opposition that protests are no longer being made against its unconstitutionality.[76]

It seems that Bristol's initial assessment of the necessity of a 'strong leader' figure for the better future of Turkey was evolving to a more uncomfortable level. His tone in the report suggests he had become noticeably worried about the extreme tendencies of Mustafa Kemal and the government under him. In responding to a request by Ruth Woodsmall, secretary in charge of YWCA, regarding the immediate effect of secularisation in all educational institutions including YMCA and YWCA in Turkey, Bristol stated: 'The Turk had gone mad on the subject of divorcing all religious influence from governmental affairs, and this included doing away with religious influences in schools and similar institutions.'[77] Clearly, the new Turkish regime was not discriminating between religions (whether Christianity or Islam) in its attempt to separate state from religion, and Bristol began being bothered by many of its policies.

After the declaration of the new regime as a republic and the signing of the Treaty of Lausanne in 1923, Kemalists focused on restructuring, refor-mulating the state and reinterpreting the Turkish nationalism. As referred to above, in 1924–5 the new government was also involved in practices to purge the political opposition.[78] Around this time, we see US diplomats intensifying their efforts to understand and assess the new regime and its constantly evolving ideology. Some of these reports were written by the staff of the High Commission and relayed to Washington. Understandably, there were many lively debates and exchanges of ideas in the High Commission in Istanbul. Among those reports, one received a commendation from Washington. This is a highly attention-grabbing report that analysed the intellectual basis of the emerging regime in Ankara. Dated 12 September 1924, it is titled 'An Intellectual; Interpretation of Modern Turkey'. The author of the report is Gardiner Howland Shaw, one of the staff members under Bristol. The long and detailed report first evaluates the Westernisation attempts in the new Turkey.

> The state of mind, which prevails at Angora, brings out concrete results of intemperate westernization. A Constantinople newspaper recently devoted a leading article to what it called 'Angoritis' [*Orient News*, 12 August 1924]. The expression is apt, for few will deny the morbid quality, which attaches to those who govern Turkey today. The disease may be German measles – as we all hope – or it may be cancer – as some of us [are] coming to fear – but [a] disease of some sort or other it certainly is. These are the symptoms of 'Angoritis': (1) Nationalism and nationalism of the narrowest and most ingrowing variety, a nationalism not sure of itself: parvenu nationalism, intolerant and suspicious, immensely self-conscious; (2) an acute sense of sovereignty constantly agonized at the thought that something may not be on the basis of complete reciprocity and unwilling to take as a matter of course those small derogations to sovereignty which occur in normal international relations; (3) a whole set of minute phobias and susceptibilities; (4) a narrow environment – Angora: an overgrown village remote from restraining influences of contact with at least a few representatives of other countries and ideas – just the environment, in short for a pathological mentality; (5) a dictatorship in fact reinforced by the military habits of thought of certain of the more prominent leaders and a democracy in theory, so far as the theory is grasped; (6) a single-track of mind of an astonishing degree of consistency which enables the taking of decisions concerning complex questions by seeing only one aspect of those questions; and finally (7) a naive faith in many Western ideas and in their universal self-motility. At the same time, nobody can visit Angora without being impressed by the amount of energy that is being expended and in

a great measure wasted . . . To summarize, if Angoritis is a disease, *it is a western disease, but the victim is an oriental*, and there has not been time for the development of acquired immunity or counter-toxins . . . I am not writing against the spread of western ideas in the East. I am seeking to point out the consequences of westernization when carried on indiscriminatingly and without regard to the time factor.[79]

The author seemingly borrowed the term 'Angoritis', a word-play to mean the disease of Angora, from an Istanbul newspaper and built his argument on this. Shaw seems to be puzzled by the speed of Westernisation frenzy in Ankara and suggests that such a hasty Westernisation has consequences; however, it might be delayed. This criticism of Westernisation by a Westerner reveals that the uncontrolled speed of the modernisation process was a source of concern. The assessment deems the new Turkish Nationalism as intolerant, suspicious, dictatorial and self-conscious. The report also gives detailed examples of the development of intellectual roots and interpretations of Kemalist nationalism. The author's conclusions do not fall too far from those of Bristol's diary entry about his conversation with Senator King in 1925.

We know that this detailed analysis of Turkey and of the ideology of the emerging regime in Ankara impressed the State Department. Under Secretary of State Joseph Grew sent a note to Admiral Bristol asking him to congratulate Gardiner Howland Shaw for this insightful analysis of Turkish intellectual life and added that reports of this nature would be most welcomed in Washington.[80]

It took another eight months for a report of this nature to be prepared by the High Commission in Istanbul. Bristol asked Howland Shaw again to author the new evaluation, which was even more stimulating in its assessment; this time it evaluated the 'reality' on the ground, not the 'ideology'. This report was sent to Washington on 22 May 1925. It stated that the earlier analysis of modern Turkey, prepared by Shaw, 'is not to be considered as a definitive evaluation of Turkish Nationalism, but rather as one bulletin or estimate of the situation true enough today but doubtless to be corrected in the light of future events'.[81] The new assessment expressly rephrased the title to 'A Realistic Interpretation of Modern Turkey'. It stated:

A good deal has happened both to Turkey and to the author of the report during the past nine months – so much, in fact, as to suggest the desirability of a re-examination of the report in the light of the situation in Turkey as it exists today and further tentative evaluation and description of Turkish nationalism.

[The difference between last autumn's report and this one] is indicated by the difference in the words 'intellectualistic' and 'realistic.' It was possible to speak of the effect of the ideas upon the first or idealistic phase of the Nationalistic movement – a phase which began its decline after the signature of the peace treaties at Lausanne on July 24, 1923, and which at least at the time of radical reforms of the winter of 1923–1924 was a thing of the past . . .

We [those in the High Commission in Istanbul] have perhaps been too prone to idealize the Nationalist movement . . . We saw Turkish Nationalism inaccurately. It was something hidden away in Anatolia; there was a mystery about it; heroism, which captivated the imagination and put to sleep the faculties of criticism and rational judgment. Let us be quite frank: we were sentimental over Turkish Nationalism. Our judgment was further warped by a close acquaintance with the blundering of Allied diplomacy in the Near East. We saw so vividly the falsity and stupidity of one side that we almost unconsciously ascribed strength and wisdom to the other side.[82]

This section testifies that there was a degree of sympathy among the members of the American High Commission towards the Turkish nationalist movement led by Mustafa Kemal. Shaw's romanticising the Kemalist movement admittedly originates from the reaction of the Allied policies in Turkey, which were considered to be counterproductive by US diplomats in Istanbul. The anger over these Allied policies, Shaw admits, coloured the diplomats' view of Turkey positively. The developments during the last eight months proved to Shaw that as soon as the peace agreement in Lausanne was signed in 1923, the government turned her attention to silencing the legal, political opposition in Ankara by despotic means. Shaw goes further into sharper criticism of the Kemalists:

The Nationalist Movement is sinking into the mud, mentally and morally, and it is sinking into the mud because it has degenerated into a dictatorship, a dictatorship, moreover, without the temporary justification of unquestionable efficiency.

Moustapha Kemal Pasha is the only reality in Turkey today; the rest has significance only in so far as it stands in some definite relationship to him or against him. The real program of the Government is to keep Moustapha Kemal Pasha in power . . . The value of Deputies, of Cabinet Ministers and of other officials is determined by the ruthless application of one criterion; will they work wholeheartedly to keep Moustapha Kemal Pasha in power; will they take orders? If so, they may be stupid, they may be dishonest, they may get drunk, but they belong to the governing machine . . .

A dictatorship, a deterioration in the quality of the governing personnel, an arresting of any real political thinking – what will be the downfall of the present regime, but the day of downfall may be indefinitely postponed and this for several reasons: (1) Moustapha Kemal Pasha is an extraordinarily able political strategist and tactician, and while a government cannot be run indefinitely on clever strategy and tactics, it can be so run for a considerable time especially in Turkey where great prestige attaches to those in power and where public opinion is unorganized, if not non-existent. (2) The Army is still apparently loyal to Moustapha Kemal Pasha, and (3) the Opposition, the Progressive Party – is in a rudimentary stage of organization.[83]

Bristol seems to agree with Shaw's assessment of the despotic tendencies of Mustafa Kemal; however, we know from Bristol's conversation with Senator William King that he thought of Mustafa Kemal's despotism as a necessary evil. Bristol maintained his faith in the future of the new regime.

We know of Bristol's support of Shaw's analysis of the shortcomings of the government in Ankara, because of an earlier report that was prepared by Shaw. This report contained Shaw's views of politics in Ankara as the seat of the government after his visit to the Turkish Grand National Assembly. On 12 March 1925, Admiral Bristol dispatched a letter to the Secretary of State and attached Shaw's analysis. Bristol assured the State Department that 'the notes present an accurate picture of Angora and the life which is led there'.[84] Shaw's report was titled the 'Angora Notes', and after giving information about the living and working conditions in the city, he goes on to present his views on politics under the subtitle 'A Medley of Politics'. What follows is from a section where Shaw presents his view of the Turkish parliament, Mustafa Kemal and politics in Ankara in a very forthright manner.

The Assembly naturally must not be taken seriously. A serious student of parliamentary life would be out of place in Angora. The Assembly is a play that goes on in order to make a few unobservant people forget what Moustapha Kemal Pasha is doing. Sometimes the Ghazi President is present while the play is going on and then, of course, the acting is even better . . .

There is only one determining factor in Angora: Moustapha Kemal Pasha. The rest, including the Assembly and the Cabinet, is chiefly camouflage. There is no semblance of democracy or of self-government at Angora. The Government is a disguised dictatorship, and often the disguise is very thin indeed. Is Moustapha Kemal Pasha patriotic? This is a hard question to answer, but there are many nowadays who contend that he has a crudely possessory attitude towards Turkey and that all he cares for is to maintain his domination over the country. Like most Turks, he has no loyalty to his subordinates—he uses them to the limit and beyond and then throws them into the discard. He cannot abide men of first-rate ability and independent views around him. He wants a chief of staff instead of a Prime Minister, and as for the rest, they are to be mere servants. He has found his chief of staff in Ismet Pasha and his servants in a gang of touches in the Assembly. The expression is not elegant, but it is an accurate description of such Deputies as Kilidj Ali Bey, Ali Bey [Çetinkaya?], Reouf Bey of Rize [not Orbay] and others . . .

Angora is an ideal environment in which a narrow nationalism can develop to its logical extreme and, in time, kill itself. This process is now going on rapidly; Turkey will not adopt the reforms and especially the secularization of Angora; therefore, these reforms and this secularization are to be forced down the throats of the Turks by Tribunals of Independence, suppressing newspapers and other kindred practices. The tragedy of it all is that there is not enough intelligence in the Angora crowd to see that Turkey is once more back in the old vicious circle of tyranny begetting revolutionary opposition, which, when it comes to power, follows in the footsteps of the tyranny which has been overthrown. Only superficially has Turkey progressed since the days of Abdul Hamid.[85]

On 6 April 1925 a memorandum from the State Department, Division of Near Eastern Affairs, was sent to Joseph C. Grew, then Under Secretary of State (later, in 1927, Ambassador to Turkey), by Secretary of State Frank Billings Kellogg.[86] In regard to Shaw's 'Angora Notes', the memorandum stated that 'Information of this sort, which is distinctly out of the scope of routine dispatches, seems to me to be unusually helpful and brings life and humor to situations, which are often treated only in a prosaic, official manner. I feel that Shaw is deserving of commendation, and I, therefore, attach an instruction to this effect.'[87] To Bristol, Kellogg responded on 4 May 1925, 'The Department has found these notes unusually interesting and helpful and requests that you inform Mr. Shaw of the Department's appreciation of his comments. Further notes of a similar character from time to time would be welcomed.'[88]

The report establishes that the US diplomatic mission in Turkey did not regard the regime as a democracy. On the contrary, one comment compares the new regime to that of the earlier despotic periods; 'Only superficially has Turkey progressed since the days of Abdul Hamid.'

Until Mustafa Kemal established himself as the unchallenged leader of the republic, we see many political activities of the Kemalists in Ankara and Istanbul. Bristol always keenly followed activities in the Turkish Parliament and continued to cultivate US relations with the new leaders of Turkey. From time to time, he met leaders of the republic to make sense of the political atmosphere in Ankara and developed his views based on primary information. For example, in dispatch, Mark Bristol includes his 'War Diary' that informs Washington of his trip to Ankara to meet Turkish ministers and also Prime Minister Ismet Pasha. An entry dated 25 April 1925 gives a transcript of the conversation that took place between Ismet Pasha and Admiral Bristol, interpreted by Mr Shaw. This meeting took place in Ismet Pasha's residence in Ankara and lasted one hour, in which Bristol brought up the subject of political opposition. Below is the translation of this conversation by Mr Shaw.

> The conversation then drifted to the difficulties of political life, especially the difficulty of handling a parliament. The Admiral asked Ismet Pasha point-blank what he thought of a two-party system. Ismet Pasha replied that two parties were clearly desirable. He made this statement; however, it seemed to me, with very little conviction. The Admiral pointed out that the advantage of having two parties was that the various questions brought up in parliament were looked at and discussed from several points of view. Ismet Pasha admitted the truth of this. He asked how many members of Congress we had in America. The Admiral replied that we had some 420. Ismet Pasha expressed the greatest horror at this and was inclined to sympathize with the United States Government, even more, when he learned that besides 420 Congressmen, we had a

number of Senators. Apparently, Ismet Pasha felt that 288 Deputies was more than sufficient as a source of trouble. He said that an opposition in a parliament was quite all right, but not an opposition, which was opposed to the Constitution and to the foundation of the society.[89]

Bristol and his translator describe the meeting as cordial and frank but seem to be surprised at Ismet Pasha's remark about seeing deputies in the Turkish Assembly as a source of trouble. It is in this meeting that Bristol received first-hand information regarding the government's unfavourable attitude towards the opposition party in Turkey. One month later, the opposition party (the Progressive Republican Party) was shut down by the government; 1925 was the year in which a Kurdish uprising took place in Eastern Anatolia and provided the Kemalists with a pretext to suppress all political and intellectual opposition.[90] During this time, the Kemalist government was unconcerned about being 'democratic' under the banner of 'saving the infant regime from its enemies'. Bristol seemed to agree with Mustafa Kemal. It is very likely that his sympathy for Mustafa Kemal came from the fact that both men were of military origin, and real politics almost always overrode romantic ideas of democracy. I cannot go as far as to suggest that Bristol supported despotism in Turkey, but he certainly understood it. Ironically, he had little patience for the despotism of the previous regime. I believe that this distinction originates from the fact that with the Kemalist despotism, the means justified the end: modernisation of the state apparatus along Western lines.

There were many statements by Bristol confirming that he saw Mustafa Kemal as a dictator, but one captures the attention as it was said to a Turkish diplomat assigned to the USA as a consul general. Celal Münir Bey, who was appointed to the US, came to visit Bristol and asked if he had any words of wisdom. Bristol reported this conversation:

> He asked me what my advice was to him in going to the United States, and I told him that a frank, open policy with Americans he met was necessary. When there was propaganda in the United States against Turkey, it was a bad policy to just deny it, especially when this propaganda was based on facts as for instance, as regards to the Laidoner Report.[91] Ismet Pasha denied that any atrocities or ill-treatment had been accorded Christians in South-Eastern Anatolia. It would have been very much better if Ismet Pasha had made some

statements explaining the situation because I knew full well that there had been mistreatment of Christians in that part of the country, but I also knew from my experience here that there were surrounding circumstances which, if explained, would not put all the blame on the Turks. I told him that he would be questioned regarding the dictatorship of Mustapha Kemal Pasha and in this case, it would be a mistake to deny absolutely any dictatorship but it could be readily explained how Mustapha Kemal was looked up to by all the Turks by virtue of what Kemal Pasha had done for Turkey and the Turkish people and therefore how they welcomed the reforms that Kemal Pasha was having put through by the Grand National Assembly . . . I don't imagine I made much impression upon Djalal Bey, but if I made any at all I am satisfied.[92]

No doubt, Bristol saw the regime in Ankara as a dictatorship and was aware of the mistreatment of the Christians. However, he saw things in their proper context. He believed that denial did not help but hindered American public opinion. The next section will present documents dealing with the significant internal affairs of Turkey.

It is incorrect to think that Bristol was critical of Mustafa Kemal's authoritarian style of governing. On the contrary, according to Bristol, the harsh treatment of his political opponents was a necessary practice. We see this attitude in the government's dealing with the aftermath of a Kurdish rebellion of 1925. In this report, Bristol comments on the newly passed reforms: 'The efficiency and expeditious manner in which the [1925 Shaikh Said] uprising was met made possible the imposition of republican reforms which otherwise might not have been practicable for an indefinite period of time. Amongst the more important of those reforms may be enumerated the abolition of Tekkes, social renovation, more particularly the forced renunciation of feudal titles such as "Sheik," and modernization of dress.'[93]

As for the draconian and infamous Law on Maintenance of Order of 1925, Bristol states:

This law, apart from its political effects, real or potential, has made for a degree of public security never heretofore enjoyed in Turkey. The reactionary outbreak, which occurred in November last and gave the government a measure of preoccupation in the regions of Marash, Cesarea, Sivas, Tokat, Keressun, Trebizond, Erzerum, Hazze and Rizeh is understood to be now under complete control.

The fact that this movement, in contrast with the Kurdish revolt, had a character more of a demonstrative protest against the government's modernization program and the abolition of the fez, than a revolt, made the matter of its suppression considerably less difficult. The Angora Tribunal of Independence charged with bringing the dissenters back into line appears to have accomplished its object in a remarkably short time, likewise with a minimum number of capital sentences.[94]

It seems that Bristol was completely in line with the government's harsh method of silencing the opposition. To Bristol, this was necessary realism to give a breeding ground for the infant regime.

Concluding Remarks

Admiral Mark Lambert Bristol arrived in Constantinople at the end of World War I, one of the most destructive human experiences in history, and immediately observed the misery on the ground in territories where fierce battles were fought. He saw how citizens of one empire, next-door neighbours for so long, became killers at each other's throats. Bristol witnessed first-hand how a major world empire sank into history and how imperialistic designs by the victors of the Great War were put into action.

How much he knew of the Ottoman Empire before he arrived is not known. But it seems that he either came to this war-torn empire with a degree of bias or immediately after his arrival developed a noticeable distaste for the dying Ottoman administration. Only a couple of months after his arrival, Bristol's reports judged that the survival of this empire would be a great crime to civilisation.

His earlier experiences also coincided with the long wait for a peace treaty. It was during this time that he also developed a distaste for the Allied manipulations, especially those of the British, which promoted selfish policies to divide the Ottoman Empire for her own interests. Bristol thought that British designs in the Middle East inevitably led to further conflict and certainly did not serve peace or the interests of any peoples in the region. As an ardent believer in the Open Door Policy of the United States, Bristol sent many condemning messages to Washington complaining about Great Britain and her imperialistic designs. He urged the State Department that the US should pay more attention to the faith of the Ottoman Empire and of the Middle East.

Otherwise, Great Britain would collect the spoils of the war in the Middle East for her own selfish interests.

Bristol was adamant in his suggestion that a partial mandate for an Armenian state would serve neither the Armenian nor the US interest but instead that of Great Britain. He believed that the Armenian mandate would not be sustainable for it required money and military power that neither the US nor other Allied Powers could afford, nor were they willing to provide. This would lead to more bloodshed in the region. The next chapter discusses this issue in more detail. Bristol was successful in convincing the State Department that if there was to be a mandate, it should be for the entire Ottoman Empire so that the competing interests of other mandate holders would not clash at the expense of the locals.

Bristol was the first to realise the potential of the nationalist movement in Anatolia, urging his superiors to pay due attention to this movement. As early as 23 November 1920, long before the Turkish War of Independence was won by the Turks, he issued a warning to Washington that the nationalists in Anatolia needed to be taken seriously. He stated:

> It is time for European countries to realize that the Kemalist movement is as near a nationalist movement as anything could be in Turkey and that this movement must be considered seriously. England, especially among the European countries, has belittled this movement and tried to make it appear as an old Union and Progress movement engineered by Enver Pasha and Kemal Pasha, backed by German interests. Also that this nationalist movement is very popular in Anatolia and represents a small minority. This is not the opinion of the Britishers here who know anything about the subject.[95]

Bristol used all his intelligence-gathering power to understand, analyse and explain this emerging movement. As a soldier himself, he felt sympathy for the Kemalist movement and established informal contacts with its leaders. Despite the fact that he despised the Ottoman administrative practices, even after the establishment of the nationalist government in Ankara, Bristol kept an equal distance to the royalists and the nationalists.

The US High Commissioner took part in the first portion of the Lausanne Conference in 1922. He was instrumental in preparing and promoting a separate proposal with the new Turkey called 'Treaty of Commerce and Amity between

US and Turkey' on 6 August 1923. Bristol lobbied fiercely for the ratification of this treaty; however, it failed in the Senate vote. The main reason for the failure of the ratification was the activities of Armenian and Greek lobbies in the US Senate. The next chapter will discuss Bristol's firm but controversial standing towards the Greek and Armenians in Turkey after World War I.

Notes

1. Thomas A. Bryson, 'Admiral Mark L. Bristol, an Open-Door Diplomat in Turkey', *International Journal of Middle East Studies*, 5.4 (1974): 450–67; 454.

2. Bie Ravndal, a Norwegian-born political officer at the embassy in Constantinople, called Bristol the 'right man for the occasion' and said more 'vessels should be added so that reasonably effective force may be within a call'; 867.00/871, Ravndal to Secretary of State, 7 May 1919.

3. 867.00/121, StaNav Constantinople (Bristol) to Simsadus London (the cable address for the American Navy in Europe), 18 March 1919.

4. 867.01/7, Bristol to Secretary of State, 23 January 1920.

5. 867.01/51, Bristol to Secretary of State, 7 May 1920.

6. Bristol noted this conversation in his 'War Diary' dated 3 January 1920, 'Bristol Papers', box 1; see also Dinç Yaylalıer, 'American Perceptions of Turkey, 1919–1927', PhD dissertation, University of Utah, 1996, p. 70.

7. See Neville Henderson's report to Mr MacDonald, 5 August 1924, in Robin Bidwell (ed.), *British Documents on Foreign Affairs: Reports and Papers from the Foreign Office Confidential Print. Part II, From the First to the Second World War. Series B, Turkey, Iran and the Middle East, 1918–1939*, 1997, p. 207.

8. 867.00/972, Bristol to Department of State and Department of Navy, 28 October 1919.

9. 867.01/153. A memorandum prepared by Bristol on 25 April 1920 was relayed to Washington by C. Vaught Engert in 1923.

10. 'Bristol Papers', entry date 23 November 1920.

11. Joseph C. Grew, *Turbulent Era: A Diplomatic Record of Forty Years, 1904–1945*, vol. 1 (Cambridge, MA: The Riverside Press, 1952), p. 496; emphasis added.

12. Bristol to Admiral Albert Gleaves, 8 April 1919, 'Bristol Papers', as cited in Peter Michael Buzanski, 'Admiral Mark L. Bristol and Turkish-American Relations, 1919–1922', PhD dissertation, University of California, Berkeley, 1960, p. 115.

13. 867.00/850, Bristol to Secretary of State, 7 March 1919.

14. 867.00/364, Ravndal to American Embassy, Paris, 14 August 1919.

15. 867.001/9, Bristol to Secretary of State, 19 November 1922.

16. 867.01/153. A report to the Department of State was relayed by C. Vaught Engert on 26 March 1923, three years after it was originally written by Bristol for the guidance of Engert.

17. 867.01/153. A memorandum prepared by Bristol on 25 April 1920 was relayed to Washington by C. Vaught Engert in 1923.

18. Edgar Browne's private papers are housed at the Hoover Institution of Stanford University; see <http://pdf.oac.cdlib.org/pdf/hoover/browne.pdf> (last accessed 28 September 2020). I did not have access to this collection and rely on Yaylalıer, pp. 93–4. Browne describes vividly how adventurous was his trip from Istanbul to Sivas with the help of Halide Edip [Adıvar], one of the noted female figures among the nationalists.

19. Browne to Crane, 25 August 1919, Browne Papers, file 3f, box 1, as referenced in Yaylalıer, p. 96, n. 6. See also Seçil Karal Akgün, 'Louis Edgar Browne and the Leaders of 1919 Sivas Congress', in George S. Harris and Nur Bilge Criss (eds), *Studies in Atatürk's Turkey: The American Dimension* (Leiden and Boston: Brill, 2009), pp. 15–55.

20. See Yaylalıer, chapter 2; also Buzanski, chapter 5.

21. 867.00/1157, Bristol to Secretary of State in a telegram dated 16 March 1920.

22. Buzanski, p. 164, refers to a report in 'The Bristol Papers' dated 21 November 1920.

23. Buzanski, p. 146.

24. Bristol to Secretary of State, dated 17 April 1920, numbered 867.00/1225. The report mentions her encounters with Mustafa Kemal and Ali Fuat twice. It unfortunately does not give much detail about the content of the interviews other than mentioning that Mustafa Kemal assured the Americans of the safety of the NER workers in districts under the control of the nationalists.

25. Şuhnaz Yılmaz, *Turkish-American Relations, 1800–1952: Between the Stars, Stripes and the Crescent* (New York: Routledge, 2015), p. 48.

26. Heath Lowry, 'I. Uluslararası Atatürk Sempozyumu, Ankara April 2, 1920– August 16, 1921', *Halide Edib Hanım in Ankara* (Ankara: Atatürk Araştırma Merkezi, 1994), p. 703.

27. Yılmaz, p. 48.

28. Heath Lowry, *Clarence K. Streit's The Unknown Turks* (Istanbul: Bahçeşehir University Press, 2011), p. 210; see also Yılmaz, p. 49.

29. Lowry, *Streit's The Unknown Turks*, p. 105.

30. The *New York Times* published an article on 4 May 1920 about the interviews by Paul Williams of the *Chicago Tribune*: 'Kemal Presents Nationalist Views; Tells

an American Interviewer He is Fighting to Free the Sultan. Counts on Other Moslems. Expects them to "Hamper the Enemy" – Says He Won't "Willingly Accept" Allied Terms'.

31. Buzanski, p. 148; Bristol to L. I. Thomas, 14 December 1919, 'Bristol Papers'.

32. Buzanski, p. 149; report for week ending 13 June 1920, 'Bristol Papers'.

33. Buzanski, p. 155.

34. 'War Diary' dated 27 January 1921, in 'Bristol Papers'.

35. The story of the Blacque family is examined in Orhan Koloğlu, *Osmanlı Basınının Doğuşu ve Blak Bey Ailesi – Bir Fransız Ailesinin Bâbıâli Hizmetinde Yüz Yılı: 1821–1822* (Istanbul: Müteferrika, 1998).

36. For more information, see <http://earsiv.sehir.edu.tr:8080/xmlui/bitstream/handle/11498/13988/001582250010.pdf?sequence=1> (last accessed 28 September 2020).

37. On 7 July 1921, Blacque Bey again visited Bristol and brought a letter from İzzet Pasha, the Ottoman Foreign Minister, insisting on Ottoman representation in Washington. Bristol's response was discouraging. The admiral told Blacque Bey that at this time such a request would not receive a favourable response; 'War Diary' dated 7 July 1921, in 'Bristol Papers'.

38. Bristol, 'War Diary' dated 28 January 1921, in 'Bristol Papers'.

39. Bristol, 'War Diary' dated 28 July 1921, in 'Bristol Papers'.

40. 867.4016/664, Bristol to Acting Secretary of State, 14 September 1922.

41. 867.4016/664, Bristol to Acting Secretary of State, 18 September 1922, enclosure 2; emphasis added.

42. 867.4016/707, telegram from Secretary of State to High Commissioner at Constantinople (Bristol), 24 October 1922.

43. 867.4016/708, Bristol to Secretary of State, 28 October 1922.

44. Ibid.

45. 867.4016/723c, telegram from Acting Secretary of State to Ambassador in France, 1 November 1922.

46. 867.4016/730 ½, memorandum by the Secretary of State of a conversation with the British Ambassador (Geddes), 10 November 1922; emphasis added.

47. 767.68119/5, telegram, Bristol to Secretary of State, 5 October 1922.

48. United States Department of State, *Papers Relating to the Foreign Relations of the United States, 1923* (Washington, DC: US Government Printing Office, 1923), vol. 2, pp. 879–1252.

49. See a letter from the Secretary of State to Senator Henry Cabot Lodge on 5 May 1924; the document is numbered 711.672/287b.

50. For an insightful essay, see John M. Vander Lippe, 'The "Other" Treaty of Lausanne: The American Public and Official Debate on Turkish American Relations', *The Turkish Yearbook of International Relations (Milletlerarası Münasebetler Türk Yıllığı)*, 23 (1993): 31–62.

51. 123.B773/73, Bristol to Secretary of State, 15 April 1924. See also FRUS, 1924, vol. 2, p. 730.

52. Ibid.

53. 711.672/280a, telegram, Secretary of State to High Commissioner in Turkey (Bristol), 21 April 1924. See also FRUS, 1924, vol. 2, p. 730.

54. 711.672/288, High Commissioner in Turkey (Bristol) to Secretary of State, 27 April 1924.

55. 711.672/308, telegram, High Commissioner in Turkey (Bristol) to Secretary of State, 9 July 1924; FRUS, 1924, vol. 2, pp. 733–4.

56. 711.672/397a, telegram, Secretary of State to High Commissioner in Turkey (Bristol), 24 February 1924; FRUS, 1926, vol. 2, p. 974.

57. 711.672/464, telegram, High Commissioner in Turkey (Bristol) to Secretary of State, 15 May 1926; FRUS, 1926, vol. 2, p. 979.

58. 711.672/465a, Under Secretary of State (Grew) to Senator Charles Curtis, 20 May 1926; FRUS, 1926, vol. 2, p. 980.

59. See Vahan Cardashian, 'American Committee Opposed to the Lausanne Treaty', in *The Lausanne Treaty: Turkey and Armenia* (New York, 1926), a collection of letters and short articles by various authors, copyrighted by the American Committee Opposed to the Lausanne Treaty and edited by Vahan Cardashian.

60. 711.672/261; the folder contains Cardashian's letter to the Secretary of State and the State Department's letter to Bristol. No signature is legible but this letter was possibly written by Allen W. Dulles. We can guess this because another letter, 711.672/2641/2, responding directly to this one, is addressed to Allen Dulles.

61. 711.672/465a.

62. Ibid.

63. 711.672/400a, telegram, Acting Secretary of State to High Commissioner in Turkey (Bristol), 24 June 1926.

64. 711.672/491, telegram, Secretary of State to High Commissioner in Turkey (Bristol), 3 July 1926.

65. We do know from the document 711.672/532a on 18 and 20 July 1926 that Turkey and the US signed an agreement on 'Mutual and Unconditional Most Favored Nation Treatment in Customs Matters'. FRUS, Turkey, 1926, vol. 2, pp. 992–3.

66. 711.672/464, telegram, High Commissioner in Turkey (Bristol) to Secretary of State, STAMBOUL (CONSTANTINOPLE), 15 May 1926.

67. 711.672/539b, telegram, Secretary of State to High Commissioner in Turkey (Bristol), 18 January 1927.

68. 711.672/640, telegram, High Commissioner in Turkey (Bristol) to Secretary of State, 19 January 1927.

69. 711.672/642, telegram, High Commission in Turkey (Crosby) to Secretary of State, 21 January 1927. The exact date of the *Milliyet* editorial is not given. However, for the communication on the subject, please also see the files numbered 711.672/640, 711.672/540 and 711.672/540a in FRUS, 1927, vol. 2, pp. 768–72.

70. 711.662/566, High Commissioner of Turkey to Secretary of State.

71. The full text was also published by the Turkish Foreign Ministry in both French and Turkish in 1927. A copy can be found in Atatürk Library, Istanbul; *Türkiye ile Amerika hükumet-i müttehidesi beynindeki münasebâtın tanzimi zımmında Hariciye Vekili Doktor Tevfik Rüştü Bey Efendi hazretleriyle Amerika mümessil-i siyasisi Amiral Mark L. Bristol arasında teati olunan notalar* (Ankara: Hariciye Vekaleti, 1927).

72. 123.B773/147c, telegram, Secretary of State to High Commissioner in Turkey (Bristol), 19 March 1927.

73. 867.00/1886, Bristol to Secretary of State, 1 August 1925; emphasis added. See also Bristol's 'War Diary' entry dated 14 July 1925.

74. 867.00/1882, Bristol to Secretary of State, 2 July 1925; emphasis added.

75. The first of a succession of Soviet secret police organisations.

76. 867.00/1870, Bristol to Secretary of State, 8 May 1925.

77. 867.00/1884, Bristol to Secretary of State, 17 July 1925.

78. See Hakan Özoğlu, *From Caliphate to Secular State: Power Struggle in the Early Turkish Republic* (Santa Barbara: Praeger, 2011). This book discusses the purging practices of the Kemalists in detail.

79. 867.401/8, Robert Scotten to Secretary of State, attached to a report by Howland Shaw, 12 September 1924; emphasis added.

80. 867.401/8, in the same folder, the letter dated 17 October 1924.

81. 867.401/10. Shaw's report was attached to Bristol's confidential report to the Secretary of State on 22 May 1925.

82. Ibid.

83. Ibid; emphasis added.

84. 867.00/1860, Bristol to Secretary of State, 12 March 1925.

85. Ibid.
86. I could not read the signature, but there is little doubt that it belonged to Kellogg.
87. 867.00/1860, memorandum to Joseph C. Grew, 6 April 1925.
88. 867.00/1860, Secretary of State to Bristol, 4 May 1925.
89. 867.00/1872, Bristol to Secretary of State, 6 May 1925.
90. See Özoğlu, *From Caliphate to Secular State*, chapter 3.
91. It was the report which was prepared by the committee headed by an Estonian politician, Johan Laidoner, describing the Mosul border of Turkey.
92. 867.00/1928, Bristol to Secretary of State, 'War Diary' dated 26 April 1926.
93. 867.00/1911, Bristol to Secretary of State, dated 11 January 1926.
94. Ibid.
95. 'Bristol Papers', entry dated 23 November 1920.

4

BRISTOL AND CONFLICTS BETWEEN TURKS, GREEKS AND ARMENIANS IN ANATOLIA

In the aftermath of World War I, the political atmosphere in the US was unquestionably anti-Turk but also decidedly uninformed about the Turk. The main reason for this was the active anti-Turkish propaganda in the US by the American missionaries once very active in the Ottoman lands and also by the Armenian and Greek diaspora lobbying activities. This chapter will examine Bristol's efforts to counter this propaganda through the reports he and his staff sent to Washington. These dispatches open up a window for the reader to follow Bristol's mindset, shaped by his belief that in this part of the world, no group was innocent and the main difference between the victim and the villain is the opportunity presented to a certain group in the fog of the post-World War I period.[1]

In an earlier chapter, we discussed the issue of Bristol's 'pro-Turk' label and his response to it. This label was and has been used to discredit Bristol's reports from Turkey without examining the validity of their content. However, the fair-minded reader can make his or her judgement based solely upon the merit of the reports relayed by Bristol to Washington. Bristol was simply a 'pro-American' who later sympathised with the Kemalist struggle to replace the Ottoman Empire, which he thought was 'corrupt'. Let us now turn our attention to the pro-Armenian/anti-Turk public opinion in the US, which will demonstrate the challenges Bristol faced in relaying any report to Washington that was not markedly anti-Turkish. This chapter will examine several documents and reports that reached the State Department first on the issue of the Armenians and then on the Greeks. It will analyse the texts of primary documents to understand and explain the evolution of Bristol's attitude towards the creation of an Armenian state, claims of Armenian massacres, and Greek minorities during the Greek occupation of Smyrna in 1919–22 and its aftermath.

The Armenians and Bristol

Admiral Mark Lambert Bristol reported on many subjects and areas in the Ottoman Empire. None, however, received the attention of his reports on the Armenians as the fate of the Armenians in the Ottoman Empire had always been one of the most controversial subjects of the twentieth century. Earlier chapters touched upon how Bristol's position on the Armenian issue earned him the title 'pro-Turk'. This section will discuss the subject in a more detailed manner and follow the evolution of Bristol's train of thought on the issues of the US mandate on Armenia, the creation of a state for Armenians and inter-communal killings during his tenure in Anatolia. In it, we can see Bristol's resentment for the old Ottoman regime. This section will bring in documents about Bristol's views on the Armenian and Muslim massacres, a hotly debated issue over the century, and his views on the creation of an Armenia as both an independent state and an American mandate.

When Bristol arrived in Constantinople, American public opinion towards Turkey was very low, thanks partly to Armenian lobbying activities headed by Vahan Cardashian, an Armenian lawyer and activist. The document below by Cardashian exemplifies the mindset of the anti-Turkish lobby in the United States:

> There are over 2,000,000 Armenians in Russian Armenia, and possibly 1,250,000 in Turkey. The Armenians belong to the Latin branch of the Indo-European family and are vigorous and progressive Christian people . . .
>
> The Turks of Turkey, who number about 4,000,000, are an irresponsible and destructive aggregation, amalgamated principally from the undesirable elements of a score of the races and tribes of the east, during the last 800 years.
>
> They are morally unfit for self-rule. With the separation from Turkey of the non-Turkish nationalities, the Turkish state, should one be left, will be short-lived. It is the consensus of competent opinion that, if the Turks were to

be placed under a civilized alien rule, they would, in the course of a hundred years, disintegrate and possibly disappear as a separate racial entity. This would be a great blessing to civilization.[2]

This view was by no means an uncommon one among the American public. Against this background, Admiral Bristol entered the picture and sent reports to Washington that did not fully corroborate the anti-Turkish lobbying activities. It is worth repeating that Bristol did not deny the bloody massacres/genocide committed by the Turkish administration in 1915, but he also insisted that Armenians and Greeks committed massacres against the Muslim population of Anatolia, and the American public had the right to see the other side of the coin. Below is an example of Bristol's view on the massacres:

> The partitioning of [the Ottoman Empire] for the imperialistic desires of European countries, including Greece, and also for the purpose of exploiting this country commercially, would be the greatest crime of the Twentieth Century. In addition to this, by cutting up this country, as it is proposed now, it will simply concentrate the races and intensify the race hatreds that now exist. It must bring about, if successful, small states having the most antagonistic feelings towards each other, not only on account of the ordinary hatred induced by race and religion but by virtue of the horrible crimes that were committed during the great war. *The Turks will never become repentant for their dastardly acts, and their hatred of the other races will be intensified by their feeling guilty and especially by the fact that they know this solution of the problem is only an excuse on the part of those who solved the problem to gain their own selfish ends.*[3]

There should be little doubt that by 'dastardly acts' Bristol was referring to the Armenian massacres of 1915. However, he was quite realistic in implying that the Armenian issue was readily seen as a tool by the Western Powers to advance their own selfish goals. The same document also realistically assesses the military might necessary to support an Armenian state:

> The Greeks in Smyrna are maintaining their rule by absolute military force and must continue to do so. They have at least 100,000 men in that territory now, 25,000 to 50,000 men in reserve ready to throw into the country. *If Armenia is to be established, there must be at least the same number of men fully*

armed and equipped. The Armenians have not these men, nor the equipment, nor can they provide them without money; therefore, in order to establish Armenia there must be a force of foreign troops of 150,000 men fully armed and equipped and the funds to maintain this force. Who is going to supply these troops and money? If these troops and money are not provided, then it means a racial war between the Turks and Armenians, in which they will simply murder each other, including women and children.[4]

There is little doubt that Bristol had strong feelings about the Armenian issue. In reference to a suggested Armenian mandate, Bristol wrote to Lewis Heck, the former Commissioner to Turkey, who had earlier left for the US State Department, pleading his point of view. It should be noted that the date of this letter is 8 July 1919; Bristol's arrival in Istanbul was 28 January 1919. In other words, it took six months for the admiral to have such strong feelings. Bristol asked Heck: 'For God's sake, get the idea out of [the State Department's] head that there is such thing as Armenia from a national point of view. I cannot imagine any greater calamity than for the United States to accept a mandatory for Armenia.'[5]

Another document reveals Bristol's frustration with the misinformation prevalent in the US:

The people of the United States as a whole fail to have any correct idea of the situation in the old Turkish Empire and refuse to believe those honest Americans, who would set them right. This is not to be wondered at because, for the past six years, the United States has been flooded with the most persistent propaganda on the part of the Greeks and Armenians that has given but one side of the story. In addition, this side of the story is a distorted and inaccurate story . . .

The mass of the Armenians in this part of the world are illiterate. There is no doubt if the Armenians could be gathered together in one locality and educated and trained, they could govern themselves like any other race; however, such a locality would have to be arbitrarily assigned, and it would probably take force to remove the original inhabitants. There is no considerable district in this part of the world where the Armenians are the majority, nor were they in a majority before the deportations took place. Therefore, in order to establish an Armenian nation, it would require large forces of foreign troops, large sums of money, probably fighting and bloodshed and two or three generations, if not more, to carry out such a project. I am sure that if our people at home who are advocating an independent Armenia would come out here and see the real facts, they would immediately change their minds. I know that this is a fact because every one of our Americans in this territory agrees with me on this point, and the great number of Americans who come out here to work for the Near East Relief Committee change their minds when they know the real facts.[6]

Clearly, Bristol was not in favour of an Armenian state for practical rather than ideological or political reasons. The following document, however, suggests that he changed his stand. In his 'War Diary' dated 27 November 1922, he gives clear evidence on how he felt about the Armenian state; here, he somehow shifts his views in favour of the creation of an Armenian state:

In a conversation, I . . . pointed out to [James Barton] that I was in a decided favor of someplace where the Armenians could find a home. *I had come to this conclusion recently*, although previously I had believed that the best solution of the problem was to keep the Armenians, Greeks, and Turks together and reform the Government and develop the Government of Turkey so that they could live together in peace and happiness.[7]

This is significant in demonstrating that Bristol adjusted his views based on the facts on the ground. In fact, his 'War Diary' in the following paragraphs mentions another meeting with George R. Montgomery, a Constantinople-born son of a missionary family:

[George R. Montgomery] started at me with a lot of old arguments that I have heard so many times that they bore me to death. They bore me because I agree with the arguments and do not need any further convincing, but simply because I will not lose all my perspective and think of nothing else but getting an Armenian nation into existence. I am supposed to be anti-Armenian, and it is necessary to convert me from my total ignorance of the subject. I told Montgomery it wasn't necessary to go all over this information and argument with me, that whereas previously, I had believed that the best thing was for the Turks, Greeks, and Armenians to live together in one country under an improved Government. *I now, due to the force of circumstances that have recently developed, believe that the only thing is to find someplace where the Armenians can be given a home and a place to go to and live and develop.* Montgomery talked along in his same old monotonous and stale way. I tried very hard not to show that I was bored and to take an interest in what he had to say. I think I succeeded very well. I told him plainly that where people thought I was against the Armenians, they were absolutely mistaken, and in my opinion, the people who had done the Armenians the most harm were those who were trying to help them . . .

I felt sorry for [Montgomery] because he has such a small point of view and can't see that though his arguments are perfectly sound, nobody is going to carry them out. Therefore, he must look for another solution that will be accepted. This seems almost impossible for him to understand, and he always comes back to what 'should be done.'[8]

What we learn from this entry is critical. Contrary to Bristol's earlier position on the Armenian issue, he clearly states that in 1922 he became convinced that Armenians should have a state of their own, and, as usual, he flatly denies that he is anti-Armenian. What he is against is the method of the Armenian lobby in the US, supported by the American missionaries by painting all the Turks red. Bristol believed that the lobbyists exaggerated, if not lied about, the conditions in Turkey for a political end, and American people had the right to know the truth. We can only speculate about what made him change his position and what the 'force of circumstances' was, but we know that between 1920 and 1922, Bristol became in favour of the creation of an Armenian state. It is possible that within two years it became clear to him that the nationalists would succeed in creating a 'nation-state' for the Turks and the Armenians would not fit in this new regime.

Bristol never denied or tried to justify the Armenian massacres of 1915 and, if the term had existed at that time, he might have qualified them as 'genocide'. What he does deny is that the systematic killings of the Armenians continued in the post-World War I period. To demonstrate this point, we can look at a US archival document. In a telegram dated 9 March 1920, Bristol responds to allegations that the nationalists in Anatolia were massacring the Armenians during the post-World War I period. In doing so, however, he acknowledges that the massacres in 1915 were, in fact, systematic. In this telegram, Bristol complains about 'misleading reports appearing in newspapers in London and Paris' regarding the Armenian massacres in 1920:

The tenor of news and comment regarding Turkish events in London and Paris press that reached here [Constantinople] dated to the end of February is quite misleading and gives wrong impressions, particularly with respect to Armenian massacres. That is deliberate propaganda to influence conference and throw dust in the eyes of the public to support the solution of Turkish problem according to selfish European national interests is possible. To judge by recent debates of the Turkish question in the House of Commons official information regarding the situation is distorted deliberately or otherwise when it reaches Europe. As typical, I refer to editorial LONDON TIMES, February 18th.

Wholesale massacres have occurred lately anywhere in Anatolia, notably Marash, and these were coincident with the nationalist attack on the French, which was provoked (?) *There is no good evidence that any Turkish element plans systematic exterminations as occurred in 1915.* Similar measures would be absolutely against any Turkish desire to preserve even a fragment of Turkish sovereignty in the present crisis, but, it is believed, would obviously be to the selfish interest of France and other nations seeking territorial gains in Asia Minor to create the impression with the public, and the Conference, that massacres are systematic and widespread.[9]

As mentioned above, what is most significant in this telegram is the fact that Bristol did acknowledge the 'systematic exterminations' of Armenians in 1915. This is clear proof that he never denied the massacre of Armenians, but wished to educate the American public of the nuances of these killings under World War I conditions. In fact, Bristol strongly believed that the protection of the Armenians could only be achieved by not provoking the Turks by exaggeration of facts or producing pure lies. He never shied away from advising Armenian officials for the well-being of the Armenians.

In his 'War Diary', Bristol records his conversation with Alexandre Khatissian, former minister-President of Armenia, in the Caucasus. He informs us that he had met Khatissian three times before in Tbilisi, and in one of those conversations he had given the Armenians of the Caucasus a piece of advice:

The advice I had given [Khatissian] was to stop all offensive operations of the Armenians in the Caucasus and to organize his country so the people could live and await the developments of the Peace Conference. I warned him that he could not count upon the Allies or any other country giving the Armenians military assistance and, therefore, the Armenians made a great mistake to stir up the Tartars and the Turks against them. I also told Khatissian at that time that, in my opinion, it would be very much better for the Armenians to take up negotiations directly with the Turks to the westward and the Tartars to the eastward and come to some agreement without depending upon outside assistance. I based this recommendation upon the belief right from the beginning that the countries of Europe had had enough war and would not undertake any more fighting, especially for altruistic purposes such as the establishment of an enlarged Armenia in the Near East.[10]

These statements clearly place Bristol as a realist, not anti- or pro-Armenian. However, being a realist is what Bristol strived to accomplish during his tenure in the Middle East. In continuation, he moved into his discussions with Khatissian on a national home for the Armenians. Bristol recorded that

Khatissian had three propositions to make in connection with a home for the Armenians. The first was a separate state in Eastern Anatolia where the Armenians could establish and govern themselves but under the suzerainty of Turkey, which would guarantee the neutrality of this new country. The idea is that this country would be a buffer state between Turkey and Russia. The second proposition was to enlarge Russian Armenia by taking territory from the Eastern provinces of Anatolia, and the third proposition was an Armenian home in the neighborhood of Cilicia. The arguments advanced were the usual ones that the Armenians had lived in Turkey for many centuries and were really the oldest inhabitants of the country and therefore were entitled to a place in Turkey for a home. I told Khatissian that *I was heartily in sympathy with the idea that the Armenians should have a place to live in Turkey, and they were entitled to such a place.* In reply to my questions, he admitted that the Turks would probably be averse to giving up any territory to Armenians and that the Allies could not be counted upon to use force to obtain from the Turks a home for the Armenians . . . There was one thing about this conference that struck me very forcibly, and that was that the Armenians have steadily bargained in regards to what they wanted. They started out with half of Anatolia for Armenia and argued just as strong then that that was their absolute right and just due. Gradually they have reduced their demands, and now they claim their just right as a little territory in

Eastern Anatolia for 700,000 Armenians. However, this figure is still about double what it should be. There are probably three or four hundred thousand Armenians that would go to a home thus provided. The Armenian is like the Jew in that he lives off of the rest of the world, and if they were all living together a good many of them, I believe, would starve to death.[11]

In the final months of 1922, Bristol was busy interviewing Armenian leaders like Khatissian. We know that he was ordered to go to Lausanne to be part of the US team to observe negotiations between Turkey and the Allied Powers. Since one of the most pressing issues of the time was the creation of an Armenian state, Bristol also wanted to know what the local Armenian leaders in Turkey thought of the issue. These interviews with the Greek Patriarch, the Armenian Gregorian Patriarch and the head of the Armenian Protestant Community were conducted by Bristol and his staff and collected in one folder.[12] The interview with the Armenian Patriarch Monseigneur Zaven was conducted by Bristol. This document does not have a date, but since it was conducted by Bristol himself, it must have been before his departure for Lausanne on 2 December 1922. The minutes must have been taken by one of Bristol's staff:

> The Admiral inquired concerning the fate of the Armenians in Eastern Anatolia. The Patriarch stated that they had been ordered to leave and that many of them were actually on the move. The Admiral then asked the Patriarch's opinion concerning the ultimate solution to the Armenian problem. Monseigneur Zaven replied that it was essential that the Armenians should be given a particular bit of territory of their own. The Admiral asked what particular bit of territory the Patriarch had in mind. Monseigneur Zaven said that two places had been selected. 1). Part of Northeastern Anatolia and 2). Cilicia. Monseigneur Zaven added that at one time, the Turks themselves had been willing to assign territory for an Armenian home. The Admiral asked whether it was likely that the Nationalist Turks held similar views. Monseigneur Zaven thought that things had probably been changed. The Admiral then inquired how this idea of a national home for the Armenians could be realized without resort to force.[13]

The Patriarch thought that diplomatic pressure at the Lausanne Conference had a good chance of success. However, he did not think 'any of the Powers would use force to bring about a solution of the minorities question':[14]

The Admiral then questioned Monseigneur Zaven regarding other possible solutions to the Armenian question. As to sending Armenians to Greece, the Patriarch thought that they would even be worse off than if they remained in Anatolia under Turkish rule. This, in his judgment, was due to the fact that the Greeks did not know how to treat foreigners, and constituted a highly homogenous population.

. . . The Admiral asked about the fate of the Armenians who left Cilicia during the evacuation. Monseigneur Zaven said that they had mostly gone to Syria or to the Islands, and while they were still refugees in the true sense of the word, they were to some extent, at any rate, earning their own livelihood . . . The settling of the Armenians in Mesopotamia and in the Arab countries Monseigneur Zaven thought would be difficult.[15]

Interesting information coming from this interview is not the fact that the Armenian Patriarch was in favour of an independent state but that in its absence if the need arose to relocate the Armenian community in Anatolia, it would be preferable to them. Zaven flatly rejected Greece claiming that the Greeks did not know how to treat foreigners, and they would be worse off under Greece than under Turkey. Settling Armenians in Arab countries, Zaven claimed, would also be very difficult.

The interview with Zenop Bezjian, the head of the Protestant Armenians, was carried out on 21 November 1922. Bristol began by informing Bezjian that the nationalist Turks gave assurances for the protection of Christians in Constantinople. However, Mr Bezjian expressed a certain degree of doubt. The admiral then asked for information regarding the future of the Armenian people in Turkey:

Mr. Bezjian emphasized the desirability of founding a national home for the Armenians in Turkey. He said that they have been here for over 2000 years and felt that they had the right to remain. He spoke of the possibilities of establishing such a home in North Eastern Anatolia but said that for his part, he felt that Cilicia would be a better place. He said that 200,000 Russian Armenians he considered henceforth belonged to Russia. He estimated the number of Armenians at present in Turkey as about 400,000. As for Armenians seeking refuge in Greece, he did not think that that would work out well. Romania or Bulgaria, but especially Romania, he thought, would be hospitable to the Armenians.

It seems that the Protestant and Orthodox Armenian leaders agreed on their first choice being an independent state and, in its absence, Greece would not be ideal for relocation; however, they differed on alternatives. Bezjian thought Romania or Bulgaria would be better choices. Understandably, Armenians were worried about the Kemalist takeover of Constantinople, since they bet entirely on the Allied countries winning the war and dividing the old Ottoman Empire.

The Treaty of Lausanne did not create an independent Armenia, and the nationalist government in Turkey solidified their control of the country. Faced with this reality, Bristol's view on an Armenian homeland in Turkey changed again three years later. In response to a direct question by US Senator William H. King, visiting Istanbul, on the possibility of establishing an Armenian homeland in Turkey, Bristol stated:

> I felt convinced that the Turks would fight before they would give up any territory for an Armenian home . . . Still, I felt that if the Armenians here were left alone, they would work out their salvation and maybe in a generation or two the Armenians would become Turkish citizens like foreigners become citizens of the United States and this, in my opinion, was the desirable condition to be accomplished.[16]

As mentioned, the change of heart is probably due to the fact that the Allied Powers left Turkey and the new Turkish regime was established in 1923. By the end of 1925, Mustafa Kemal was in firm control of the country. Bristol thought that the best solution for the Christians of Turkey was to integrate into the new Turkey as equal citizens. This is a clear indication of his flexibility in responding to the political developments on the ground. One can conclude that he did not have set ideas about the formation of an independent Armenia.

As previously mentioned, in 1925, Bristol stated his updated opinion on the Armenian state to US Senator King. In that sense, the report is a significant document where the admiral notes Senator King's visit and his conversations on the Armenians. The entry dated 18 July 1925 records a conversation between the senator and the admiral. In response to Senator King's opinion that the Turks should give territory and compensation to the Armenians, Bristol stated:

> I told the senator that I was quite in sympathy with the [idea] which he had that Turkey would give a certain territory for an Armenian home, but as I explained before, I believed Turkey would not give up any territory to this

end without fighting. The Senator with a deprecatory motion of the head stated that, of course, we were not going to fight for such a home. I told him when it came to a question of Turkey giving any recompense for Christian properties destroyed willfully or otherwise, I had always been met with certain statements which I had to admit were true . . . I told [the senator] that when I had tried to argue with the Turks along this same line which I had done many times they always met my argument with the statement that the Armenians in Eastern Anatolia during the war had ruthlessly destroyed Turkish property when the Russian army advanced in Eastern Anatolia. I told him that I knew this from Russian sources and also from Americans who were in that part of the country at the time. In the Mosul territory, an American told me that the Armenians with the Russian army had destroyed and killed so that there was not a cat or dog left in the country when they retreated. In the Caucasus just after the Armistice, the Armenian Government carried on a systematic driving out of the Moslems, and in one territory, particularly the Moslems had been cleared out for fifteen miles on either side of the railway from Erivan to the Persian frontier. During the Turco-Greek war, the Greeks, with their own soldiers, had carried on a systematic program of destruction along the southern shores of the Sea of Marmara. The facts in the case were established by foreign eyewitnesses, by the refugees, some 15,000 arriving in Constantinople, and by pictures and reports of an Inter-Allied Commission.[17]

In line with the previous document above, we see that Bristol was convinced of the new regime's resolve in not giving up any territory for the Armenians. It is important to note that his opinion is not based upon any emotional motivation, but solely on realpolitik. At this point, he strongly believed that fighting for an independent Armenia in Turkey would not be in the interest of the Armenians as they would be exposed to possible military operations or other interference by the Turks. The admiral quite correctly assumed that a large foreign military force needed to be stationed here to protect the fragile would-be Armenian state. Since there was no commitment from any of the Western Powers, Bristol believed that the best possible solution for the Armenians was to live in a new state with the Turks, a state where their lives and rights would be protected.

Such a line of realism (but also perhaps optimism) was undoubtedly not appreciated by those who favoured an Armenian state and lobbied for it. Therefore, it is easy to understand why the supporters of an Armenian state labelled Bristol as pro-Turk (see Chapter 1). However, I hope that independent readers will appreciate Bristol's reasoning against Armenian independence. Besides, he was adamant about the one-sided propaganda of Turkish atrocities against the Christian 'races'. On every occasion, he did not shy away from stating that Armenians and especially the Greeks committed similar crimes, and they should not be overlooked as well.

Partisan scholarship, even in the twenty-first century, does not refrain from directly attacking Bristol's stand on the Armenian issue. Robert Shenk, in an essay, blames Bristol for selling humanity for US commercial interests, by criticising the missionary reports describing the suffering of the Christians in the region. To Shenk, Bristol was covering up for the Turks. He writes:

> [US missionaries'] dilemmas were often exacerbated by the lack of understanding, demeaning attitude, and outright cover-ups perpetrated by the American head official in the region, Admiral Mark Bristol in Constantinople . . . Of course, Bristol himself had never been deep inland in Turkey, and certainly never had to deal with utterly soulless Turkish officials completely on his own . . . But what drove Bristol to his belittling of so many of the relief workers he dealt with and to his policy of hushing up the widespread atrocities that were once again taking place throughout much of continental Turkey? . . . It was his utterly shortsighted zeal for American commerce that he supported with alacrity from the start of his tour of duty in Turkey that so blinded him to other realities—like suffering humanity.[18]

Shenk was criticising Bristol's knowledge of the situation, suggesting that he had never been 'inland', a term that is not fully described. Bristol indeed travelled beyond Constantinople all the way to Tbilisi. This is a rather weak attempt to criticise as Henry Morgenthau, Bristol's predecessor and champion of the Armenian cause, was also not a traveller to the hinterland. Unlike Morgenthau, Bristol's staff and intelligence sources were diverse and very much in a position to collect information from the region. Bristol's opinion of the Near East was largely based on the intelligence reports he received from his ship captains, who were also ordered to go 'inland' and report. He also gathered information from other Western travellers, officials and missionaries. US commercial interests were surely a factor in Bristol's position towards the Armenian issue; however, they were not the determining one.

The admiral genuinely believed that inciting Armenians against the Turks or vice versa would not help the Armenian well-being since no outside force would help Armenians when faced with Turkish retaliation. Like that of Shenk's, there are many attacks on Bristol's view of the Armenians and their character, which were undoubtedly orientalist in nature. These attacks on Bristol in the current scholarship, however, do not take into consideration the fact that he was not the only American official holding such views. In fact, on his tour to Batum and Constantinople in order to see the situation for himself, Bristol's superior Vice Admiral Harry Shepard Knapp, Commander of the US Naval Forces Operating in European Waters (Chief of Naval Operations), wrote the following:

> [T]he Armenian character in no way palliates the crimes that have been committed against the Armenians, nor should cause any diminution of sympathy of the suffering and underfed Armenian population. That sympathy, however, would be much greater if the estimate of the Armenian character were higher. Armenians here in Asia Minor are represented to me to be a very thrifty, commercially astute, and personally miserly and mean people who penetrate everywhere, by their great business capacity, get practical control of business affairs, especially in the way of a larger business. From what Colonel Haskell tells me the wealthy Armenians do not appear to be exerting themselves nor manifesting any liberality of spirit for the benefit of their less fortunate countrymen, but on the contrary, seem to be entirely willing to accept everything that the generous people of the United States will do for them, and even to endeavor by devious methods to get hold of supplies sent out and then sell them to whomsoever has the necessary funds to pay the prices asked, whether Armenians or foreigners. Furthermore, it seems to be the belief of people who know the Armenians well; *if they were in the majority and had the power, they would as ruthlessly slaughter the Turks as the Turks slaughtered them, as indeed they have already done.* Summing up I should say that the general opinion of the competent observers hereabouts is that the Armenians are conducting very skillful propaganda for material outside help and for political support that has achieved a result far in excess of their deserts and that the real Armenian character is not understood by the generous people of the United States and England who are making such earnest and honest endeavors in their behalf.[19]

Vice Admiral Knapp's view clearly shows that Bristol was not alone in describing the Armenians as as ruthless as the Turks but in a more disadvantaged position to display it. This view of stereotyping the 'Eastern people' regardless of race and religion was indeed 'orientalist' in nature, as Edward Said described the term in his seminal work *Orientalism*.[20]

Bristol was keen on informing the American public of the other side of the coin where, in his words, Armenians were not Christian 'saintly martyrs'.[21] When he travelled to the US, he made his views known boldly and unapologetically. Reflecting on past events, Admiral Bristol gave a speech at the US Army War College in 1925. In the speech, he mentioned many atrocities committed in the region, and he did not spare the Armenians:

> Now going back a little, I want to say just a few words about the atrocities. So far as atrocities are concerned, I don't think any of the races in the Near East has it over the rest. Just after I got there [to the Near East], I had a rude awakening. In Armenia, that is the Russian Armenia, for 20 versts[22] each side of the railway, the Armenians cleaned out the Moslems, drove them out, and those who did not get out were killed or left to starve. When the Greeks landed in Smyrna, they shot up the place until they were stopped by the advice of the Allies. In Cilicia, the French had a foreign legion of Armenians. These Armenians used to pay off old scores against the Turks by twitting them and every once in awhile shooting up a man. The Turks retaliated, so whenever an Armenian was caught outside the French lines, he lost his life.[23]

Needless to say, such statements did not win the admiral any favour among the Christian missionaries. Here, I would like to add that Bristol's opinion of the Kemalist movement in 1922 evolved into a more respected level towards the end of his tenure in Turkey. For all critics of Turkey, Bristol stated:

> Nearly everybody believes that [the Turks] will not be able to take care of themselves and that they will be financially, economically, and most probably socially ruined without the Christian races. I believe that necessity is the mother of invention, and therefore when the Turks are thrown on their own, they will have to paddle their own canoe or else they will sink, and if they sink and are destroyed, that will dispose of the 'horrible Turk.' If there is anything in him the necessity will bring it out, and under adversity, he may build up a government of the people, by the people for the people, and then other races will drift back into this country in the same way that they drifted into America; or they will become established in other countries and then can demonstrate that they never wanted to live with the Turk. Well,

there is one thing anyway that we must face; the Turk is in power, and he has an army, and he'll fight . . . If our people are not ready to fight for what they claim, then they should not keep talking about impossible things. They make matters worse.[24]

This research repeatedly documented that Bristol always tried to be neutral in the very polarised political environment. He never changed his stance on the fact that there were systematic massacres against the Armenians during the World War I period. The Turkish massacres of Armenians during the War of Independence era (1919–22) were not systematic, unlike those in 1915. However, Bristol also pointed out Armenian killings of the Muslim population during and after World War I. This position did not change during his tenure. What did evolve was his solution to the Armenian sufferings. In his earlier reports, Bristol subscribed to the idea that the entire Ottoman Empire should be maintained under a US mandate. The dividing of the empire could not help the Armenians, but living under a multi-ethnic/religious empire whose political and administrative institutions were modernised would be the best hope for the Armenians.

After 1919, Admiral Bristol was more sympathetic towards the idea of the creation of an Armenian state somewhere in Turkey and the Caucasus region. When the Kemalist/nationalists achieved winning the war and declaring a new state, Bristol's suggestions matched with this political reality and suggested that the Armenians should live in the newly established state as full citizens. After the new regime was established in Turkey as a republic, Bristol was hopeful for the future of Kemalist Turkey and supported it as a modern, secular, Western-oriented state that could allow Armenians to thrive in the new regime. Towards the end of his tenure in 1927, his reports did not contain much information regarding the Armenians. He was a close observer and admirer of the Kemalist regime's ability to pull a new state out of the rubble of the corrupt Ottoman Empire. The distinction here is vital. I believe that after the creation of the new state as a republic, Bristol became an admirer of the emerging Turkish regime, not a pro-Turk. As another chapter shows, he criticised the reforms and the Kemalists when he saw fit.

During the Lausanne negotiations, Bristol was a staunch supporter of signing a peace treaty with the emerging Turkish regime. When he realised the objection to such a treaty in the Senate, he sent a letter to the Secretary of State, dated 3 January 1924.[25] What Bristol wrote in this letter shows that the emerging Kemalist regime was feeling the shame of the Armenian killings under the previous regime:

> The most serious charge laid at the door of Turkey by those who desire to exclude her from the pale of civilization is in connection with the cruelties practiced upon the Armenians by the Turks acting under official orders, and in pursuance of a deliberate official policy. It may, however, be illuminating to quote in regards to them the following words taken from a pamphlet on the Turco-Armenian question issued in 1919 by the National Congress of Turkey. This pamphlet stated: No doubt, the forcible transplantation of an entire people at short notice is a cruel measure. But considering the circumstances involved in a war in which her very existence was at stake and in which she had to strain every nerve to avoid defeat, Turkey found herself confronted with an internal enemy acting in support of, and inclusion with, the external and employing the most desperate and ferocious means to bring about her fall. While the great majority of Armenians of both sexes and all ages were engaged in this task, was she to sacrifice the supreme interest of the state, its preservation, [and] welfare, this at a time when by the operation of the war, the laws of humanity in their general exception were suspended?
>
> The guilt of the unionist organization [Committee of Union and Progress], which conceived and deliberately *carried out this infernal policy of extermination and robbery*, is patent. Its leaders rank among the greatest criminals of humanity. The Turkish people bows its head. It does so in grief for the Armenian people and in shame for itself. It has recognized and is fulfilling the obligations under which this situation places it. But it repudiates all moral responsibility in connection with the action of its unworthy leaders whom it has disowned.[26]

It is conceivable that many members of the National Congress of Turkey, who were seemingly anti-CUP in the 1919 Constantinople, later became members of the Kemalist movement. This report of the mentioned pamphlet to Washington indicates that Bristol was keenly aware that the anti-CUP establishment in the Ottoman Empire also acknowledged the killings of Armenians by the state, but refused to accept responsibility. Bristol's argument for the signing of the treaty was that the post-CUP Turkey accepted the crimes committed by the previous regime and was ready to move along with other nations to the next chapter in world history. It is significant that in 1919 Armenian massacres were acknowledged in the Ottoman Empire. We know that the issue became taboo in the later period, and such acknowledgment was revoked.

In any case, Admiral Bristol always sympathised with the sufferings of the Armenians and the Turks; however, such sympathy only occasionally existed towards the Greek population of Anatolia, and especially the Greek occupiers of Western Anatolia. In the next section, I will focus on the event that shaped Bristol's view of the Greeks – that is, the Greek occupation of Smyrna and the north Aegean region that resulted in the Greek atrocities towards the Muslim civilian population. Bristol was a primary source for details of these events as he was appointed as the US member to an Inter-Allied Commission to investigate the atrocities in the region in 1919. Let us now turn our attention to this issue.

The Greeks and Bristol

We know that Admiral Bristol never had sympathy with the Greek invasion of Western Anatolia. One of the main reasons behind his distaste for the Greeks was the attitude of the Greek minority in the Ottoman Empire and the Greek army that invaded Smyrna in 1919, events he himself witnessed. He repeatedly warned Washington that the Greek occupation was a bad idea and fuelled the Turkish resistance, which gave birth to the success of the Kemalist movement in the region. Bristol shared his opinion with Josephus Daniels, Secretary of the Navy: 'It was the landing of the Greeks in Smyrna and the prospect that the Vilayet of Aidin would be ceded to Greece that started the Nationalist movement . . . The Nationalists have maintained their control and increased their influence throughout Turkey by keeping alive the Greek and Armenian threats against the partition of their country.'[27]

What Bristol did not know, however, was that his own president, Woodrow Wilson, was heavily involved in the decision-making process of the Greek occupation of Western Anatolia. President Wilson's little-known support for the Greek invasion of the area is a significant fact for the historians. This support also indicates that Bristol was unknowingly in stark disagreement with his own President. We have an archival document to demonstrate this point. In the US archives, the document numbered 867.00/179 contains the minutes of a meeting, catalogued as 'top secret', which informs us of the dialogues among the 'Council of Four'[28] members about the occupation of Smyrna in 1919. The meeting took place in Lloyd George's hotel room in Paris. What is noteworthy here are the statements by the American President Wilson encouraging the Council for the Greek occupation. The date for the meeting was 6 May 1919, only nine days before the Greek landing at Smyrna. Those present at the meeting were President Wilson (USA), Lloyd George, General Wilson, Rear Admiral Hope (Great Britain), Clemenceau (France) and Venizelos (Greece). The following section of the minutes demonstrates the point:

> President Wilson said that he supposed that the [Mudros] Armistice gave the Allies the right to send troops [to Smyrna].
>
> Venizelos said that more than 30,000 Greek citizens in the town of Smyrna were in danger from the Turks.
>
> President Wilson said that this provided a very good reason for protecting them.
>
> General Wilson said that it was true the Allies had the power to land the troops, but the Italians had [also the same] right.
>
> Venizelos pointed out that the Italians had landed in Adalia without consulting the Allies.
>
> President Wilson said that if Greek troops were sent, the Italians could hardly land troops unless they intended to break with the Allies. After discussions, the Supreme Council agreed to the immediate dispatch of Greek troops to SMYRNA and the occupation of that town by purely Greek forces. Lloyd George asked if Venizelos had warned the Greeks to keep the matter quiet, and received a positive response.[29]

President Wilson was not only aware of the looming occupation but in fact played a major role in strategising the landing. He strongly suggested that the Turks should not be warned about the Greek landing until the last minute. President Wilson agreed that warning the Turks 'would be the correct procedure. But if the Turks were warned too far in advance, they would make preparations.' He suggested that 'no communications should be made to the Turks until the [Greek] troops were on board' and heading for the landing.[30] Nine days later, the occupation began by order of the Allies without the knowledge of Italy and the Ottoman Empire until the last minute.

Accordingly, the Greek administration was established in Smyrna and speedily began to expand towards the north and the hinterlands, which triggered what was later known as the Turkish War of Independence and the formation of the new Turkish Republic. The Greek armies remained in the Ottoman territories until 1922. Admiral Bristol witnessed the Greek military administration with great distaste. He became very critical of the Greek occupation and the attitude of the Greek minorities in the Ottoman Empire. He was later appointed to the Inter-Allied Commission of Inquiry on the Greek occupation of Smyrna and the adjoining territories; let us now turn our attention to this commission and its findings in order to understand the origin of Bristol's negative opinion of the Greeks.

The Greeks and the Inter-Allied Commission of Inquiry[31]

Tensions between the Greeks and the Turks in Smyrna were rising prior to the Greek occupation of the city on 15 May 1919. A report by Lewis Heck, a US Commissioner in Constantinople, to the Secretary of State dated 11 March 1919 clearly points out the already tense relations between the two communities a short time before.[32] This report is significant, especially to understand the context in which Bristol formed his views about the Greeks in the following years. Therefore, I begin this section by quoting this document. Heck, after informing the Secretary of State of the in-fighting for Smyrna between Italians and Greeks, describes the relationship between the local Turks and the Greeks in the following manner:

> The present situation between the Greeks and the Turks in the Smyrna region is very tense. The Greeks have grave and well-justified grievances against the Turkish government. [Greek] claims to a just and an equitable form of government have to receive the most serious consideration. Nevertheless, . . . it must be remembered that . . . as a whole, the Greeks are in the minority everywhere outside of Smyrna . . . even before the deportation of 1913. The attitude of the Greek population at Smyrna and of the Greek officers [stems from the belief that] the Smyrna region will be given to Greece.[33]

As for the Turkish attitude towards the Greeks, Heck claimed that the Turks' feeling of mistrust towards the Greek government found its roots in the harsh treatment of the Turkish population in Macedonia. The Turks, concluded Heck, 'will not retire any further and . . . rather than to do so, they will resist a Greek government to the last man. They undoubtedly have an organization with a view to such resistance and have stocks of arms and ammunition ready.'[34] Furthermore, Heck predicted the following:

> So far as I can ascertain the feeling of the local Greek population in Smyrna they are unanimous in desiring to get rid of the Turkish rule and of being incorporated in the Greek Kingdom. There was one prominent Greek of Smyrna, only with whom I talked confidently, who expressed a doubt as to the wisdom of that region being given to Greece. As stated above, it seems certain that the Greeks are bringing in some supplies of arms and ammunition, and numerous local incidents which occurred in which either Greeks or Turks have been killed are an indication of the intensity of the situation. If, in the course of a generation, the Greek elements succeed in overwhelming the Turkish element, the question will have to settle itself without serious complications, but if the region is given to the Greek government as matters stand today, it is quite likely that serious and even bloody consequences between the two elements would result.[35]

We know that the Greek occupation of the region began on 15 May 1919 with disastrous consequences. We also know that Admiral Bristol temporarily came to Constantinople to relieve Heck on 7 May 1919, just a week before the Greek landing.[36] He must have received first-hand information about the Greek occupation of the city and its shortcomings. It is during this time that Bristol formed his views on the Greeks in Turkey. The landing of Smyrna stirred many hard feelings within the Ottoman Empire. The horrifying stories of Greek occupation and alleged atrocities committed by the Greek troops outraged the Muslim population. Within a short time of this occupation, the US State Department was flooded with complaints of atrocities committed by the Greeks. The accusers were mainly Turks, but Peter Buzanski points out that there were some American residents of Smyrna who also complained.[37]

The news travelled to the Paris Peace Conference fast. On 15 July 1919, the Sheikh-al-Islam of the Ottoman Empire, Mustafa Sabri Efendi, complained to the conference and asked the formation of an 'Inter-Allied Commission' to investigate the crimes committed by the Greek troops. Three days later, Clemenceau and other Allied leaders endorsed the request, and by the end of the first week of August, Italy, France, Britain and the United States had appointed their members to the commission. They were as follows: for the United States of America, Commodore Mark Bristol; for France, Brigadier Georges Bunoust; for Britain, Brigadier Robert Hugh Hare; for Italy, Lieutenant-General Alfredo Dall'Olio. Lieutenant Luigi Villari was appointed Secretary-General. The following officers were also attached to the Commission: for the US, Lieutenant Robert S. Dunn, Lieutenant Stewart (later replaced by Lieutenant Jones) and Mr Caessbrough (Turkish interpreter); for France, Lieutenant Rumerchne, Sub-Lieutenant Vitalis (Greek interpreter) and Sub-Lieutenant Dugoureq; for the British Empire, Major Thomson (Turkish interpreter), Captain Harris and Lieutenant Higham (during the Commission's stay in Asia).[38]

Between 12 August and 15 October the commission held forty-six meetings, twenty of which took place in İzmir. The rest were held in the areas on the Aegean coast where the alleged Greek atrocities took place. The first and the last meetings were organised in Istanbul. The main methodology of the commission in gathering information was to conduct interviews with the locals, which resulted in 175 of them. The witnesses included Turks, Greeks, Americans, Frenchmen, Italians and Englishmen, as well as Armenian and Jewish minorities of the empire.

At the initial meeting, it was agreed that the presence of a Greek officer at the meetings of the commission would make Turkish witnesses reluctant to speak freely and vice versa. When they finished all hearings, one fact emerged: Greeks and Turks blamed the atrocities on each other. Therefore, the commission would tend to give the greatest importance to the testimony of those who were neither Turk nor Greek.

The final report consisted of three parts. The first part was titled 'Accounts of Events'; it narrated the terrible events that took place between 12 August and 6 October 1919. The second part dealt specifically with the persons responsible for the incidents under the title of 'Establishment of Responsibilities'. The third section was 'Conclusions'.

Under the section titled 'Accounts of Events', the report lists forty-seven points, sixteen of which defined the incidents before the Greek occupation of Smyrna. The second section blamed the Greek Military High Command and some specifically named officers who failed to keep the order as it was the responsibility of the occupying force. The commission also accused Turkish authorities, who failed to take necessary steps to prevent the escape of the prisoners before the landing.

In the section titled 'Establishment of Responsibilities', the authors of the report made several 'statements of facts', which had been established during the inquiry between 12 August and 6 October 1919. Overall, they listed forty-seven points, the majority of which put the blame on the shoulders of the occupying force, Greece. However, there was also criticism of the Turkish side, especially the Turkish irregulars. The following is the summary of several points made by the commission:

> Since the Mudros Armistice in 1918, Christians have not been in danger in the Turkish province of Aydin, and fears of Christian massacres were unjustified. The situation in the *vilayet* did not justify the landing of Allied troops in Smyrna. On the contrary, the situation worsened after the Greek landing due to the state of war existing between the Greek troops and Turkish irregulars. On 15 and 16 May, countless acts of violence and looting targeted at the Turkish people and their homes took place in the town. Many women were raped. Some people were murdered. The acts of violence and looting were committed for the most part by a mob of Greeks from the town, although it has been proven that soldiers also joined in and that the military authorities took no effective measures to stop the acts of violence and looting until it was too late. The committee took the pain to state: 'the accusation made by Sheikh-ul-Islam is not entirely justified.' However, 'the occupation, the purpose of which in principle was only to maintain order, actually has all the appearances of an annexation.' Therefore, the majority of the blame goes to the Greek army.[39]

In an attachment to the report, Colonel Alexander Mazarakis, the Greek liaison of the committee, objected to some of its conclusions. His letter to the committee dated 11 October 1919 challenged its findings. Mazarakis stated:

1. The military occupation was imposed to restore order, to rescue what remained of the Christian population, which was persecuted, exiled and massacred for five years, and to prevent a resurgence of Turkish extremism;
2. All the events, which had regrettable consequences, took place after Turks had attacked the Greek army;
3. Not only did the Greek authorities act promptly throughout to restore order, but I even venture to suggest that they treated and continue to treat the Muslim population favourably;

4. Even the lack of foresight on the part of the Greek Command in Smyrna can be explained to a certain extent in view of the fact that neither Greece's representative nor the representatives of the Entente in Smyrna expected the Turks to attack, and thus took no effective measure to move the Turkish troops and prevent the people from gathering and going about their business;

5. Perfect order reigns in the zone occupied by the Greek army, whilst there is complete anarchy outside this zone.[40]

The four-member committee was not impressed by this letter but, regardless, included it in the report. The report's conclusions insisted that the majority of the blame should go to the Greek forces of occupation, despite the fact that it spelled out several incidents where the Turkish authorities were at fault. It should be underlined that the British, American, Italian and French members of the committee all signed the document, and the conclusions were unanimous. This fact is very significant because the report was later kept out of publication and circulation and accused of being biased. As will be seen below, this angered Bristol, who cried foul in the name of being fair to all sides.

The last part of the report was titled 'Conclusions Put Forward by the Commission'. It bears the date of 13 October 1919.

1. The situation which has arisen in Smyrna and in the *vilayet* of Aydin following the Greek occupation is strained because:

(a) The occupation, which had as its principal purpose merely the maintenance of order, has, in reality, assumed all the forms of an annexation. The Greek High Commissioner alone exercises an efficacious authority. The Turkish authorities, who have continued to carry on their functions, no longer have any real power. They no longer receive orders from Constantinople, and, on account of the almost complete disappearance of the Turkish police and gendarmerie forces, they no longer have the means necessary for the execution of their decisions.

(b) The occupation imposes extensive military sacrifices upon Greece, which are out of proportion with the mission to be fulfilled if this mission is temporary and should have only maintenance of order as its purpose.

(c) It is incompatible in its present form with the return of order and of peace for which the populations, threatened with famine, have great need.

2. The Commission deems:

(a) That if the military occupation of the country is to have as its sole purpose the maintenance of security and public welfare, this occupation should not be entrusted to Greek troops, but to Allied troops, under the authority of the Supreme Allied Commander in Asia Minor.

(b) That the occupation by the Greeks alone should not be maintained unless the Peace Conference is resolved to announce the complete and definite annexation of the country to Greece. In such a case, freedom of action should be left to the Greek Commander *vis-a-vis* the Turkish forces.

(c) That the pure and simple annexation as above stated would be contrary to the principle proclaiming the respect for nationalities, because in the occupied regions, outside of the cities of Smyrna and Aivali, the predominance of the Turkish element over the Greek is incontestable. It is the duty of the Commission to observe the fact that the Turkish national sentiment, which has already manifested its resistance, will never accept this annexation. It will submit only to force, that is to say, before a military expedition, which Greece alone could not carry out with any chance of success.

3. In view of these conditions, the Commission proposes the following measures:

(a) To replace as soon as possible all or part of the Greek troops by the Allied troops much fewer in number.

(b) If, in order to safeguard Greek self-respect, it is decided that a part of the Greek troops may cooperate in the occupation, distribute these troops in the interior of the occupied regions in order to prevent them from coming in direct contact with the Turkish national forces.

(c) As soon as the occupation by the Allies has been completed, it requires the Turkish Government to reorganize its gendarmerie under the direction and command of Inter-Allied officers. This gendarmerie should be constituted as soon as possible to assure order in the entire region with the purpose of replacing the Allied detachments.

(d) At the same time, as the reorganization of the gendarmerie, the Turkish Government should be required to restore its civil administration.

4. The heads of the national movement, having on many occasions stated that their opposition was only directed against the Greeks, the measures proposed should dispose of all grounds for armed resistance on their part and return to the central government of Constantinople the authority which it no longer has. Nothing should then prevent the disbanding of the irregular troops. In the case of the contrary, the Entente will finally be able to know what faith it can place in the protestations of loyalty made by the Turks, both by the leaders of the national movement and by members of the Government.

The commission unanimously signed these conclusions, which clearly was not intended by Lord Earl Curzon of Great Britain in 1922. Curzon was responsible for creating the Commission of Inquiry and including the Americans to participate in it. We know that after much debate in the US, Admiral Mark Bristol was instructed to chair the commission. It is clear from Bristol's reports to Washington that the main aim of Curzon was to pressure Turkey for the upcoming peace negotiations, not necessarily an honest attempt at fact-finding.

The problem for Curzon was that Admiral Bristol was very much interested in the facts. In his report, Bristol advised the US Secretary of State as follows:

We should bend every energy to ensure not only critical examination of events in Anatolia during the past six months but primarily the fullest publicity for a report which shall place these events in their proper historical, political, and religious perspective. To accomplish this, it will be essential to take cognizance of the Smyrna investigation of 1919 and the Allied investigation of 1921 into Greek atrocities of Allies . . . The Commission will find information from native sources unreliable and one-sided and will, therefore, necessarily rely on first-hand information principally upon American missionaries and relief workers in Anatolia. Practically none of these workers have been in territory under Greek control, so their evidence will almost entirely be confined to acts in territory under Turkish control. Unless, therefore, our representatives on Commission insist upon proper perspective, we will find the American name in Turkey publicly identified with one of the several conflicting partitions of views of the Turkish question now held with obvious results of entangling the United States in Near Eastern political intrigue.[41]

In other words, Bristol was warning that unless the commission remained neutral in uncovering all the atrocities from independent sources (relatively speaking, of course), the report would not be treated as fact and would tarnish the non-partisan image of the US in the Near East.

This was obviously not what Great Britain wanted. Bristol, in a separate report, implied that Curzon wished to accomplish three things with his proposal of a commission:

1. Secure a good ground for breaking off negotiations with the Turks and withdrawing concessions made in the last peace proposals; the Turks refuse to accept the commission of inquiry.
2. Get the Allies together in their Turkish policy on a platform from which it would be very difficult for any dissent. He presumably wants the United States to participate not only for the reason of impartiality stated in his telegram but also because it would be difficult for France to refuse to join if we should do so.
3. To quiet the pro-Greek pro-Armenian sentiment in England, which is very strong.[42]

In reality, Bristol was questioning the humanitarian aspect of the proposed commission and highlighting the political goals behind it. Let me add that Bristol in the same document suggested mediation between the Greeks and the Turks; otherwise, he warned, the Turkish atrocities towards the Christians would continue, especially in the hinterland where the Allies did not have any control, and where many Christians resided.

As discussed, the Inter-Allied Inquiry did not produce a result that could be embraced by Great Britain or Greece. It listed atrocities committed by both sides and concluded that the Greek side bore the most responsibility.[43] However, the Turkish side was also on the receiving end of some criticism. Interestingly, despite the fact that the Allied Powers commissioned the report, Lloyd George of Great Britain convinced his colleagues in other Allied countries that this report should never be made public. When asked in the British House of Commons, he stated that the report was not fair, for no Greek was a member of the inquiry.[44]

The Allies' Attitude towards the Report

'The Council of Heads of Five Great Powers' discussed the findings of the commission on 8 November 1919. The general tone was to ask the Greek side for their defence of the incidents caused by the Greek occupation. Venizelos, the Greek Prime Minister, upon receiving the chance to talk, said that this report should be considered null and void and that another commission of investigation should be established. His objection seemed to be directed towards the methodology of the investigation rather than the findings. He claimed that it was not fair that the Greek representative, Colonel Mazarakis, was not present at the meetings of the commission where the testimonies of the locals were recorded. General Bunoust of France strongly opposed Venizelos's accusation that the commission's work was biased and that Greece was not treated fairly. After all, the commission had unanimously agreed that neither the Greek nor the Turkish representatives should be present when the testimonies were taken simply because those who were before the commission would feel uncomfortable about being entirely open and frank. In fact, Colonel Mazarakis's objections were presented to the commission in a report that is also attached to the final report in which he made seventeen points in an attempt to refute the findings. Furthermore, the commission, after reading the Mazarakis rebuttal, was unanimous in stating that there were no grounds for modifying the commission's original report. When pressed to accept responsibility for the crimes committed under the Greek occupation, Venizelos conceded that some excesses might have occurred, but they could be readily explained by the unfavourable conditions under which the Greek landing of Smyrna took place and by the fact that those who were found responsible were brought to justice by the Greek government. At the end of the meeting, Venizelos was asked if he was aware of the danger that the Turkish side would increase their attacks. He proudly answered that Greece had an army of twelve divisions with 325,000 men, an army stronger than it was at the time of the Armistice. Mustafa Kemal had only 70,000 men. He had nothing to fear. After further discussions on the following days, the Council in Paris issued a letter to Venizelos and, on the one hand, condemned the atrocities that had taken place under Greek occupation because of the Greek misrule of the territories; it also legitimised the occupation of Aydin, in addition to Smyrna. Consequently, the Council did not take any specific measures to prevent further atrocities by the Greek army, which would soon start marching towards other parts of Anatolia.

Regardless, for Admiral Bristol, the work done to fulfil the mandate for the commission helped shape his views of the Greeks at that time. In that sense, the interviews conducted by the Inter-Allied Commission were significant for the purposes of this study. This certainly explains why Bristol had negative perceptions of the Greek invasion of the Smyrna region.

We know that the report was not made public, and this made Bristol uneasy about the fairness of the post-World War I settlement. He claimed, 'the conclusions and recommendations of the Smyrna investigation have been published in all papers in Constantinople; therefore, I suggest that the facts, established conclusions and recommendations should be given to our papers and published in America. This is to ensure accurate information to our people and not information colored by European interpretation of the true facts.'[45]

Bristol always regarded the suppression of the report as unfair. Reflecting on the issue at a meeting with his staff in 1922, he showed his distaste for the outcome of the report, noting:

> At the suggestion of one of the secretaries [at the embassy], I describe the work of the Committee of Investigation on the Greek occupation of Smyrna. I defined the relationship, which existed between this investigating committee, composed of representatives of Great Britain, France, Italy, and America, with the Greek representative designated to assist in this investigation. I also pointed out that the Turkish representatives were designated by the Turkish government upon the request of the committee. When my attention was drawn to the fact that Mr. Lloyd George has probably stated that the report of the investigation could not be published because it was not fair, due to the fact that the Greek representative had not been allowed to be present at the meetings of the committee and offered a defense for the charges brought against the Greek government and Greek people, I pointed out that this investigation was not a Court where charges were made and, therefore, there had been no defense or prosecution, but the simple investigation of the conditions in connection with the occupation of Smyrna and the surrounding territory by the Greek troops. In my opinion, this investigation was conducted in the fairest possible way, and all the facts that were established were real facts and unanimously agreed to. I

stated that in my opinion, I could not imagine a fairer and squarer investigation than that one had been. It was all tommyrot for Mr. Lloyd George to make such an excuse for not printing this report. It was simply a case where he did not desire to have the facts brought out. Certainly, if four people had agreed certain facts had been established, no question of a Greek representative defending charges brought against his government could affect these established facts. The reason we did not allow either the Greek or the Turkish representatives to be present was because we desired to have the witnesses free from any intimidation and thus obtain the real truth if possible. Everybody knew perfectly well that if the Greek representative was present, none of the natives would dare to say anything detrimental to the Greek occupation, because they would be certain to be persecuted if not made away with afterward.[46]

As mentioned, Bristol's first experience with the Greeks was through the Greek occupation of the Western Aegean coastline. He must have been so deeply disturbed by what he learned and experienced in the Commission of Inquiry that in 1920, in a letter to George Horton, the American Consul General in Smyrna, Bristol was very direct in blaming the Greeks and the British. He stated:

> The selfishness of these European countries is almost beyond imagination. The latest combination of British and Greeks to spoil this country [Turkey] for their imperialistic and commercial advantages is not much less than a crime. Then, if one considers the old principle of 'To the victor belongs the spoils,' one cannot understand why the Greeks should be given so much of the spoils. It would seem that the despicable conduct of Greece at the beginning of the war has been forgotten.[47]

In response to Bristol's accusatory message, George Horton began his letter by claiming that he is not a philhellene or anti-Turk, but in the region, the Greek administration is fair and just towards the Turks. However, we do know that in 1926, after his resignation from the State Department, Horton wrote a book titled *The Blight of Asia: An Account of the Systematic Extermination of Christian Population by Mohammedans and of the Culpability of Certain Great Powers; with the True Story of the Burning of Smyrna*.[48] Horton's distaste for the Turks and admiration for the Greeks is very visible in this book. Significantly, he was very deferential towards Bristol in his book, even knowing that Bristol felt exactly the reverse.[49]

Bristol did not alter his position towards the Greek minorities even after the Greek army was defeated and left Smyrna in September 1922. In his 'War Diary', sent to the Secretary of State on 31 October 1922, less than two months after the Turkish takeover of the area, Bristol recorded a phone conversation with Dr Esther Lovejoy of the American Women's Hospital Association, who had just returned from Smyrna and wanted Bristol to know the horrific scenes she had experienced in terms of the living conditions of the Greek refugees on their way out to Greece. Although acknowledging that there was sporadic kindness from the Turkish officials towards the Greek women and children in Smyrna who were waiting for their turn to leave the country, Dr Lovejoy was deeply disturbed by the Turkish treatment of the Greeks left in the town. Admiral Bristol's response to the doctor was a clear indication of his attitude towards the Greek invasion and the terrible after-effects of the event. In his entry to his diary dated 2 October 1922, Bristol recalled:

> She was so impressed by the scenes and all the surrounding circumstances that she could not give any thought to the fact that these refugees had themselves committed outrages upon the Turks when they retreated from the country, and it was their own race as soldiers who had burned all the villages, devastated the country, driving their own people to the seafront, where they are now refugees, and the Greek Army had deserted them, leaving them at the mercy of the Turks, whose vile passion and worst characteristics had been stirred up by what the Greeks had done in retreating from the country.[50]

Bristol's distaste for not only the Greek occupying forces but also the local Greeks who helped the occupation is very noticeable, and his fury seems not to distinguish the Greek civilian population at first glance, but in fact he was very critical of the 'vile characteristics' of the Turks as well. This statement also supports Bristol's general attitude towards the people, in general, living in this part of the world. However, he believed that the Greek occupations and the mistreatment of the Muslim population were the main reasons for the massacres that took place afterwards.

For Bristol, the occupation of Smyrna was a big mistake which claimed 30,000 victims and fifty million pounds of Turkish money for the Turks and devastated the land.[51] According to Bristol, even the idea of Greek rule in the former Ottoman territories was a big error in judgement. C. Vaught Engert informed the Index Bureau in Washington by attaching a memorandum by Bristol dated 25 April 1920 in which the admiral shares his views on the Treaty of Sèvres negotiations. Engert claims that the attached report is 'the most complete statements of Admiral Bristol's views and policy at the time'.[52] In it, Bristol states, 'There is not a majority of Greeks in western Asia Minor as there is no justification for Greek rule. And, above all, there is not a majority of Hellenistic Greeks in this country; therefore, [Greeks should not be allowed to rule].'[53] The same report goes into more detail about how Great Britain encouraged the Greeks in Western Anatolia to occupy the Aegean for their own selfish reasons. Bristol repeatedly warned Washington against European imperialistic designs and Greece's role in them. He states:

> The partitioning of this country for the imperialistic desires of European countries, including Greece, and also for the purpose of exploiting this country commercially, would be the greatest crime of the Twentieth Century. In addition to this, by cutting up this country as it is proposed now, it will simply concentrate the races and intensify the race hatreds that now exist. It must bring about, if successful, small states having the most antagonistic feelings towards each other, not only on account of the ordinary hatred induced by race and religion but by virtue of the horrible crimes that were committed during the great war.[54]

Bristol's views on the Greek issue strengthened the impression that he was pro-Turk and biased, and therefore his reports and analyses should not be trusted. It is, in fact, a calculated move to paint the Bristol reports as unfair and biased by the Allies and the Greek and Armenian lobbies in the West so that one-sided reporting would gain more traction, especially in the US. However, even the later scholarship tended to read his reports in the same dim light. Peter Buzanski, whose dissertation should be considered a starting point for Bristol research, questions the fairness of Bristol. Buzanski, dealing with the Smyrna occupation and its aftermath, presents an accurate narrative of the facts based on the archival material; however, he could not avoid leaving a questionable bias against the final report of the Inter-Allied Commission of Inquiry. This is especially visible when he discusses the accuracy of the minutes of the sessions. After presenting Venizelos's objections on the final report on the grounds that no Greek representative was allowed in the questioning of the witnesses, Buzanski takes issue with the report based on his 'assumption' that the minutes were taken by Robert S. Dunn, Admiral Bristol's intelligence officer.[55] Buzanski, without showing any hard evidence, suggests that there were grammatical and syntactical mistakes in the text, which indicated a journalistic style, which also indicated that they were written by Dunn. Since Dunn is a pro-Turk and an anti-Greek, this is another unqualified statement, and since the translation must have been entrusted to him, he probably had a mighty opportunity to manipulate the testimonies to show the Greek side in a much darker light. This is an interesting deductive logic as such minutes were read and approved by three other representatives of the commission, namely the British, French and Italian members. Also, a counter-report by the Greek liaison, Mazarakis, did not raise any such objection regarding Dunn's pro-Turk tendencies. The same is also true for Venizelos, who was blamed for the shortcomings of the Greek occupation of Smyrna. Venizelos's statements fail to point out what Buzanski assumes in the Inter-Allied Commission of Inquiry's final report. Buzanski concludes his section on the Smyrna occupation by stating: 'Admiral Bristol was fortunate indeed that the Smyrna report confirmed the High Commissioner's prejudices.'[56] There is no need to state that the word 'prejudice' is a loaded one and in itself carries all the traits of 'prejudice' unless clearly supported by the facts. I will not go into great detail discussing the unqualified statements in portraying Bristol as unfair as many of his other statements and actions regarding the Turks might indicate otherwise. My reasoning for highlighting Buzanski's dealing with this section in his dissertation is to prove that the subject matter has always been highly politicised.

On 14 January 1921, in a private letter to Charles Crane, a former member of the King-Crane Commission, and then the American Minister in the Legation in Peking, China, Bristol reflected on the Inter-Allied Commission of Inquiry: 'It still seems that all the work that your Commission [The King-Crane] gave so much attention to amounts to nothing. In the same way, the International Commission on the Smyrna Occupation has been relegated to the secret archives. In the same way, the Harbord Report, except for a few extracts, has not seen the light of the day. I wonder when we come to pitiless publicity and do away with secret negotiations? Until such time comes, I haven't much faith in any League of Nations, International League, or any other similar institutions.'[57]

The Burning of Smyrna

One of the most notable events that took place in Anatolia in relation to the Greeks was the fire in Smyrna that swept the entire city four days after the recapture of the city by the Turks. Admiral Bristol was in charge of the rescue efforts, and the following was his initial observations of the fire:

> The following information has been received from destroyers and individuals who were in Smyrna during the fire. Shortly after noon on 13 Sept., the fire started in the Armenian section of the city and, fanned by a southeasterly breeze, wiped out the entire city except the Turkish quarter.
>
> The cause of the fire is unknown and probably cannot be definitely determined. The Turks charge Armenians with having set the fire, while others believe that the Turks started the fire as part of a plan to rid Turkey of the Christian minorities.
>
> Turkish soldiers were observed to be spreading the fire by means of rags soaked in kerosene. Refugees to the number of about 300,000 crowded the quay and were hemmed in between fire and water, and for a time, it was believed that all would perish. The heat of the fire, which could be felt on ships in the harbor, was so intense on the quay that the refugees took cover under water-soaked carpets or blankets or any other of their belongings, which would protect them from the intense heat and keep sparks from their bodies. A few jumped into the water and swam to ships in the harbor where they were cared for. Others were drowned attempting to crowd into caiques or other small boats along the quay. This panic-stricken mob feared to sway from the quay, as it [was] believed that Turkish machine guns were planted at either end. This belief proved to be unfounded.
>
> All men-of-war in the harbor evacuated their own nationals. About 150 naturalized Americans and wives and children of the native Americans were evacuated to Piraeus by the USS. SIMPSON. Consul General Horton went with the SIMPSON to take care of these refugees. After the fire had swept down to the waterfront, the vessels in the harbor attempted to evacuate the refugees regardless of nationality, as their lives were considered to be in immediate danger. Facilities for evacuation, however, were entirely inadequate, and only a small portion of the refugees were removed before it became apparent that they were no longer in immediate danger of their lives.[58]

This was one of the most descriptive and level-headed accounts of the event; most of the others are predictably emotional. We see that Bristol was not quick to blame the Turkish side for the fire. The very likely reasoning for this was his experience of dealing with information at the Inter-Allied Commission of Inquiry and his conviction regarding the manipulated information coming from all sides.

Several years later, Bristol reflected on the Greek occupation of Smyrna and the suspicious fire that had swept the city. This speech gives clear evidence of his views on the Greeks and his assessment of the manipulated or fabricated information that was freely circulated among the Western public about the Turkish/Greek conflicts. He stated:

In the Smyrna district, when the Greeks made their advance in the summer of 1921, they sent their ships along the Black Sea to the Pontus district, and there was some thought that the Greeks would land there and make an attack from the rear. So the Turks started to deport all the Greeks from the coast and treated the deportees horribly. I protested to them about the humanity of the thing, etc., and it did do some good but not very much. [The Turks] would say to me, 'What are we going to do? These irregular bands are organized in the mountains, they are being furnished arms and munitions by the Greek ships, and the Greeks in the villages are transporting the supplies to the bands in the hills.' I knew that to be true, though I never let them know it. Just before the final showdown of this war on the south coast of the Marmora, the Greeks started to clean out the territory and make it a Greek territory. That is a scheme they have: to occupy a place and drive out the people. They cleaned out all the Moslem villages there. One of our destroyers reported one morning seeing 24 villages burning as observed from the ship as it came along.[59] This thing got so bad; the Allies had to do something and sent a mission down to investigate. I asked for a copy of the report, but they would not give it to me, but they allowed me to talk to one of the British generals who showed me all the photographs and gave me his notes. The photographs showed the villages burning and bodies mutilated. Greek troops took part in these outrages.

Just as soon as I heard of the Turkish offensive in 1922, I sent destroyers to Smyrna. I heard a month before that this was to happen. It is funny how information leaks out in the Near East, but it does, so I was prepared for it. The attack started about the 25th of August, and the Greeks got out of Smyrna on the 8th of September, and the Turks came in on the 9th. A representative of the Nationalist movement, to whom I had delivered a note about committing atrocities as soon as this advance started, came to me in Constantinople. I said, 'What are you going to do?' He said, 'We are going to drive the Greeks into the sea.' I said, 'That is a pretty big proposition, isn't it?' He said, 'No, we will be in Smyrna on the 9th of September.' And they did march into Smyrna on the 9th. They knew their people and knew if they ever broke through, the Greeks could never stand against them. As the Greeks left, they burned every village – they drove the Greeks out of Greek villages or had the priests induce them to leave, and burned the villages so they could not go back. From my point of view, I don't think such destruction was justified. If it had been in advance through a country to cut the lines of communication or make the country unproductive for the carrying on of operations, it would have been different, but this systematic destroying of the country does not seem to be justified. It was done systematically for every house was burned, the mosques were bombed, and the large buildings were bombed.

When the Turks occupied Smyrna, some of their troops had never been in a civilized place in their lives, and they had been all stirred up by the propaganda of their own leaders and the destruction and outrages they had seen in following up the Greek retreat. Still, they occupied it in a very efficient way. But, they did not provide patrols, so there were robbing and looting by all races, and Turkish soldiers were seen in their uniforms taking part in it. I do not believe the Turks burned Smyrna deliberately; it was a city they wanted to capture and a big prize, so why burn it! There is a good deal of talk that the Greeks burned the city, but there is nothing to definitely prove that the Greeks burned it. When the fire started, it just swept the city. There was a strong wind, so strong that it broke the lines of our destroyers that were tied up at the dock, so you can imagine it was blowing hard. Then, they have no fire department, and the fire started in a city built mostly of wood and narrow streets, there was no chance of stopping it. Our destroyers were there from the 5th of September. They sent ashore landing parties and occupied certain American buildings, assisted refugees, and moved about all over the city and suburbs. From all the different sources of information I can get hold of, I have come to the conclusion that during the first days of the occupation of Smyrna by the Turks, two or three thousand were the total number of people killed. When the Greeks occupied Smyrna under absolutely peaceful conditions, the number killed was something like 800. So you can see how propaganda stories are circulated in that part of the world.[60]

On many occasions, Bristol made statements and relayed reports on the Smyrna fire and other fires that swept the countryside. One of Bristol's intelligence officers in Smyrna, Lieutenant Commander J. G. Wars, sent the following report to Istanbul:

> Fire started in the Armenian quarter of the town, and it was feared the whole town is in danger. The American consulate has been burned. This fire commenced on the 13th. The refugees have been evacuated by all concerned. One of our destroyers took a load of 600 to Salonica. The Greek population of Anatolia was advised by either their priests or by Military Commanders to evacuate, and when the Greek troops evacuated the villages, they burned them. The Anatolian Greeks are infuriated with the Hellen Greeks for delivering them once and then advising them to evacuate and leaving them in the plight of a refugee with no place to go.[61]

Bristol was making his conclusions based upon reports like the one above. He also collected first-hand information himself for the events that took place. Therefore, there should be only a marginal doubt about the reliability of the information he relayed to Washington. His conclusions, of course, can be scrutinised; however, it is deeply unfair to suggest that Bristol's facts were fabricated.[62]

After the Greeks lost the war and escaped Turkey from the Smyrna harbour, the Greek population in Turkey was in panic mode as they expected reprisals. After the ceasefire agreement with Greece in Moudania on 14 October 1922, there were many questions and uncertainties over the future of the Ottoman Greeks. Bristol himself was trying to find out from the Greek Patriarch the desire of the Greek community in Turkey. An interview with the Greek Ecumenical Patriarch was arranged for 22 November 1922; however, since Bristol was leaving the next day for Lausanne, the interview was conducted by the staff in the High Commission:

> The first question to His Holiness Monseigneur Meletius IV concerned the future of Christians in Turkey. He replied that 'it was absolutely essential to retain in favor of the non-Moslem communities in Turkey those rights and privileges which had been accorded to them voluntarily by the first Sultans who came in contact with Christian communities.' . . . His own idea apparently is that Constantinople and the territory adjacent should be nominally

under Turkish control, but actually in charge of some international organizations to be composed, for instance, of Swiss or Dutch.

The Patriarch was later asked if he would agree with the idea of transferring the Patriarchate to another location; the answer was negative for this was an ecumenical institution and had to be at the center to assure constant contact with other churches and people. Meletius added, 'if the Nationalists assumed unrestricted control of Constantinople, there was every probability that the Patriarchate would be transferred.'[63]

Meletius was hoping to impress upon the Americans that some special rights and privileges should be maintained for the Christian communities of Turkey. He was not in favour of transferring the Patriarchate. The Patriarch seemingly was worried about the consequences of the Kemalist possession of Constantinople. Meletius was firm in his statement that his office should remain in Istanbul under international protection.

We know that Armenians and Greeks not leaving but residing in Turkey was also Bristol's desire. He was hoping that the Ottoman Greeks under the leadership of the Patriarch would remain in Turkey and integrate into the new regime. Bristol was not successful in convincing the international community that the Greeks would stay. Soon after Turkey winning the war against Greece, a population exchange was proposed for the Greeks in Anatolia and the Turks in Greece. Bristol was originally against the idea, but later he realised the benefit of such a move. He confided to US cadets in the military academy in his speech in 1925, stating:

> As regards minorities, the scheme for the exchange of population was proposed to me in my office in the embassy in Constantinople by Dr. [Fridtjof] Nansen, High Commissioner of refugees for the League of Nations, who also sent one of his agents working with his commission, to try to get me to advocate the exchange of population at the Lausanne conference. I told Dr. Nansen it was a crime to suggest that kind of an idea in that part of the world. He tried to demonstrate to me how successful it had been in Macedonia. I begged him not to propose that scheme. At the Lausanne conference, you can imagine my surprise when Doctor Nansen was introduced by one of the plenipotentiaries of the Allied Nations to propose a scheme for the solution of the minorities question, and the scheme for the exchange of population was there proposed. The exchange of population, so far as Anatolia is concerned,

has most probably turned out to be the best, though. The Greeks themselves were scared to death ... The Turkish hatred for them has been worked up to a murderous attitude, and if they had not gotten out of there, it probably would have been a great many of them killed. In addition, there would have been a pestiferous interference in the affairs of the people, which would have driven them out. The refugees going to Greece have been a godsend to Greece in one sense of the word. At first, there was terrible suffering, but the Greek leaders admit now that the refugees they got from Anatolia have been a decided economic benefit to the country. As regards Turkey, it was a benefit to her because the people she got out of Greece are industrious and hardworking, and also many of them are artisans. The exchange of population applied to Constantinople was based on the principle that all those who were established there in 1918 would be allowed to remain, but all others must be exchanged.[64]

The initial request for the population exchange came from the Greek Premier Eleftherios Venizelos and was promoted by Fridtjof Nansen, High Commissioner for Refugees for the League of Nations. The Turkish government in Ankara concurred, and the agreement was signed by both countries on 30 January 1923 in Lausanne. The compulsory order was issued by both countries forcing over 1.5 million people to leave their homes. Bristol was in general against the idea of removing Christians from Turkey; however, in 1925 he admitted that population exchange probably saved many lives.

Nevertheless, Admiral Bristol's view of the Greeks did not change for the better. In a letter to Admiral William S. Sims on 18 May 1919, he stated: 'the Greek is about the worst race in the Near East.'[65] Bristol did not waver from his view of the Greek army and the local Greeks' attitude towards the Muslim population of the Aegean coast. After the population exchange in 1923–4, and the formation of the Turkish Republic, Bristol always reflected on the period of the Greek occupation of the Smyrna region with distaste and never sympathised with the Greek point of view.

Conclusion

Following the end of World War I, Admiral Mark Lambert Bristol, the American High Commissioner in the Ottoman Empire/Turkey, witnessed a significant period in which there was a transition from the Ottoman Empire to the Republic of Turkey. This period was also significant because Western interference created the new political alliances and borders. In this period, one of the most significant events used by the Western Powers was the issue of Armenian massacres committed by the CUP administration. As in many other Western countries, the plight of the Armenian citizens of the Ottoman Empire found a very compassionate reception among the American public. However, some of the information received and propagated in the US was viewed as 'manipulated' by Admiral Bristol, who saw it as his duty to portray as realistic and objective a picture of the situation as possible. Since some of the reports he sent to Washington and his conclusions on the Armenian issue contradicted the picture painted by the Armenian lobbyists and many NER mission workers, Bristol was labelled as pro-Turk and anti-Armenian. This section has aimed to shed light on this politically oriented labelling of Bristol, presenting documents to show that he was a realist and a fair-minded observer. He never denied that wholesale Armenian massacres took place, but he also pointed out the suffering of the other groups. This was readily seen as a calculated distraction from the question of the Armenian massacres (the term later evolved into 'genocide'). Bristol later sympathised with the emerging nationalist movement; however, he did not compromise his integrity. In fact, his conclusions evolved with the fast-changing situation in the Middle East. On the issue of an Armenian state, for example, he first opposed, then accepted, and later gave up the idea that an independent Armenian state in Anatolia was to be granted; he always had questions about its sustainability and benefits for the Armenians themselves. This evolution in his thinking indicates the strength of the admiral's position. Bristol was constantly assessing the ever-changing situation on the ground for the Armenians and adjusting to it. He strongly believed that an independent but unprotected Armenia could not serve the interests of the Armenians in Turkey. Those who lobbied for it in the West, and particularly in the US, either wilfully manipulated the information or else were clueless about the situation in the region. It is this reasonable objection that earned Bristol the hatred of Armenian lobbyists and, in later periods, anti-Turkish groups. I hope that this section gives clues to the just-minded reader about his integrity and, more significantly, his realism. Bristol devoted his loyalty to the interests of his country but also to what he perceived to be fair.

The Greek minority of the Ottoman Empire was another issue that took up much of Bristol's time. As soon as he arrived in the Ottoman territories, he witnessed the Greek occupation of Smyrna and parts of the Aegean coastline. His views on the Greek minority in the Ottoman Empire were different from those of the Armenian. For Bristol, the Armenians and the Greeks may have betrayed the Ottoman Empire during the Great War, and they suffered a great deal as a result of it. However, it was for the Greeks that he lacked much sympathy. It is probably because, during his tenure in Constantinople, Bristol witnessed the Greeks' occupation and local Greeks' support for it. After World War I, many Armenians enlisted with the French forces in Southern Anatolia and were on the offensive towards the Muslim populations in their areas; however, the damage to the local population was limited. The Greek occupation on the Aegean coast was much more destructive. Bristol was also disturbed by the wholesale massacres committed by the Turks, especially towards the Armenians. He always referred to the mass killings in 1915 as systematic massacres, perhaps because the term 'genocide' had not yet been coined. What distinguishes Mark Bristol from his predecessor, Henry Morgenthau, is that Bristol believed the Turks were not the only villains in these conflicts. An entry to his diary demonstrates his view rather aptly. Bristol recalls his conversation with A. J. Allen, the ex-governor of Kansas:

> The fact that all the races in this part of the world did not know the difference between falsehood and truth that so far moral character was concerned, they were all much alike and as regards committing atrocities and other outrages all the races acted very much alike, and it was only the question of which one was in power at any given time. I explained the way that the Armenians, for the first two years I was out here, persecuted the Moslems in Armenia, how the French troops used Armenian soldiers in Cilicia and had to disband them on account of their behavior towards the Moslem natives, and how the Greeks had committed all kinds of atrocities and devastated the country in Anatolia. I explained that the Turk was all that you painted him and that there absolutely were no excuses for the outrages they committed, except that it must be borne in mind that the Armenians and Greeks, Ottoman subjects, were not loyal to the government, did rebel against the government and, therefore, in the legal sense of the word were traitors, and if the Turks

had deported these people to detention camps during the way and treated them properly, nobody could have said anything. [Allen] asked me if the massacres of the Armenians and Greeks in these deportations were ordered by the government. I told him I believe that in a measure they were and that in my opinion, these deportations were part of a scheme to rid Turkey of the Christian races. I further stated that the Greeks and Armenians had a large number of their people in America and these people were the cleverest in the world at propaganda whereas the Turks had very few people in America and in general they were fatalist, accepting conditions without whining or protest, and were not given to even making propaganda in setting forth their case before the world. Thus, in the United States especially, we heard everything bad about the Turks and nothing good, while at the same time, we heard everything good about the Christian races and nothing bad. Thus they had an absolutely one-sided picture of the situation out here.[66]

Notes

1. This is not a phrase that Bristol himself coined but a popular saying in Turkish: 'Bu topraklarda mazlum, zalimliğe gücü yetmeyen midir?' 'Or is the victim the one who failed to be the villain in these lands?'
2. 867.4016/390, letter from Vahan Cardashian to President Woodrow Wilson, 15 September 1918.
3. 867.01/153, C. Vaught Engert to US Index Bureau; emphasis added. Engert sent an earlier report given to him by Bristol explaining his views prior to the signing of Sèvres (26 March 1923).
4. Ibid.; emphasis added.
5. Bristol to Lewis Heck, 8 July 1919, Office of Naval Records and Library, Naval Records Collection (NRC), box 709, as cited in Peter Michael Buzanski, 'Admiral Mark L. Bristol and Turkish-American Relations, 1919–1922', PhD dissertation, University of California, Berkeley, 1960, p. 111.
6. 867.01/51, Bristol to Secretary of State, 7 May 1920.
7. 867.00/1583, 'War Diary' dated 27 November 1922; emphasis added.
8. Ibid.; emphasis added.
9. 867.00/1154, telegram from Bristol to Secretary of State, 9 March 1920; emphasis added.
10. 867.00/1583, report from Bristol to State Department, 30 November 1922.
11. Ibid.; emphasis added.

12. 867.4016/810, Frederic R. Dolbeare, Acting United States High Commissioner, to Secretary of State, 1 December 1922.

13. Ibid.

14. Ibid.

15. Ibid.

16. 867.00/1884, 'War Diary' dated 17 July 1925.

17. 867.00/1886, Bristol to Secretary of State, 18 July 1925.

18. Robert Shenk, 'Ethnic Cleansing, American Women, and the Admiral: Deep in Anatolia during the Turkish Nationalist Revolution', in George N. Shirinian (ed.), *Genocide in the Ottoman Empire: Armenians, Assyrians, and Greeks, 1913–1923* (New York and Oxford: Berghahn, 2017), pp. 187–213.

19. 867.00/1285, Vice Admiral Knapp, Commander of the US Naval Forces Operating in European Waters (Chief of Naval Operations), 11 June 1920; emphasis added. Vice Admiral Knapp sent similar excerpts to the Secretary of the Navy, the Secretary of State and even the President of the United States.

20. 'The unisons are made between general categories and what they contain. An Oriental lives in the Orient, he lives a life of Oriental ease, in a state of Oriental despotism and sensuality, imbued with a feeling of Oriental fatalism'; Edward Said, *Orientalism: Western Conceptions of the Orient* (New Delhi: Penguin, 2006), p. 102.

21. 867.00/1541, report from Bristol to Secretary of State, 23 August 1922. Bristol states: 'I was absolutely against one-sided reports which gave the atrocities committed by the Turks and led our people at home to believe that the Christian races are saintly martyrs of Christianity.'

22. A Russian measure of length, about 1.1 km (0.66 mile).

23. 867.00/1914, Bristol's speech at the US Army War College, titled 'Conditions of the Near East', 6 October 1925.

24. 867.00/1883.

25. 711.672/250, from Bristol to Secretary of State.

26. Ibid.; emphasis added. Bristol was certainly referring to the pamphlet titled *The Turco-Armenian Question: The Turkish Point of View*, issued by the National Congress of Turkey (Constantinople: Société anonyme de papeterie et d'imprimerie, 1919). We know that the National Congress of Turkey was an umbrella group of more than fifty political and cultural organisations in Istanbul. Bristol's quotations are accurate and come from pages 83 and 116.

27. 867.00/1335, Secretary of the Navy Josephus Daniels relays Bristol's assessment to the Department of State, 25 August 1920.

28. Also known as the Big Four or the Four Nations, it refers to the four top Allied Powers of World War I and their leaders who met at the Paris Peace Conference in 1919. It was composed of Woodrow Wilson of the United States, David Lloyd George of Britain, Vittorio Emanuele Orlando of Italy, and Georges Clemenceau of France. However, in the minutes I examined, the Italian representation was replaced by the Greek Prime Minister Eleftherios Venizelos in their 6 May meeting. We know that the Allies had secret discussions even among themselves and Italy was absent in some significant negotiations.

29. 867.00/179, 'Minutes of a Meeting of Council of Four', Paris, 6 May 1919.

30. Ibid.

31. Report of the Inter-Allied Commission of Inquiry on the Greek Occupation of Smyrna and Adjacent Territories, Appendix A to HD-87, Constantinople October 14, 1919, in US Department of State, *Papers Relating to the Foreign Relations of the United States, The Paris Peace Conference, 1919*, <http://digicoll.library.wisc.edu/cgi-bin/FRUS/FRUS-idx?type=turn&id=FRUS.FRUS1919Parisv09&entity=FRUS.FRUS1919Parisv09.p0054&q1=inter-alliedcommissionofinquiry-onthegreed> (last accessed 28 September 2020), p. 44 onwards.

32. 867.00/859.

33. Ibid.

34. Ibid.

35. Ibid.

36. 867.00/870, from Paris to Secretary of State, 7 May 1919: 'During the absence of Heck in Constantinople the commission has designated Admiral Bristol temporarily as Chief political officer of the United States in this city and he has been requested to submit from time to time telegraphic and written reports on the conditions in Constantinople.'

37. Buzanski, p. 52.

38. Ibid.

39. Report of the Inter-Allied Commission of Inquiry on the Greek Occupation of Smyrna and Adjacent Territories, Annex II, in US Department of State, *Papers Relating to the Foreign Relations of the United States, The Paris Peace Conference, 1919*.

40. US Department of State, *Papers Relating to the Foreign Relations of the United States, The Paris Peace Conference, 1919*. The Council of Heads of Delegations: minutes of meetings 6 November 1919 to 10 January 1920, p. 838 onwards.

41. 867.4016/529, Bristol to Secretary of State, 9 June 1922.

42. 867.4016/502, 'Memorandum on Earl Curzon's Request for American Participation on a Commission to Investigate Turkish Atrocities', 15 May 1922, prepared by Mark Bristol.

43. 867.00/192, 'Greek Lootings of Turkish Houses in Smyrna', 18 May 1919, Constantinople. This is a telegram by Admiral Bristol to American Mission in Paris (for the peace negotiations) which stated: 'Greeks, Smyrna, reported looting houses, making many arrests, occasional street fights, few killed. Christian population inland apprehensive, Greeks undertook task beyond their power. New Ministry under Ferad (Ferid?) probably coalition and less unfriendly to Entente.' Another report by Bristol on 17 July 1919 indicates that Turks and Greeks were killing each other (867.00/315). Bristol also reports Turkish atrocities; for example, a report numbered 867.00/325 and dated 19 July 1919 claims that the Turks nailed horseshoes on to the wounded Greeks. The same report also indicates that inter-communal rivalry was not just between the Turks (Muslims) and the Greeks (Christians); Bristol claims that Catholics were the main rivals of the Greeks.

44. Buzanski, p. 69.

45. 867.00/1096, letter from Bristol to Secretary of State, 28 January 1920.

46. 867.00/1542, Admiral Bristol's 'War Diary', sent to Secretary of State; report dated 31 August 1922. Bristol's entry is dated 21 August 1922; he talks about his experience in the Commission of Inquiry to his staff at the US Embassy.

47. 867.00/1301, 29 May 1920. Bristol's letter was attached to George Horton's report to the Secretary of State with his own response.

48. (Indianapolis: Bobbs-Merrill Company, 1926). In this book, Horton admits his great distaste for the Turks; see 'Introduction'.

49. George Horton sent several other messages directly to Washington, skipping Bristol. In one of those reports, Horton described a meeting with the Greek High Commissioner in Smyrna, Mr Sterghiades, who on 17 December 1920 confessed that he was pessimistic about the Greek administration at Smyrna. Horton acknowledged that 'the life of the Greek mandate [at Smyrna] may be short . . . the country had undertaken in the present venture far too much in view of its resources and administrative ability' and there were too many conflicting international interests. 867.00/1374, George Horton to Secretary of State, 22 December 1920.

50. 867.00/1561, Bristol's 'War Diary' addressed to the Secretary of State on 31 October 1922.

51. 867.00/986, report dated 6 November 1919.

52. 867.01/153, dated 26 March 1923.

53. Ibid. Bristol retained this view after his tenure in Turkey.

54. Ibid.

55. Robert Dunn later published a book where he discussed his professional life: *World Alive: A Personal Story* (New York: Crown Publisher, 1956).

56. Buzanski, p. 72. Interestingly enough, Buzanski three years later in an essay on the subject refrained from making such accusations towards Dunn and had a much more favourable view towards the final report. See Peter M. Buzanski, 'The Interallied Investigation of the Greek Invasion of Smyrna, 1919', *The Historian*, 25.3 (May 1963): 325–43.

57. Oberlin College, 'Henry Churchill King Papers', RG 2/6/1, box 20.

58. 'Report of Operation' for the week ending 17 September 1922, 'Bristol Papers'.

59. Here, I can include an interesting observation by Earle Russell, American Vice Consul in Charge dealing with the Turkish refugees, albeit in the Aegean region: 'As is customary with all Asiatics, the Turkish inhabitants of Aidin buried a good deal of their money and jewelry in the cellars of their houses.' We do know that the Greeks carried out the same practice after they left Turkey. The author of the report calls it 'a common Asiatic practice'. See 867.00/1342, 20 August 1920.

60. 867.00/1914, Bristol's speech at the US Army War College, titled 'Conditions of the Near East', 6 October 1925.

61. 867.00/1548, Bristol to Secretary of State, Intelligence Report, 21 September 1922. The report was prepared by Lieutenant Commander J. G. Wars, Intelligence Officer, and forwarded by Bristol.

62. For a good accusatory statement, see Shenk, p. 188.

63. 867.4016/810. Meletius was also asked about the position of the Turkish Orthodox community: 'After the Patriarch was asked about his opinion of the Turkish Orthodox Church. He declared that the Kemalists had found small groups of Greeks and Armenians in the vicinity of Sivas and Caesarea who used habitually the Turkish language, and out of those groups for their own purpose they had endeavored to fashion some ecclesiastical organization . . . Monseigneur Meletius mentioned 15,000 as the number of the Orthodox Turks. [He added that the Patriarchate] expected a great deal from the United States.' Interestingly, the High Commission was aware of the Turkish Orthodox Church which would potentially blur the Greek Orthodox demands from the Lausanne Conference and Bristol may have wished to know what the Patriarch himself thought of that community.

64. 867.00/1914, Bristol to Secretary of State, 2 February 1926.

65. Buzanski, p. 128, n. 89.

66. Bristol's diary indicating his conversation with Mr A. J. Allen. The initial 'A' might have been a typo; it is possible that the full name was Henry Justin Allen, who served as governor of Kansas between 1919 and 1923. In a report from Bristol to Secretary of State, 867.00/1658. The document is dated 2 May 1923; however, the conversation took place on 5 April 1923.

5

POLITICAL AND HUMAN LANDSCAPES OF TURKEY IN DIPLOMATIC REPORTS

This chapter aims at drawing a picture of Turkey immediately after World War I using American diplomatic correspondence prepared particularly by Admiral Bristol and his subordinates. It presents US documents mainly on the plight of the people (both Muslim and non-Muslim) of the Aegean, Central Anatolia, the Black Sea regions and Constantinople. The latter part of the chapter will chronologically introduce documents dealing with significant political events, such as the abolition of the Sultanate, and later Caliphate, in Turkey. The reader will also be introduced to lesser-known documents on the personal life of Mustafa Kemal, such as his divorce and his personal belief system. Admiral Mark Bristol and his team were travelling to Ankara and reporting their views of political and intellectual life in the city; therefore, the second half of the chapter is devoted to selected documents on the lesser-known internal affairs in Turkey, seen through the eyes of American diplomats. Let us begin with the reports portraying daily life in some Ottoman cities and inter-communal relations after World War I.

Description of War-torn Cities and Inter-communal Relations

World War I created a sizeable volume of displaced people in Anatolia. The predicament of the population of the area has been exploited for many different political discourses in the following decades up to the present. The primary goal of this section is to demonstrate the living conditions of the people of the defeated Ottoman Empire and inter-communal relations while waiting for the signing of a peace treaty.

Like many other Ottoman cities, Constantinople, the capital of the Ottoman Empire and the seat of the Caliphate at the end of World War I, was in dire condition. When the Mudros Armistice was signed on 30 October 1918, hopes for the peace treaty and for a return to normality were very high in the Ottoman Empire. However, the stillborn Treaty of Sèvres was not signed until 10 August 1920. The interval of twenty-two months proved to be very difficult for the inhabitants of the empire. Several reports describing the living conditions in Constantinople vividly demonstrate the pain and suffering of the locals. The first report that will be presented here is very detailed and was prepared for the Americans who entertained the idea of travelling to Constantinople. The report, dated 26 December 1918, two months after the signing of the Mudros Armistice, was transmitted by American Commissioner Lewis Heck to the Secretary of State; however, the author of the report is Luther R. Fowle, a member of the ABCFM[1] in Istanbul. The title of the report is 'Living Conditions in Constantinople'.

> For adults in good health, the question of living conditions in Constantinople is merely a question of money. Food of most kinds can be had in abundance by those who can pay for them—but the mass of the people is suffering much. The charge for a board in the American Colleges that used to be $200 per annum before the war is now $1.000, and at this rate, the College suffers a loss. Pension for a single person costs from $150 to $200 per month and is found with difficulty. American families already established in Constantinople and keeping house for themselves most modestly expend over $100 per month per head. To live in good hotel costs about $450 per month for board and lodging.
>
> Costs in cents of certain staples are as follows: <u>per pound</u>
>
> Sugar $1.75, rice .90, white beans .45, kerosene 1.00, cheese 1.20, cooking butter 3.50, meat 1.60, flour .50, wheat .35, potatoes .25, milk .50.
>
> Eggs .18 apiece, rubber galoshes $30.00, shoes $75.00, spool of thread $1.50, man's suit of clothes $200.
>
> In February 1918, the Ottoman Minister of Finance stated in the Parliament that prices had increased since the beginning of the war two thousand percent for foodstuffs, and this still holds true. The ratio of gold to paper

currency is four to one. Hence, if gold can be imported, the increased cost of living drops from 2000 percent to 500 percent.

No serious epidemic exists at the present time, but the city is very dirty, and the service of various public utilities—water, lights, trams, etc.—is most irregular and often cut off owing to the lack of fuel. It is to be expected that the entry of the Entente Forces will make possible an improvement in this regard.

The above is the situation, as it existed on December 7th, five weeks after the signing of the Armistice. There is no prospect of improvement in the immediate future. The Entente Forces are importing all their own foodstuffs, thus avoiding local prices almost entirely.

Children and adults without a definite work to do should not go nearer to Constantinople than Egypt or Italy until after May 1919.[2]

We do not know the significance of the date of May 1919. But the advice is sound, requesting children and unnecessary personnel to stay away from the capital at least another year. We can speculate that Fowle was expecting the peace treaty would be signed, and the city would go back to normality in terms of prices. A significant point in the report is the hyperinflation rate of 2,000 per cent due to blockade and uncertainty since the beginning of the Great War. The same folder contains another report with more detailed information about daily life in Constantinople. This report was penned by Lewis Heck on 30 January 1919, a month after Fowle's report.

Heck also points out the great increase in the cost of living in Constantinople and concludes that the 1,000 per cent increase in July 1917 was a combination of the following: (1) scarcity of supplies; (2) difficulties of transportation; (3) inflation of the currency and (4) inability to replenish stocks of imported goods due to the blockade.

> The main special cause was the action of political and even governmental agencies concerning the market in certain staple lines and in charging very high bribes for means of transportation . . . The bread is the only foodstuff which has been rationed with a degree of success. During the summer of 1917, the 'vessika' or ration bread was extremely poor, consisting of cornmeal mud [?] for days at a time. In the autumn of 1917, the control of rations was taken over by the military authorities, and conditions were at once improved owing partly to the new crop and to the better organization affected under military control.

This improvement did not last for a long time, and by the summer of 1918, the quality of bread was almost as poor as in the previous year.

Apart from bread, there are distributions of sugar, cheese, matches, olives, and potatoes, but these articles were never given out with any regularity or in any considerable [quantity]. Three-quarters of a pound of sugar per head used to be distributed about one piaster in three months at a charge of the 20 piasters an oke . . .

In order to maintain the local water, electric light, tram and ferry services, the city of Constantinople requires about 1200 tons of coal a day. The Germans used to send here from Germany an average of about three hundred tons of coal and coke a day. After the Armistice, these supplies from Germany were not only cut off and local stocks exhausted, but owing to the disorganization of the Turkish military department, most of the workmen, who were under military discipline, stopped work at the mines of Zonguldak. It is also reported that German officers stationed there caused much damage to the machinery of the mines before they left. As a result, there was a period of about three weeks without electric light. It was at this time that public order was at its worst when the disorderly elements were encouraged by the darkness of the streets. There was much shooting in the streets at night, and often several men were killed in one night. There were a number of political murders at the same time. This situation is now much better; the authorities have decided to disarm the population of the city, but this measure will not be carried out with any degree of efficiency in the prevailing circumstances . . .

Since the latter part of December, it has been possible to maintain the electric light service more regularly so that now it does not go out for a very long period. The electric tram service has stopped running since the beginning of December chiefly from lack of coal and also because the company does not wish to resume operations until the Municipal authorities permit a decided increase in its tariffs (as much as 400 percent.)

The water service was poor all through 1918, as the pumping apparatus at Lake Dercos was out of order, and the water flowed for only a few days each week. Now there is water for several hours each day, but only a small supply and none can be used for street cleaning.

The Bosphorus and other boat services are limited by lack of coal, and boats are always dangerously overcrowded, although so far there have been no accidents. The service of the railways in both Asiatic and European Turkey is also limited because of short supplies of fuel . . .

Persons returning to Constantinople are very much increased by the great number of people in the street who seem to have no occupation. This is due first to the fact that everybody must go on foot and also to the fact that trade and industry are almost at a complete standstill . . .

During the war and especially the last two years, some very great fortunes have been made in this country by people who were either in the government or who had the right sort of connections with men in authority. The figures for the amounts made by many persons are fantastic when one considers the utter misery and destitution of 95 percent of the whole population. [They keep their money in Germany and Austria] . . .

The ordinary Municipal services of the city, such as the removal of garbage, cleaning the streets, etc., are very poor and the city is generally in a filthy condition, both the street and the people themselves, who have been obliged to keep on wearing the same clothes for several years due to lack of textiles . . .

With all the poverty prevailing in Constantinople, it is nevertheless in certain ways one of the best-stocked cities in the world for those who have money to pay high prices. There are very few commodities which cannot be obtained here if a sufficient amount is paid.[3]

This report vividly describes the desperation of people in Constantinople, the capital city of the dying Ottoman Empire. The bread was rationed, and the distribution was problematic. Water was scarce, which not only caused a shortage of drinking water but also posed great problems in personal hygiene. The garbage collection was poor, and the city was filthy. It seemed only by luck that there was no major outbreak of infectious disease. Due to coal shortages, transportation was almost at a standstill; boats across the Bosphorus were overcrowded, inviting deadly accidents. Irregular power outages due to limited coal production, which caused blackout nights, made the streets breeding grounds for criminal activities. During the daytime, people used their legs as a means of transportation, and hence streets were full of people in miserable clothing walking to their destinations. Yet, the author of the report indicates that the city is one of the best-stocked in the world for those who can pay the high prices. If the capital of the empire was in such a dire situation, comparisons could only be imagined for other non-prominent Ottoman towns. It is during this troubled period that Ottoman citizens waited for the signing of a peace treaty to normalise their lives, at least to a degree.

It is not easy to find such a strikingly detailed report describing the post-war realities in the imperial city in the US archives. However, there are plenty of others, collected mainly from the ship captains of the US Navy under Admiral Bristol's command or missionaries describing other locations. These reports are usually collected from port towns, and their main aim is to depict the conditions of the non-Muslim populations. For example, the following document describes Samsun, a Black Sea town, in April 1919, just one month before Mustafa Kemal's landing there on 19 May. This event is considered to be the commencement of the Turkish War of Independence. Just before Mustafa Kemal landed at Samsun, the following was the situation according to a US captain of a warship:

> We found conditions in Samsoun[4] quite encouraging. In place of the five thousand, reported to be starving in the streets, we found that the soup kitchens were handling the cases of the destitute and that while the prices were high, they had already commenced to fall and no actual famine existed. For example, eggs, which we had understood were non-existent, were selling lower than in New York.
>
> We took two automobile trips, one on land, one along the coast, and found a surprising number of sheep and the land, which appears to be exceptionally rich, fairly well cultivated. The political situation was quiet, unquestionably owing to the presence of 200 British troops. There are, however, 2000 armed Greeks in the nearby mountains who are a decided menace and who refuse to surrender until a government is established, which would assure their safety when disbanded.
>
> No massacres were reported at Saumsun, but deportations of large numbers took place under conditions which resulted in great sufferings and loss of life. We saw some of the Greek villages, which have been completely destroyed. This was done by government troops on government orders. It seemed to be confined to certain districts said to be among the most prosperous in this region. More or less contraband trade in rifles had been carried on between the Russians and Greeks in the district in question.[5]

Compared to similar reports from different towns, this one portrays a less desperate picture of a post-World War I town in the defeated empire. However, the reader should keep in mind that the author of the report was prepared to see a lot worse and was pleasantly surprised by anything less than complete destruction.

What can we get out of this report? For one thing, the existence of soup kitchens indicates that there was a degree of social and political order. The report credits the 200 British troops with this. In other words, when Mustafa Kemal and his friends landed in Samsun, there were 200 British troops stationed in the city. We are not aware of any attempt to arrest Mustafa Kemal and his associates simply because their nationalist intentions were not yet known to the British. We also learn that some Greek villages around Samsun were destroyed, the report claims by government troops. One can safely assume that it was the government in Istanbul which was responsible for the destruction, as the government in Ankara had not yet been established. Questions over why, when and how the royal government in Istanbul destroyed the Greek villages remain to be answered. We can assume that this destruction took place during World War I, after which Istanbul was occupied and the Ottoman administration was not in a position to order such destruction.

This report also states that Greek bands 2,000 strong were armed and had taken up in the mountains, which indicates that tensions between the Greek population and the Turks were high, despite the fact that conditions in the city were calm. Such bands on the mountains of Samsun indicate that either the Greeks needed protection against further destruction, or they were readying themselves for an uprising with the aid of the Allied occupation of the area. We can only speculate as to which was the case.

Another noteworthy take from this report concerns the issue of the Russian arms deal. The information on the rifle trade between the Russians and the Greeks is significant since we know that soon after, the Russians were the sole suppliers of rifles for the Turkish nationalists. It is possible that the Russian weapons purchased by the Greeks were of Tsarist origin, as we do know that the remnants of the Imperial Russian Army had stockpiles of weapons around Trabzon. It would be interesting to know if, indeed, it was the Bolsheviks who sold weapons to both the Kemalists and the Greek bands.

All in all, until the occupation of İzmir, the political mood in Anatolia seemed to be subdued, and people's lives were on hold. Muslims and non-Muslims were waiting for the signing of a peace treaty with the prospect of getting back to a level of normality. Nevertheless, it should not be hard to assume that inter-communal relations were quite tense. However, things would change overnight for the worse with the occupation of İzmir on 15 May 1919. For this occupation, we have Admiral Mark Lambert Bristol's accounts as the US High Commissioner who chaired the committee for investigating atrocities committed by both Greeks and Turks in İzmir. As mentioned above, four days after the occupation of İzmir, Mustafa Kemal landed in Samsun and initiated the war against the Allied and Greek occupation of Turkey. Within a three-year period, the Greeks were pushed back from Western Anatolia, culminating with Turkish forces recapturing İzmir on 9 September 1922. However, the occupation of İzmir by Greece and the great welcome they received from the local Greek population disheartened the Turks and triggered an unfortunate chain of events, which fuelled the Turkish War of Independence and resulted in the Greek population of the empire leaving their homeland for Greece. Let us now look at the situation in Anatolia after the Kemalist victory in 1922.

Non-Muslims of Anatolia after the War of Independence

The US archives are full of reports complaining about the mistreatment of Christians, especially Greek Orthodox and the Armenian population. Yet, an overwhelming majority of them were prepared by those who were party to the conflicts. In other words, these reports by American missionaries, understandably, used the local Christian population as their primary source. Since the missionaries were embedded with the local Christian communities and had very limited access to the Muslim communities, these reports by their own nature did not paint the whole picture. The US diplomats relayed these reports to Washington without critically examining the reliability of them. This practice ended with Admiral Mark L. Bristol, who insisted on preparing or sending reports by paying attention to their dependability. As mentioned, Bristol put himself in a more advantageous position by expanding his network of intelligence. For example, when discussing the Armenian plight with Bishop J. H. Darlington, Bristol countered the argument that Cilicia was mostly Armenian and that this information was based soundly upon carefully prepared birth records. Bristol stated that 'this was all true, but there was one thing that the Patriarch did not inform the Peace Conference, and that was the record of deaths, so the records of the population based on births was correct, but it was not correct as regards the population of the district'.[6] The reason I quote this conversation is to show the reader how detail-oriented and fair-minded Mark Bristol was. He asked his staff to be as neutral as possible.

With this instruction at hand, Bristol's staff, which included diplomats as well as his ship captains in the Navy, prepared many reports describing the political and human conditions of Anatolia. Below we have Bristol's Trade Commissioner's report describing life in Ankara after the nationalist movement established itself in 1923:

> Angora has changed a great deal since I was there in 1921. There are a great many shops and hundreds of additional soldiers . . . During my stay there, I observed many Armenians and Greeks in the city walking on the streets and going about their business as they have always done. I saw both Armenian and Greek priests on the streets, and they apparently had all the liberty that anyone also had and went their ways unmolested. Two of the Greek priests called at the Assembly building on Mustapha Kemal Pasha on Thursday, May 17, and were received by him just minutes before I paid my respect. I went up on the hill within the walls of the old fortress, where I know there was an old Greek church more than 600 years old. I found that it was in no way destroyed, and services were held regularly and that the old priest who was there in 1921 was still there. I saw him personally, and on entering the church found one Greek woman engaged in prayer.[7]

This report interestingly describes the inter-communal relations as at a level of normality in Ankara around 1923. Business life seemed to be improving. If this was the situation in the new capital city, was it any different in other less prominent towns? In the same folder, we have the reports prepared by the ship captains under Bristol patrolling the Black Sea. Among those, a report by J. B. Rhodes, the captain of the USS *Litchfield*, describes the refugee situation in several coastal towns:

> Unieh [Ünye], Turkey
> There are about 350 refugees here, 300 of who are Greeks and the rest being Armenians. The conditions are good, about half of them having means of their own and all are working and earning their food. There are no refugees in nearby villages, and there have been no new arrivals lately. They live in different houses around the city, depending upon where they work. There is very little disease, as all refugees are vaccinated. No refugees are leaving the

city either by steamer or going into the interior. There are about 150 Greek bandits in the hills, but as they never come into the village, they are very little cause for worry to the Turk.

Fatsa, Turkey

In the village, there are about 1300 Greek and 100 Armenian refugees. The conditions are good. About half are working; many have means of their own, and a few are in need of food. About 400 refugees have recently arrived at Fatsa. They live in Greek houses. There is practically no disease among the refugees. A doctor inspects daily and administers to the sick if there are any. All refugees have gone to a nearby village for work, but none have left the city by steamer. There are no bandits around Fatsa.

Kersunda [Giresun?], Turkey

There are about 300 refugees here, most of whom are Greeks. Conditions are good; most of the refugees are working. There is no disease among them, and all have been vaccinated. None have left the city by steamer, but a few have gone into interior villages to look for work. There are no bandits in or near the city.[8]

If nothing else, these reports indicate that non-Muslims still existed in towns despite the fact that the level of trust between the communities was at an all-time low. This mistrust is visible in the existence of Greek bandits in the Black Sea mountains as late as 1923.

In reference to inter-communal relations, we have another report by the commanding officer of a different US ship, the USS *Edsall*, that also gives us a bit of information about Muslim refugees. Admiral Bristol relayed this report to Washington the same way he did others; the date for this particular one is 6 June 1923. Commander Robt. T. Young prepared the report in which he stated that

There were also Turkish refugees offside of Inebolu. Mr. Crutcher of the Standard Oil sent a wire to [Constantinople] requesting authority to afford relief to those refugees. The reply from the Near East Relief came five days later on 12 June 1923, indicating that for those Turkish refugees, grits, flour, and clothing were being shipped. Rushdi Bey, President of the local Red Crescent, will wire to have foodstuff landed, get it through customs, and have automobiles ready to take it inland.[9]

This account is significant because it is one of the rare reports indicating that Muslims were also displaced and in need of relief work, and also that some form of help was given to them by the Near East Relief via the US Navy.

The same commanding officer, Robt. T. Young, reported from the Trabzon harbour on 8 June 1923. Accordingly, we learn that the US missions fed 2,764 refugees a day.

> Mr. Grant [an NER representative] informed me of the refugees. There are only two cases of typhus and no smallpox. He further informed me that tomorrow, 9 June, the Vali would issue a proclamation prohibiting the sale of tickets to Greeks and Armenians to sail [out of] Trebizond . . . Mr. Grant first informed me it is because of the conditions in the refugee camps at Constantinople; that the steamers would not take refugees only as far as Constantinople, and due to conditions in Constantinople, the authorities did not desire anymore to come there. I did not know of any unwarranted conditions existing in Constantinople at departure, so later brought up the subject of the reason again. He then informed me, he believed it was a proc-lamation desired by the Turks. *The reason, the Armenians and Greeks are the artificers (skilled workers), and the workmen, and they are absolutely essential at Trebizond. This was coming more towards the real reason.*[10]

This is another piece of information contradicting the claims that the new administration wished to expel all non-Muslims in Anatolia. The need for artisans in Trabzon seems to be a factor in not allowing the Greeks and Armenians to leave the city. Interestingly, during this time, the population exchange activities between Turkey and Greece were still continuing.

The same ship arrived at Ineboli (İnebolu), another Black Sea port town, on 14 June 1923 to deliver the goods for the Turks. The members of the US Navy and the NER workers delivered the goods to the hinterland. Below is the diary entry of the commanding officer, Robt. T. Young, describing the situation:

> The welcoming at Ineboli was most cordial. On arrival ashore, we were met by Turkish officials and went to the Mayor's office, and at about 14:30 started for Kure . . . Kure is about 7 miles inland by sea, but 55 kilometers by road. The trip was made in a Fiat bus and a Ford. Kure has an elevation of 1200 meters, and the road, although an excellent roadbed, showed poor upkeep, consequently far from the satisfactory condition.

On arrival at Kure, the citizens and small children were drawn up in a line as a reception committee. They were most grateful indeed for the relief.

The facts of the relief are as follows:

Population of Kure	1700
Families	380
Houses and buildings burned	116
Homes remaining approximately	25

Relief afforded: 14000 pounds of grits, 7000 flour, and 1600 pounds clothing.[11]

Judging from the ratio of burnt buildings to standing ones, we can conclude that the Turkish towns were badly damaged, and the wars also put the Muslim population of Anatolia in a desperate situation, nearly as much as their non-Muslim fellow citizens. The main distinction was that Muslims' desperation was not highlighted in US reports as much as that of non-Muslims. The Near East Relief extended its help to Muslims, for which Admiral Bristol received some criticism in the US, but much praise in Turkey.[12]

In addition to the commanding officers of US ships, the US High Commission also collected information from missionaries, businessmen and visitors. For example, Robert M. Scotten, chargé d'affaires *ad interim*, relayed a report by Mr C. B. Wylie, a member of the Constantinople office of the Standard Oil Company, to the general manager, Mr Campbell. This report, prepared on 6 August 1924, describes the author's inspection trip through Anatolia. From it, we understand that the religious minorities, particularly Greeks and Armenians, were leaving Turkey en masse in 1924. Wylie reported:

> I was greatly interested throughout the trip to ascertain the Turks' feelings towards foreigners in general and Americans and Jews in particular. In the southern part of the country, there is undoubtedly a strong anti-foreign feeling which covers all nations and races, but French and Armenians in particular. This applies to the towns of Adana, Aintab, Marash, and Ourfa. It was in this region that the French carried out an exceedingly stupid policy of occupation with Armenian troops.
>
> In Aintab, Marash, and Ourfa, regular sieges were undertaken with the bombardment of the towns, later followed by the evacuation of the French troops and massacre of Armenians. In Ourfa, not an Armenian left, while in

Marash and Aintab, there are a few who are connected with the American institutions . . .

It was naturally among the Armenians that our missionaries found fertile ground for conversion, schooling, and general education. These people are now faced with the fact that there are no Armenians left and that their future work must be with the Turks. However, the Turks are suspicious; they remember the close association of the missionaries and the Armenians, and they see the Armenians still in the compounds of the institutions.

Throughout the interior, from Diarbekir to Sivas, there are here and there a cluster of Armenian families in which the women and children are preponderant, but their ranks are rapidly thinning, and it can be safely assumed that by the end of the year not a single Armenian will be left in Anatolia . . . In order to get away, these people are selling their real property (they have nothing else) at prices that defy all competition. For instance, a fine fertile little garden valued at Ltqs gold 500 went for Ltqs gold 30, and the purchaser made Ltqs 15 on the deal by cutting off the 45 trees and selling them for Ltqs 1-each. Of course, the value of the garden was destroyed.

In Northern Anatolia, where the Greeks were the strongest, those that are left are rapidly being shipped in the exchange of populations, and this operation should be completed within a couple of months. We shall then witness a real, true Turkey for the Turks. A few Levantine French and Italians will be left, but their number is negligible.

Every town visited was from one quarter to three quarters in ruins. Villages ranged from three quarters to complete wrecks. The havoc caused in the interior is really indescribable. It should be borne in mind that the ruined towns and villages back in Smyrna had been in the theatre of warfare or trampled over by a retreating defeated army, but the section covered by my trip was at no time in the war zone, except the towns of Aintab, Kars, and Erzeroum.

The havoc and destruction [have] been caused by the Turks themselves, who will destroy a $ 5000 house by tearing out the roof . . . for firewood . . .

[The Turks] don't want foreigners resident among them, but in no way do they object to their visiting their country or traveling through it. This feeling is not as intense as it was a year ago, and will no doubt continue to decrease with time. In many points, we found expressions of regret that the Armenians and Greeks had gone. A year ago, the expression of such a feeling or thought would have been considered as treason and dealt with accordingly.[13]

This document in 1924 shows indications that in Eastern Anatolia, when the nationalist victory became certain and hopes for a European or US mandate were dashed, non-Muslims were leaving en masse, afraid of reprisals following their cooperation with European (mainly French and Greek) forces. Clearly, many Muslims were taking advantage of the plight of exposed and vulnerable Christian locals, such as the selling of a farm worth 500 Turkish pounds for thirty. It is quite possible that intimidation tactics were utilised by the locals to force out their Christian neighbours for material gain. What is beyond ordinary in this report is that in the last paragraph Scotten informs us, 'In many points, we found expressions of regret that the Armenians and Greeks had gone.' Although certainly in the minority, these kinds of statements in reports prepared by the US observers support my claim that the situation after World War I was a lot more complicated than one can readily understand and appreciate. This settled and nuanced point does not allow us to make blanket statements about the inter-communal relations in Anatolia beyond the fact that many mass killings of non-Muslims took place during World War I.

Internal Affairs of Turkey in US Diplomatic Correspondence

Reports filed from Istanbul to Washington also inform us about the internal affairs of Turkey. Some of this information is valuable in that it is not available in Turkish sources. Therefore, the historian working in the early years of republican Turkey can make use of such information in reconstructing history. What follows is information that is mostly not available in Turkish sources.

In the transition period between the collapse of the Ottoman Empire and the rise of the Turkish Republic, one can readily claim that one of the most defining moments was the separation of the office of the Caliphate from that of the Sultanate, and the abolition of the latter in 1922. This was a colossal event not only for Turkish or Middle Eastern but also Islamic history.

The Abolition of the Sultanate and the Last Sultan Vahdettin

The Ottoman dynasty ruled the empire over six centuries until 1 November 1922, when the Turkish Grand National Assembly passed a law (numbered 308) abolishing the Sultanate. Soon after, on 17 November, Vahdettin, with his immediate family and a small entourage, left Istanbul with a British warship, HMS *Malaya*. This was supposed to be a secret operation, but Bristol was informed the day before that such a plan to remove the Sultan was progressing. In his diary, Bristol claims that he did not relay this information to Washington immediately simply because he did not believe it.

> The fact that I knew of the Sultan's plans for departure the night before he left was a source of great surprise to British officials when they heard later of my knowledge of the fact. In this connection, I desire to add that the English were much deceived in believing that they could pose as the defender of the Moslem faith by giving refuge to the ex-Sultan. I had the opinion for a long time that the Nationalist Turks had an understanding with the rest of the Moslem world before [deposing] the ex-Sultan. Likewise, I believe they were very much pleased to get rid of him in the way that they did by his seeking refuge with the British and leaving the country. This is only another instance of the way in which the British have so generally backed the wrong horse in handling Near Eastern affairs.[14]

Bristol mentions that the British were not happy to learn that the secret operation was not so secret after all. The nationalists were happy that the Sultan left, and the British inadvertently helped the Ankara government a great deal with this move. It was very easy to discredit the ex-Sultan after this escape and label him as 'traitor'. Bristol reported to Washington that Refet Pasha, the representative of the Ankara government in Istanbul, later 'went to the Allies and thanked them for having taken the Sultan away because they had removed a rather difficult situation for him'.[15]

We do know that the last Ottoman Sultan later claimed that he only temporarily left the empire (see below), but he was unable to convince anyone. Bristol was also correct that the Islamic world was not predisposed favourably towards Vahdettin. A missionary report, prepared by the ABCFM, quotes an Arabic language newspaper as saying that, as early as 1918, the mosques in Mecca did not mention Vahdettin's name in the Friday sermons: 'This decisive event which marks the definite separation between Mecca and Constantinople has been expected and demanded during the [past] several months.'[16]

Another significant document dealing with the rivalry between the dynasty and the new government in Ankara coincides with the aftermath of the abolition of the Caliphate in 1924.

The Abolition of the Caliphate and the Last Caliph Abdülmecid

After Vahdettin's escape, his cousin Abdülmecid was elected as the new Caliph in 1922 with the condition that he would refrain from participating in any political activity. However, as soon as he was declared the new Caliph by the nationalist government, Ankara became suspicious of his political activities. This was not without reason. Abdülmecid was in close contact with foreign diplomats, with oppositional figures, with Istanbul journalists, and even with Rauf Bey [Orbay], a member of the nationalist cabinet in Ankara. In the British archives, there is a document transcribing a conversation between the Caliph and a British diplomat. The report, dated 29 August 1923, was penned by the British High Commissioner Neville Henderson, who informed London that the Caliph was in favour of someone friendly to the British interests ruling Constantinople.[17]

Mustafa Kemal was following the actions of the Caliph closely; therefore, it was not a surprise to foreign diplomats in Turkey that the Caliphate was abolished on 3 March 1924. The law, numbered 431, stipulated that members of the Ottoman dynasty also left the country. After this development, we see that the last Sultan Vahdettin, who had until then been quiet, sent a letter to the US president, Calvin Coolidge, to interfere on his and his dynasty's behalf. It is significant because from 1922, when he was deposed, until 1924, when the Caliphate was abolished, the deposed Sultan did not write any such letter to anyone. In his letter, Vahdettin reiterated that the Ankara government did not have the authority to depose him and abolish the Caliphate:

> My departure from the empire is temporary and does not mean that I gave up on my birthright over the Sultanate and the Caliphate. It is a frivolous act to state that such rebellious and unruly group as those in Ankara have no authority to decide the faith of these institutions [the Sultanate and the Caliphate]. A small group of military and some other people, whose religion, origin, and homeland are questionable, do not possess the authority to separate the Caliphate from the Sultanate and isolate and abolish them, partly by force, partly by ignorance and oversight by forcing 5–6 million innocent Turks. This can only be done by the committee of Islamic scholars appointed by the whole Islamic world since it is a decision that concerns the entire world. As the *ulema* know well, such decisions that are against the Islamic sharia are null and void . . .

In addition, the illegal measures of the government, such as exiling my dynasty abroad and confiscating their property and private belongings, are against human rights. I would like to kindly request you and your government help in this regard.[18]

Let us first state that Vahdettin sent a similar letter on that date to the French President Alexandre Millerand.[19] We can only speculate as to why Vahdettin waited two years to express an open and international objection to the Ankara government. It is quite possible that the removal of the dynasty and the abolition of the Caliphate crushed all his hopes for return. In addition, the harsh language towards the Ankara government in this letter is a clear indication that Vahdettin understandably did not have any warm feelings towards the new regime and its leaders. We do know that no action was taken by President Coolidge or other world leaders in response to Vahdettin's request.

Bristol was also closely following these developments. As mentioned above, his intelligence apparatus was quite effective in Turkey; he knew a week in advance that Mustafa Kemal was going to abolish the Caliphate. Bristol sent a report by his military attaché, who was following 'a conference of Turkish Army Chiefs in Smyrna'. This conference was held on 15 February and was presided over by President Mustafa Kemal Pasha, Ismet Pasha (Prime Minister) and Fevzi Pasha (Chief of General Staff), along with other high-ranking military personnel. The declared aim of this conference was 'to study the strategy and tactics of the campaigns of August–September 1922, against the Greeks'.[20] Another military intelligence attached to Bristol's report reveals that at least France and the US knew of the decision reached to abolish the Caliphate before all members of the Turkish Grand National Assembly. The brief, titled 'Possible Political Significance of the Smyrna Conference', was as follows:

It is generally assumed that the Conference of Turkish Army Chiefs under Mustapha Kemal Pasha, held at Smyrna February 15th–22nd, was concerned secondarily, if not primarily, with politics. It is probable that the Marshal-President desired to know the attitude of the Army, particularly the Army Chiefs, under certain political eventualities.

The French claim to know of certain political topics which were discussed at the Conference, the most important of which is the abolition of the Caliphate. They think that Mustapha Kemal had made up his mind to abolish the Caliphate, which is always rival to his power and that he wanted only to assure himself of the loyalty of the Army. This assurance, they think, was given him at Smyrna.

The French also think that other political questions were discussed at Smyrna, such as the new Constitution, the Syrian frontier, Mosul, etc., as well as important military questions.

Mustapha Kemal obviously desired to confer with his military chiefs at some point distant from Angora and the National Assembly. Although Angora is more central than Smyrna, and although he was returning to Angora this month (he returned immediately after the Conference), he took advantage of his visit to Smyrna to call the Conference there.[21]

The issue surrounding the Kemalists dealing with the Caliphate was very prominent in Bristol's reports to Washington, although the inner dynamics of it are not very well known to historians of the twentieth century. We find other significant details of the Kemalist approach to the Caliphate. For example, we see that the US High Commission in Istanbul was visited by Osman Fahreldine [Fahrettin] Bey, private secretary of Seyyid/Sheikh Senoussi, who was instrumental in legitimising the War of Independence in the eyes of the Muslim public in Anatolia. Bristol reports:

> It is well known that Sheik Senoussi played an important part as an advisor on religious matters during the earlier phases of the Nationalist Movement in Turkey. He had approved the abolition of the Sultanate and the establishment of a Caliphate with purely spiritual powers. He had also, it seems, in general, been sympathetic to various other reforms tending to the modernization of Islam in Turkey.
>
> Shortly before the abolition of the Caliphate and the expulsion of Abdul Medjid last March, Moustapha Kemal Pasha, in an interview with Sheik Senoussi, offered him Turkey's support in Caliph on the condition that the seat of the Caliphate is outside of Turkey. This offer the sheik refused. He made it plain that he favored the retention of Abdul Medjid as Caliph with spiritual powers at Constantinople; . . . as a result, Ankara canceled his allowance.
>
> He has, however, come further than a mere expression of opinion. He thoroughly disapproves of the abolition of the Medresses (teleological

schools) and of the present anti-clerical policy of Angora generally. He has used his influence to postpone the Pan-Islamic Congress, which the Indian and Egyptian Muslims desired to convene at Cairo in order to examine the whole question of the caliphate, and he is in sympathy with an organization which has as its avowed objects the return of Abdul Medjid to Constantinople and his restoration as Caliph. It is hoped that Prince Omar Toussoun, who has been collecting funds for Abdul Medjid, will give financial support to the organization. There is some reason for believing that the Ulema of the El Azhar Mosque would not be averse to playing a leading role in any movement having to do with the restoration of Abdul Medjid. Fahreldine Bey has been in Constantinople working for the organization, and he is leaving shortly for Angora and the Eastern Vilayets with a similar purpose in mind . . .

The French, who have been intriguing with Abdul Medjid, have offered a considerable sum of money to the Sheik Senoussi if he will use his influence among Muslims in accordance with French interests. He has refused to have anything to do with such a proposal. He has also declined to approve a secret treaty negotiated by his nephew with Marshall Allenby because this treaty would commit him to support King Hussein as caliph and to engage in pro-British propaganda throughout the Muslim World generally . . .

It is obvious that the information contained in this dispatch is to be accepted guardedly and judgment suspended for the present as to its value. Nevertheless, it is generally conceded that the anti-clerical policy of Angora has been carried too far and that much discontent, especially among the hoja-softa class, has resulted. This discontent is not a serious menace unless it is organized and provided with a leader or leaders. The importance of such a leader is, of course, something that may happen any day. Furthermore, the present situation lends itself ideally to foreign intrigue. It is being gossiped around Constantinople, for instance, that the French would like to install Abdul Medjid in Syria as Caliph and ruler of that territory under their protection. The carrying out of any such program would naturally attract many discontented Turks to Syria and would prove a standing menace to Nationalist Turkey.[22]

The date for this report is 17 June 1924, just over three months after the abolition of the Caliphate. If this information about Mustafa Kemal's offer for supporting Sheikh Senoussi for the office of Caliph is correct, it would prove that Mustafa Kemal was not against the office of the Caliphate but the holder of the office, that is, a member of the Ottoman dynasty. The reader should not miss the detail that the offer to Senoussi was made *before* the decision to abolish the Caliphate. If Senoussi had accepted the offer, there was a good chance that the Caliphate might not have been abolished. This is stunning information if correct, of course. Bristol was careful in warning Washington that he could not confirm or deny the reliability of this information. In some Turkish sources, Mustafa Kemal's offer to Senoussi appears to be for the office of the Şeyhülislam (technically the Mufti of Istanbul), not the Caliph.[23] This report, however, is very clear in indicating that the issue was that of the Caliphate.

What is also significant in this report is the information about the existence of a secret organisation, which was busy with counter-revolutionary activities. Some of the names associated with this organisation were understandably the functionaries of the old Ottoman regime, but some of them, quite astonishingly, were members of the Kemalist regime.

> [Fahreldine Bey] mentioned the following as already connected with the organization:
> Izzet Pasha, formerly Grand Vizir
> Refet Pasha
> Ali Riza Pasha, formerly Grand Vizir
> Kemal Bey, Minister of Supply in the Union and Progress Government
> Yousouf Kemaly Bey, former deputy from Mersine
> Selahedine Adil Pasha, Military Commandant of Constantinople in 1923
> Zeki Bey, Deputy of Gumushane
> Hoja Sabri Effendi, formerly Deputy from Afium [Afyon] Karahissar
> Houloussi Effendi, formerly Deputy from Konia
> Ahmed Bey, Notable of Diarbekir
> Adbul Fetteh Effendi, Notable of Van
> Halil Effendi, Notable of Van
> Abdul Vatab Effendi, Notable of Van[24]

In this list, there are notable names, especially Refet Pasha, who was a close friend of Mustafa Kemal and a significant figure in the War of Independence. He was the commander to whom the British handed over Constantinople.

Bristol informs us that Osman Fahrettin Bey, private secretary of Ahmed Cherif El Senoussi, returned from his trip to Mersin and Ankara and visited the High Commission several more times. The admiral notified Washington that firstly the conversation revolved around this secret committee for restoring Abdülmecid as the Caliph in the Pan-Islamic Congress in Cairo. Osman Fahrettin Bey further informed Bristol that the secret committee's ultimate objective was the overthrow of the current government in Ankara. The future constitutional monarch would be either the deposed Abdülmecid himself or Selim Efendi, the eldest son of Abdulhamid II. Bristol narrates the information he gathered:

A meeting of political leaders of the movement was held a short time ago at Erenkeuy. Some twenty-five persons, including Raouf Bey [Orbay] and Refet Pasha [Bele], were present. Raouf Bey spoke at length in favor of a constitutional monarchy for Turkey along English lines and declared that the republican form of government was not suited to Turkey. Refet Pasha said they had been willing to follow Moustapha Kemal Pasha as a military leader in the war against the Greeks, but they did not propose to follow him and his 'gang' in a political dictatorship. He said the National Assembly should rule the country, not Moustapha Kemal Pasha. The tactics of these political leaders are characterized by great caution. They have taken little or no action heretofore desiring to await the coming into effect of the Lausanne Treaty in order to avoid the danger of placing Turkey in a disadvantageous position towards the powers. They are now very discreetly spreading propaganda by means of agents who are working in various parts of Anatolia. Abdul Kader Bey, for instance, [who] got into trouble with the Tribunal of Independence at Constantinople last winter, is at present at Adalia working for the movement. The first definitive move will be to force the dissolution of the Assembly and holding of new elections that will doubtless return an even larger number of unruly Deputies than there are at present.

Then will be the time for bringing out the idea of a constitutional monarch. It is interesting to note that it is proposed to bring back but one member of the House of Othman – the one selected as constitutional Monarch. The others will not be allowed to return but will be pensioned. Fahreldine Bey states that recently Moustapha Kemal Pasha has become alarmed over the possibility of serious trouble on account of the religious situation and is, therefore, doing all in his power to enlist the Sheik Senoussi in support of the government. He has within the past few weeks proposed to the Sheik that, if he will use influence to pacify the religious elements in Turkey he, Mustapha Kemal Pasha, will send a delegation to the Cairo Pan-Islamic Congress to work for the election of Sheik Senoussi as Caliph. In the event of these efforts being successful, Mustafa Kemal Pasha would be agreeable to Sheik's residing at Constantinople in his capacity of Caliph. The nature of Sheik's reply to this proposition is not yet known. As further evidence of goodwill towards the Sheik, Mustafa Kemal Pasha, upon request, has pardoned Hodja Mehmed Askeri, who was condemned to death for opposing the government policies.[25]

This part of the report is extraordinary for the possibility that, if correct, it proves that Rauf Bey [Orbay], who was the first Prime Minister of the nationalist government, was, in fact, working against the regime. We do know that around this time, Rauf Bey and Mustafa Kemal Pasha had different methods for achieving the future of the new republic. However, this document labels him not as a republican but as a constitutional monarchist who was part of the anti-regime organisations. The same is true for Refet Pasha, who was a very close childhood friend of Mustafa Kemal Pasha.

It is interesting to note that this secret committee would bring back only one member of the dynasty to install as a monarch; the rest would be pensioned abroad. Understandably, they did not want to go back to the old Ottoman power structure but wished to create a new administration not too different from that of the Committee of Union and Progress. The monarch would be only a figurehead. This information needs to be confirmed with another independent source; however, the circumstantial evidence corroborates this information. There is information in the US archives to point out that Refet Pasha was not entirely in the Kemalist camp for the political direction of the country.

For example, a very interesting entry in Bristol's 'War Diary' comes from 25 October 1923, four days before the declaration of the new regime as a republic and a little over four months before the abolition of the Caliphate. Refet Pasha was in Istanbul, unaware that the republic would be declared in four days' time, and the discussions over the abolition of the Caliphate were not yet prominent. During this time, the legal and political status of the new Caliph, Abdülmecid, vis-à-vis the president of the Grand National Assembly, Mustafa Kemal, was a source of confusion, particularly for the diplomats in Istanbul. On this subject,

Bristol records in his diary a conversation between Robert Scotten, a member of the US diplomatic mission under Bristol, and Refet Pasha, who was then the representative of the Ankara government in Istanbul:

> I [Mr Scotten] tried to ascertain Refet's view as to the relative rank of the Calif and the 'head of the State.' I stated that it was conceivable, for instance, that a ship of war might be in Constantinople when the head of the State arrived and it would be necessary to fire a salute both to him and to the Calif, and I asked him what he conceived to be the proper salute to be rendered to each one. He laughed uproariously and stated, 'Fire as many guns as you wish for that spiritual gentleman up there in the palace at Dolma Baghche. Give him all the honors you choose, but don't salute the head of the State at all. Leave that poor fellow alone.' He said, 'He is simply a man who is unhappy enough to have fallen into a disagreeable job and who in a few years may have to be riding on a tramcar again.[26]

This conversation is significant in demonstrating that a certain level of confusion about the relative rank of the Caliph existed. It is also possible that the question was geared towards understanding Ankara's attitude towards the Caliph. However, this piece of information is even more significant for scholars whose research is on the internal power struggle in Turkey. We know that Refet Pasha, one of the leaders of the Turkish War of Independence, joined the ranks of the opposition party (the Progressive Republican Party) in 1924. This information plainly demonstrates his rivalry with Mustafa Kemal in 1923. If not a direct confirmation, this information can provide us with circumstantial evidence for the claim put forward by Osman Fahrettin Bey, who mentioned his name among anti-republican people associated with a secret organisation a year later. The reader should be warned, however, that the evidence is not conclusive. It is possible that Refet Pasha and Rauf Bey, who may have harboured such sentiments, were indeed not republicans despite the fact that the oppositional party they established along with Kazım Karabekir was named the 'Progressive Republican Party'.

Financing the War of Independence

One of the least known aspects of the emergence of the new Turkey is the financing of the new state. There are several documents that can give us concrete evidence to see at least partly where the nationalists received funding. There is no need to repeat that the Ottoman state was bankrupt and taxing the already poor citizens only partially remedied the situation. Bristol's reports give us information regarding this issue as well.

For example, a dispatch to Bristol includes a report prepared by the US Military Attaché, which was also forwarded to the Secretary of State. This report, dated 5 March 1924, two days after the abolition of the Caliphate, of the *Evkaf* (pious foundations) and of the religious courts (*Şeriat Mahkemeleri*), reveals the following information:

> The property of the *Evkaf* passes to the State. This property has an estimated potential value, according to Turkish authorities, of 2,000,000,000 Turkish pounds (a little over a billion dollars). It is thought that with the passing of this property to the State, it will be increased in value, because it has been very badly administered in the past and also because the State can now enlarge the rights of inheritance, thus increasing the value of all property.
>
> In abolishing the Ministry of Religious Affairs, which replaced the old Sheikh-ul-Islam, the State takes over directly all religious affairs. The Government has already, within a few days of the passing of the law, forbidden the majority of the hodjas to wear their distinctive turbans and gowns, and prescribed the form of prayers to [unreadable word] in the Mosques on Friday replacing the name of the Caliph by that of the Republic. The appointment of all religious officials will rest with the State, and it may be supposed that the State will, in that way, attempt to control them. It is said that police permits will be required of all who desire to preach in the Mosques during the forthcoming Ramazan (holy month).[27]

The estimated one billion dollar figure cited for the value of the transferred *Evkaf* property was little known about. One should keep in mind that the national budget for 1925 was approximately eighty-four million US dollars. In other words, this figure indicates that the estimated value of the *Evkaf* was approximately twelve times more than the annual budget of the state. Clearly, by renting or selling this property, the government tapped into a great sum of money that was not available to the Ottoman state.

On the subject of police permits for local imams to preach in the mosques, we do not know if this was a rumour or if the government was able to successfully implement it at the time. It is not difficult to guess that such a policy could not be implemented beyond the city centres. Yet, it would still be very interesting to know if this policy was put into action at all for that particular holy month, or if it was more permanent.

An earlier document gives us another set of figures dealing with the Indian Muslims' cash donation to the Turkish nationalist movement. The folder numbered 867.00/1694 includes a report dated 19 July 1923 sent to Washington by Avra M. Warren, the US Consul in Karachi. According to this report, the Indian Muslims sent aid to 'the Angora Turks in their national aspiration by the purchase of guns, airplanes and other military equipment', and 'the Muslim response [to the Kemalist movement] was general and generous, and 36½ Lakhs of Rupees, about $1,180,000, was raised during 1921 and 1922 and entrusted to Seth Chetani, the Chairman of the Central Kalifat Committee, to be forwarded to the Angora government'. There were rumours, however, that only a small portion of the monetary gift had ever reached the Kemalists. The report further indicates that after a thorough review, 'it appears that of the total 36½ Lakhs collected, only 19 Lakhs, or a little more than half, has been sent to Angora'.[28] Later Seth Chetani accepted responsibility for the 'misappropriation' of the fund. We knew that the Kemalist movement in Ankara until the abolition of the Caliphate received funding from Indian Muslims, but this document gives us specific information regarding the sum of money that the Ankara government received from India. The figure that reached Ankara was around $600,000, which is a significant sum for a movement that desperately needed cash in 1921–2. This information is also important in explaining the view of some of Mustafa Kemal's close friends, such as Rauf Bey [Orbay], who were in favour of maintaining the office of the Caliphate.

At this point, we can include another report by the US Military Attaché written eight days after the abolition of the Caliphate. This report indicates that Mustafa Kemal sent a telegram to the Indian Muslims, assuring them that the dignity of the office was preserved in the Turkish National Assembly.[29] Clearly, he was conscious of the value of the financial contributions of Indian Muslims. The very same report points out a compromise in the language of the law abolishing the Caliphate (Law #431). According to this report, the original language of the law was 'the Caliph was deposed, and the Caliphate abolished'. Later this language was modified to state: 'The

Caliph is deposed. As (or since) the Caliphate is included in the meaning and signification of Government and Republic, the office of the Caliphate is abolished.'[30] The report further claims that 'The modification is obviously a compromise, but its meaning is far from clear. Before its adoption, the Assembly had rejected a proposal to merge the Caliphate into the Republic. Yet, if the adopted modification means anything at all, it means that this merger is recognized by the Assembly.'[31] In fact, the daily *Tanin* suggested that such vague language makes available the possibility that if the Assembly sees fit, it can appoint a Caliph again, and that this language goes against the very nature of the separation of religion from the state.[32] In my judgement, the vagueness of the language was intended to blur the radical action taken by the Turkish Grand National Assembly and to soften the reaction of the Islamic world. However, if Osman Fahrettin Bey's communication is correct and Mustapha Kemal offered his support to elect Sheikh Senoussi in the Cairo Pan-Islamic Conference as Caliph, the *Tanin*'s claim of the possibility of bringing back a friendly Caliph was not far-fetched. Regardless, there is no report in the US consular reports to document that the Indian Muslims continued to contribute financially to the Kemalist movement after the abolition of the Caliphate.

Concerning international financial contributions to the Kemalist movement, on 24 March 1923 Bristol relayed earlier information that he had received directly from Princess Chevekiar, the first wife of the Egyptian King Fuad I (r. 1917–36). During a personal meeting with Bristol, the Princess claimed, 'the ex-Khedive had given the Turkish Nationalist Government 50,000,000 Turkish paper pounds to assist them in their cause.'[33] This amount equals roughly twenty-five million US dollars and, if correct, it amounts to another sizeable sum that the Kemalists received from the international community. It also shows that Egypt was trying to undermine the authority of Great Britain by supporting the Kemalists.

The Private Life of Mustafa Kemal

His Divorce

American diplomats were also interested in the private life of Mustafa Kemal, one of the lesser-known aspects of which was his divorce. On this subject, we have the following report sent to Washington; what is significant in these reports is the fact that many of them went against what was published in the Turkish press. One of Bristol's staff reported the following:

> There are unconfirmed but well-believed rumors of a serious break in the marital relations of the President of the Republic, Moustapha Kemal Pasha, and his wife, Latife Hanoum. It is stated that for a year, their relations have been very strained due to the fact that Moustapha Kemal is addicted to drinking . . . His private physician called his attention to the deplorable results which such a life would have on his health and the effect which it might have on his already weak heart. As a result of this advice, he is stated to have almost ceased drinking, but about a month ago, he fell into his old bad habits even to a greater extent than previously, which led to scenes with his wife who could not bear the existing conditions. It is reported that last week there was a violent quarrel between them subsequent to which Latife Hanoum telegraphed her mother Madame Ouchaki Zade at Smyrna that she could not remain at Angora longer and begged her mother to come and fetch her. Her mother came to Angora and remained only one night leaving the following day with her daughter for Smyrna. Latife Hanoum not wishing to see her husband before her departure left alone . . . Ismet Pasha was unsuccessfully urging her to remain. [One reason given by the Turkish press was that] his wife has failed to produce an heir to the president.[34]

We know that Mustafa Kemal married Latife Hanım, who was from the notable Uşakizade family of İzmir, on 29 January. From the couple's divorce certificate, we learn that Mustafa Kemal informed the Prime Minister of the divorce on 11 August 1925, one day *after* the US report informing Washington. This fact is a clear indication of US intelligence-gathering success. The divorce was officially registered on 15 August 1925.[35] Although Crosby informs Washington of this event as an 'unconfirmed rumor', he was indeed correct. This leads us to believe that the other, more significant information on Latife's departure with her mother from Ankara is also correct, suggesting that Latife Hanım may have initiated the separation and divorce.[36]

Mustafa Kemal's Views on Religion

Although the following document comes from a period slightly after the tenure of Mark Lambert Bristol, it is significant enough to mention it here as it describes Mustafa Kemal Atatürk's religious beliefs and his views on the religious establishment. The report, dated 17 March 1933, was sent from Charles H. Sherrill to the Secretary of State. Sherrill was the US Ambassador to Turkey between 1932 and 1933, and he was also preparing a book on Mustafa Kemal.[37] The report below was not published in his book.[38] The document I have is slightly faded, and a couple of words were not legible. However, Mustafa Kemal's candid explanation of his views on religion to a foreign diplomat have utmost significance for the reader and need to be quoted in full to see the entire context. Ambassador Sherrill reports:

> During my three-hour interview yesterday afternoon with the president of the Republic Ghazi Mustafa Kemal, and while discussing eight chapters of my biography of him, which he is going over with me, there came up the question of religion in Turkey. I remarked that I had given considerable study to the development under the Turkish Republic of the Moslem religion and would like to know for the purpose of my biography so much as he was willing to tell me either for publication or not of his own point of view upon the subject. He went into the matter in considerable detail, indicating which portions he thought would be of public interest and which not. It appears that when he was six or seven years old, his mother wished to send him to a dame school,[39] where the teacher would not only give him lessons in the [unreadable] but would also teach him the Koran, which meant learning long Arabic passages by heart. His father, on the other hand, preferred that the boy would go to a lay school, where no religious instruction was given. Although the father finally prevailed, the boy was duly entered in the dame school by his mother with the attendance ceremonies usual in Salonica, where they lived. The next day the father took the boy to the lay school, where he continued his studies. This made his mother most unhappy that she wept a great deal, so at the boy's suggestion, the religious instructor at the dame school came to the family home and gave him the Koran instruction which his mother desired. This latter only lasted a month, but at least it satisfied his mother. That was all the religious instruction he ever enjoyed.
>
> He completely denies the generally accepted belief that he is an agnostic, but alleges that his religion goes so far as to believe in the existence of God, all-powerful, the creator and ruler of the Universe. He further believes that mankind needs that belief in such a God. To this, he adds that it is good for mankind to make appeals to this God in the form of prayers of some sort. He

stops there. He then asked in some detail why I was a convinced protestant Christian, and I gave him my reasons therefore, which do not belong in this report, except for my general comment that he seemed thoroughly warmest in his question, all of which showed he had already given considerable thought to religion.

He then went on to tell me of the condition of the Muslim religion as he found it when he came to power ten years ago as president of the new Republic he erected. He found it necessary to abolish the Sheik-ul-Islam and also the medresses (schools where little but the Koran was taught), the religious courts and the Qadis who presided over them, the hodjas and all the priesthood, including the various dervishes. He said that all that remained of this elaborate priestly structure after the Ottoman Empire were the imams, who, as muezzins, gave the calls to prayer from the minarets and led the prayers within the mosques.

I asked him what, if any, religious instructions for the youth of Turkey after he had swept away as completely all this structure he had just described. He said that he had replaced the unsatisfactory medresses with a complete primary and secondary educational system throughout the country, all leading up to the already existing University, etc.; that in both the primary and the middle schools religious education was given to the student of telling the story of Muhammad and of his wise principles of better living which the Koran inculcated, and to that religious history he had caused to be added similar information about that other great religion described in our Old and New Testament and also that in the Buddhist religious books.

He and I then made a comparison of this modern Turkish religious instruction with the sort given by the average Sunday school in the United States. Then I inquired if such instruction as our Sunday schools gave could be successfully afforded by Friday morning classes under women in the Halkevis or People's Houses throughout the country, he seemed very doubtful of success for such an idea, but said that it was a novel one and would receive his consideration. The thought of women teachers for this purpose evidently appealed to him, for this would avoid any possibility of politics or the intervention of party partisans of the hodjas or such other troublesome possibilities.

In this connection, we spoke freely of the recent Bursa incident,[40] seeing that it was engineered not by Turks but by three foreigners, an Albanian, a Bulgarian, and a Russian. He even intimated that it might have been instigated by the Third International. I complimented him on the political skill with which he had changed that possibly bothersome political movement into a merely linguistic question because it solely concerned substituting Turkish for Arabic in the public call to prayer. This brought him to speak of why and how he had pushed the modern translation of the Quran from Arabic into Turkish, and this opened quite a new vista upon that subject. He maintains that when the Turkish people come to know the real meaning of some of the Arabic prayers they have long been reciting, they will be disgusted with themselves. He cited one Arabic prayer taken from the Koran in which Muhammad praised that his uncle and uncle's daughter may be consigned to the infernal regions for something they have done.[41] 'Imagine a Turk taking any interest or getting any religious Inspirations out of reciting such a prayer as that,' said he. The more he developed this line of thought, the more I was forced to the conclusion that he is pushing the use of the Koran in Turkish largely to discredit the Koran with the Turks.

He made the broad and somewhat surprising statement that the Turkish people are really not religious in any way, and alleged that the people who still go to the mosques only do so from habit or because attracted to the mosque by a vocal rendering of the prayers. I very respectfully dissented from his conclusions in this regard and told him my experience when my wife and myself, on the invitation of two Turkish friends of his, had, on the late afternoon of January 23, repaired to the mosque of Santa Sofia to witness the so-called 'Night of Prayer.' I told him how crowded it was with the ten thousand worshippers (20% of which were in military uniform) and of the intense and absorbed [concentration] which each and all of these worshippers, for one solid hour, gave to the prayers, which each one was directly addressing to the God whose existence the Ghazi himself acknowledged. My request for the explanation of those numbers, of that devotion, and of that personal absorption only brought from him more statements of his opinion as to the limited part which the Turkish government should play in affording the youth of Turkey the opportunity to know about religion. It was quite clear by the time he had finished that he does not now believe in going further in that regard than the historical instruction upon the three great religions now being given in the secondary schools and also in the small theological section of the university. But he certainly does not agree with the Soviet idea of abolishing all religion. He insists that the principle mosques should be carefully kept up by the government and should be used for the purposes for which they were originally consecrated. He believes in the ethical teachings of all of the three great religions, but more on ethics than on religions.

Then I commented that I thought that his own religious belief was incomplete without the addition thereto of frequent expression of gratitude to the one God for the blessing he vouchsafed us. He seemed surprised but interested but said he would certainly give consideration to that idea, if only because of its novelty to him. He expressed the desire to speak with me further upon this subject, which rather surprised me because such intimate friends of his as Yusuf Akçura Bey have constantly warned me that if I talk about religion with him, it would surely impair his relations with me, which relations he was kind enough to call our friendship. He was good enough to say at the conclusion of this part of our conversation that he had never gone before so fully into the matter with a foreigner, certainly not in expressing his own personal beliefs.[42]

After this lengthy quotation, it is important to highlight what Mustafa Kemal said and the significance of his words. First of all, we know of Mustafa Kemal's early education, but the detail here on the disagreement between his mother and his father about the religious vs secular education their son Mustafa should receive must be appreciated. Secondly, what is noteworthy here is that despite many claims by his opponents about Mustafa Kemal's being an atheist, he denies first-hand that he is even an agnostic, and he reiterates that he believes in the existence of God.

Ambassador Sherrill's observation of Mustafa Kemal's approach to Islam is extremely significant. Sherrill concludes that Mustafa Kemal 'is pushing the use of the Koran in Turkish largely to discredit the Koran with the Turks'. In other words, the ambassador's impression was that the president was not a strong believer in Islam or any other monotheistic religion. He saw them as a collection of moral codes which need to be taught. It is indeed very difficult to gather any other meaning from Mustafa Kemal's statements. It is, however, a mistake to define Mustafa Kemal as anti-religious. On the contrary, even if he was not a believer in religion per se, he was aware of the benefits of religion for humankind. Mustafa Kemal clearly states that he was against the Soviet style of getting rid of religion, acknowledging the positive role of religion in society. His hostility was not against Islam but the Islamic establishment as a source of political power. Therefore, the idea of religion being taught by women might have appealed to him.

Possibly to diminish the influence of the Islamic professional establishment that he identified as the main source of social and political problems, Mustafa Kemal wished to teach the moral value of all three monotheistic religions, and surprisingly he adds Buddhism. His sympathy for Buddhism might have originated from the limited political interest of this belief system on society. Sherrill's interview with Mustafa Kemal provides us with one of the most significant primary documents delving into his religious beliefs, which were not discussed openly.

Bristol and Mustafa Kemal

Bristol and Mustafa Kemal met personally at least twice. On 18 February 1926, Bristol describes his second personal meeting with Mustafa Kemal in Ankara. He was attending a reception in the Russian Embassy in the afternoon when he heard the rumour that the president, Mustafa Kemal, would come. Mustafa Kemal did come at midnight:

> About 12 o'clock the President accompanied by Kiazim Pasha, President of the Assembly, entered the ballroom and accompanied by several other men and women occupied a private room off the ballroom. I was quite surprised when a little later, Kiazim Pasha came and took me to the inner room and introduced me to the President. The latter was very cordial and had me sit down near him, and he talked for some time using one of the Turkish officials as interpreters from Turkish to French. I talked to him twice after that during that evening. One-time, Safvet Bey was the interpreter and the next time Tewfik Rushdi Bey. The President talked a good deal about the inception of the Nationalistic movement with the Congresses held at Erzeroum and Sivas. He asked about General Harbord and spoke in a complimentary way of the gentleman. He pointed out that Turkey could not understand why America, which had never been at war with Turkey, seemed to be the last country to show her friendship for Turkey. He expressed personal regard for me as a comrade stating he was talking to me as a comrade and not as a diplomat. As he did most of the talking, and naturally, I could not interrupt him, I did not have much to say. In addition to this, with the noise and confusion of the adjacent ballroom, it was hard to carry on a conversation. I made appropriate remarks in regard to the honor I felt at meeting him, stating the interest I had in his career from the first time I met him in Constantinople seven years ago up to the present

time. I referred to the establishment of a new civil code as another great step which he had assisted his country in making towards modernization and civilization. He seemed particularly pleased by this reference.[43]

Bristol notes that he had met Mustafa Kemal in 1919 in Istanbul. This meeting had possibly taken place before Mustafa Kemal's arrival in Samsun on 19 May, after which he did not go to Istanbul until 1927. Under what circumstances they met we do not know; however, it could have been very interesting to know how, where and why an Ottoman general and an American diplomat met in Istanbul in 1919.

Let us finish this chapter with another significant document regarding the publication of Mustafa Kemal's famous book, *Nutuk* ('The Speech'). This was regarded as the official history of the Turkish War of Independence, detailing the war from the viewpoint of Mustafa Kemal, the founder of the republic. It was originally delivered by the president in the Republican People's Party Assembly between 15 and 20 September 1927. What is significant in the following document is that Mustafa Kemal asked his trusted people to contact Bristol about the publication of his forthcoming speech even before any knowledge of it was made public. The meeting took place on 23 May 1927, four months before the speech was read in Ankara by Mustafa Kemal, taking thirty-six and a half hours over five days. Bristol reported:

> Instructed by Ismet Pasha, Nusret Bey called on me this morning requesting my personal and confidential recommendations with reference to giving publicity in America to the Ghazi's forthcoming resume of what he and his party have accomplished since his assumption of the direction of affairs political in Turkey subsequent to the Armistice of Mudros and with a view to final publication in book form. Nusret Bey requested an expression of my personal recommendations, but I was non-committal. The president's speech to which Nusret Bey had reference will cover about one thousand pages. I urgently recommend that this matter be brought to the attention of the American Press with a view to assigning a representative to Angora no later than July 1st. Such a representative will doubtless be granted personal interviews with Mustafa Kemal Pasha, which has seldom been accorded in the past. I would further recommend that a man of much tact and discretion with a thorough knowledge of the French language be sent. It is evident someone from Europe must be assigned to get here in time. Please instruct at the earliest moment.[44]

I was not able to locate the State Department's response to *The Speech*. However, the Ottoman archives have a record that the State Department appointed someone from the Associated Press to come and discuss the publication of *Nutuk* in the US.[45] By asking for publicity for the book in the US, it is possible that Mustafa Kemal was hoping to tell his story of the rise of the Turkish Republic to the American public and policy-makers. The contact regarding the issue was made before the signing of the US–Turkey agreement in 1926. It is possible that the Turkish side wished to bring Turkey to the attention of the US policy-makers; therefore, it might have been a diplomatic move.

Concluding Remarks

After the conclusion of the Great War, the Ottoman Empire, one of the longest and richest empires of world history, was coming to an end. This chapter began by presenting reports describing daily life in the capital city, Constantinople, and inter-communal relations in the empire, waiting for peace. After the foreign occupation of Istanbul and İzmir, and especially after the Turkish victory over the Greeks in Western Anatolia, how did the delicate balance between the Muslim and non-Muslim communities in Turkey change? The reports sent to Washington also shed some light on this question.

In the following section, the chapter presented documents dealing with some significant political events in the Turkish Republic. These documents were selected based on their possible impact on early Turkish Republican history. Some of them had not been published anywhere before. Documents on the abolition of the Sultanate and Caliphate tell a different story from that of the official narrative. The reports on the foreign financial contributions to the Kemalist movement are of particular significance as it was an unknown issue. There were many rumours about Mustafa Kemal's private life published in the diaries of his contemporaries; the documents in this section contribute to this unconfirmed information. Mustafa Kemal's views on religion are also very informative for the reader.

The subsections in this chapter cohere to present a picture of Turkey and the internal affairs in the emerging nation. In this chapter, the majority of the documents were prepared by the High Commission's staff and are descriptive in nature.

Notes

1. The American Board of Commissioners for Foreign Missions was the first foreign mission agency in the US. It was officially chartered in 1812.
2. 867.50/1, Lewis Heck to Secretary of State, 26 December 1918.
3. 867.50/1, Lewis Heck to Secretary of State, 30 January 1919.
4. The text sometimes spells it 'Saumsoum'. In modern Turkish it is spelled 'Samsun'.
5. 867.48/7, report by H. A. Hatch, 11 April 1919.
6. 'Bristol Papers', Library of Congress, box 2. Bristol's 'War Diary', dated 24 June 1920.
7. 867.00/1685, Julian E. Gillespie, US Trade Commissioner's trip to Angora, 23 June 1923.
8. 867.00/1685, 'Summary of Refugee Situation', 1 June 1923.
9. 867.00/1685, report from Robt. T. Young to Bristol.
10. Ibid.; emphasis added.
11. Ibid.
12. Isabelle T. Dodd informed Admiral Bristol with a note by Ualide Hanum (Halide Hanım), a graduate of Constantinople College, a school established by the American Friends of the Near East to educate girls. The note, dated 18 February 1919, stated that the admiral's declaration of Americans' helping people in Turkey with no regard to race or religion was most welcomed. The Turkish student told Ms Dodd, 'Do thank [Bristol] and tell him that he is the first Christian who has said it openly and it has melted the hearts that were bitter and hardened . . . We will never forget it.' 'Bristol Papers', box 1.
13. 867.00/1817, Scotten to Secretary of State, 15 August 1924.
14. 867.00/1584, Bristol to Secretary of State, 7 December 1922.
15. 867.00/1914, Bristol's War College speech, 2 February 1926.
16. The excerpt can be found in a letter from H. H. Leslie to Dr Burton, 9 May 1918, ABCFM papers, Bilkent University collection reel #33.
17. *British Documents on Foreign Affairs: Reports and Papers from the Foreign Office Confidential Print. Part II, From the First to the Second World War. Series B, Turkey, Iran, and the Middle East, 1918–1939*, ed. Robin Bidwell, pp. 138–9, document number E8826/199/44; Hakan Özoğlu, 'İngiltere'nin İstanbul'daki Yüksek Komiser Vekili Nevile Henderson'un Raporu: Halife Abdülmecid'le Görüşme', *Toplumsal Tarih*, 225 (September 2012): 78–80.
18. The transcription of the letter is as follows. I am grateful for the assistance of Robert Dankoff and Cornell Fleischer.

Amerika Cemahir-i Müttefika Resisi Mösyö Coolidge Cenablarına

Vukuat ve hadisat-ı siyasiyenin bilcümle ledüniyatina nüfuz ve vukuf-u siyasiyeleri derkar olan zat-ı asilaneleri nezdinde ne gibi esbab ve savaik-i mücbire tahtında makarr-ı saltanatımı bir müddet-i muvakkate için terk etmekte muztar kalmış olduğum malum olduğu bedihi olmasıyla bu babda arz-ı hal ve tafsilata lüzum görmüyorum.

Bu müfarekat bil ırs vel-istihkak haiz olduğum saltanat ve hilafet makamından feragatımı mutazammın olamayacağı bedihi ve aşikar olub Ankara meclisi gibi bir fitne-i bağiyenin buna dair vuku bulacak bilcümle mukarreratı keennehüm lem yekün hükmünde olduğu vareste-i arz ve beyandır. Ez cümle hilafet-i İslamiyenin saltanat-ı Osmaniyeden tecrid ve tefriki ve hilafetin külliyen ilgası gibi dini, kavmiyeti, vatanı meşkuk ve mahlut askeriyeden ve sınıf-ı saireden mürekkeb bir şirzime-i kalile ile kısmen cebir ve ikrah ile ve kısmen cehil ve gaflet ile sevk edilen beş altı milyonluk masum Türk kavminin daire-i salahiyeti dahilinde olmayıb bu ancak bütün alem-i İslam tarafından tayin olunan erbab-ı ihtisasdan mürekkeb bir meclis-i akd ve icma-ı ümmet ile hal ve fasl edilecek bir mesele-i uzma ve alemşumuldur. Ulema-ı İslamın malumu olduğu vechiyle ahkam-ı şer-i şerife mugayır mukarrarat her ne makamdan sadır olursa olsun mahkum-u akamettir. Bundan maada ahval-i hazırede meşhud olduğu ve cümle alem-i İslamda neticesi pek vahim olabilecek bir teheyyüm-ü azim ikağına müstaid ve mesele-i saire-i siyasiye, asayiş-i düvel ve milel üzerine tesir-i azmi kaviyen melhuzdur.

Başkaca erkan-ı hanedanım aleyhinde Ankara meclisi tarafından bu kere ittihaz edilen nefy ve tagrib ve müsadere-i emlak ve emval-i hususiye ve şahsiye gibi fuzuli tedabir ve mukarrerat-ı azayı hanedanımı hukuk-i insaniye ve şahsiyelerinden tecrid mahiyetinde olmasıyla bu babda zat-ı asilaneleri ve hükümet-i cumhuriye tarafından bilfiil imkan dairesinde vaki olabilecek mazhariyetin pek kıymetdar telakki edileceği müstagni-i beyandır.

Bilvesile devam-ı afiyetlerini cenab-ı Hak'dan niyaz ederim.

Mehmet Vahdettin Han Sene 13 Mart 1924

This document is registered in the US archives as 867.00/1788. The letter is dated 13 March 1924 and was sent to Calvin Coolidge via Sheldon Whitehouse from the US Embassy in Paris. Whitehouse notes that this letter was given to him by Reşat Halis, former Ottoman Ambassador to Bern, who was one of the signatories of the Treaty of Sèvres. The translation is mine. For more information, see also Hakan Özoğlu, 'Sultan Vahdettin'in ABD Başkanı Coolidge'e Gönderdiği Bir Mektup' [A Letter by the Last Ottoman Sultan Vahdettin to Mr Coolidge, the President of the USA], *Toplumsal Tarih*, 142 (October 2005): 100–3.

19. Jean-Louis Bacque-Grammont and Hasseine Mammeri, 'Sur le pèlerinage et quelques proclamations', *Turcica*, 14 (1982): 226–47.

20. 867.00/1776, report dated 27 February 1924, Bristol to Secretary of State. The first report, attached to Bristol's report, by the unnamed military attaché was dated 9 February 1924.

21. 867.00/1776, report dated 27 February 1924, Bristol to Secretary of State. This particular intelligence brief was dated 25 February 1924.

22. 867.00/1801, Admiral Mark Bristol to Secretary of State, 19 August 1924.

23. See Timuçin Mert, *Atatürk'ün Yanındaki Mehdi* (Istanbul: Karakutu, 2006), p. 145.

24. 867.00/1801, Admiral Mark Bristol to Secretary of State, 19 August 1924.

25. 867.00/1812, Bristol to Under Secretary of State, 26 July 1924.

26. 867.00/1745, Bristol to Secretary of State, 23 October 1923.

27. 867.00/1782, Bristol to Secretary of State, 12 March 1925.

28. 867.00/1694, Avra M. Warren to Secretary of State, 19 July 1923.

29. 867.00/1782, Bristol to Secretary of State, 12 March 1924.

30. 867.00/1782, 11 March 1924. The report was titled 'Modification in the Law Abolishing the Caliphate'. The Turkish original of the article 1 is the following: 'Halife halledilmiştir. Hilafet Hükümet ve Cumhuriyet mana ve mefhumunda esasen mündemiç olduğundan Hilafet makamı mülgadır.'

31. Ibid.

32. Ibid.

33. 867.00/1681, Bristol to Secretary of State, 24 March 1923.

34. 867.001K31/2, Sheldon Crosby to Secretary of State, 10 August 1925.

35. Necmi Ülker, 'Mustafa Kemal Paşa'nın Evliliği', in Latif Daşdemir (ed.), *Az Bilinen Yönleriyle Atatürk* (İzmir: Ege University, 2004), p. 28.

36. Rıfat Bali edited a volume titled *New Documents on Atatürk: Atatürk as Viewed through the Eyes of American Diplomats* (Istanbul: ISIS, 2007). Andrew Mango wrote a 'Foreword' in which he disputed the reliability of the documents on the divorce of Atatürk and Latife. Bali published the same documents that I presented above and more. Mango states that 'In some cases, the authors cited by Rıfat Bali were ill-informed', yet he fails to substantiate this claim. Bali published Latife Hanım's unknown interview with the *Boston Advertiser* (p. 26) damning Mustafa Kemal in the harshest terms. Mango judged it as 'an obvious forgery' (p. 10); however, his reasoning for this conclusion is less than satisfactory. One cannot conceive of any Turk, let alone a person as patriotic as Latife, speaking about 'a group of young, hysterical, empty headed Turks, surrounding Atatürk'. We do know that there were false reports in the US press about Mustafa Kemal,

and this might be one of them. However, Mango's reasoning is not sufficiently documented to dismiss the report entirely. I have not seen any report in the US archives addressing this article published in the US.

37. Charles Hitchcock Sherrill, *A Year's Embassy to Mustafa Kemal* (New York and London: C. Scribner's Sons, 1934). The book was translated into Turkish several times: *Gazi Mustafa Kemal Hz. Nezdinde Bir Yıl Elçilik*, trans. Ahmet Ekrem (Istanbul: Muallim Ahmet Halit Kitaphanesi, 1934); *Bir Elçiden Gazi Mustafa Kemal*, trans. Alp Ilgaz (Istanbul: Tercüman Yayınları, 1973); *Mustafa Kemal'in Bana Anlattıkları* (Istanbul: Örgün, 2007); *Bir Amerikan Büyükelçisinin Gözünden Gazi Mustafa Kemal* (Istanbul: Karakaya, 2017).

38. The Turkish translation of this document was published by Rıfat Bali, 'Amerikan Büyükelçisi Charles H. Sherrill'in Raporu: Atatürk'ün Dine Bakışı', *Toplumsal Tarih*, 153 (September 2006): 14–19. Bali fails to give the document number but refers the reader to the microfilm collection.

39. The reference is possibly to the *sübyan mektebi*, where the instruction was heavily on religious studies.

40. The Bursa incident was a protest of the public in Bursa against reciting the *Ezan*, the call to prayer, in Turkish, not Arabic. It took place on 1 February 1933 after the Bursa Ulucami imam did not obey the government warning and recited it in Arabic, leading to his arrest. The Office of Religious Affairs, or the *Diyanet*, issued the order of reciting the *Ezan* in Turkish on 18 July 1932. The government arrested many people after the protest. On 17 June 1950, the new Democrat Party government issued a declaration stating that the mosques could recite the *Ezan* in Arabic.

41. The reference may be to the *Tebbet* Surah of the Koran in which the Prophet Mohammad's uncle was exiled; see Bali, p. 19, n. 8.

42. 867.001K31/62, Sherrill to Secretary of State, 17 March 1933.

43. 867.00/1918, Bristol to Secretary of State, 18 February 1926.

44. 867.00/1969, telegram from Bristol to Secretary of State, 23 May 1927. The report was marked as 'Extremely Confidential and Personal for the Secretary of State from Admiral Bristol'.

45. President's Ottoman Archives, collection HR. İM. 257, on 2 June 1927.

6

AFTERTHOUGHTS AND CONCLUSIONS

In the nineteenth century, the Ottoman Empire left behind her past glory and was in a speedy decline. The US, on the other side of the globe, was an emerging power extending influence rapidly towards her side of the world. The diplomatic interaction between one rising and one declining world power also represented the attitude of the New World towards the ageing last Islamic empire. The US's interaction with the Ottoman Empire was not one of competition or domination in the nineteenth century but of economic expansion and missionary activities. As the nineteenth century concluded, the US would soon realise that her competition would mainly be with her Allies, especially France and Great Britain. Nevertheless, the recognition of the need for US competition with the Old World imperialists became most noticeable, especially in the aftermath of World War I. It was exclusively due to the reports of Admiral Mark Lambert Bristol that the State Department became keenly aware of British designs for the Middle East and her wealth.

Until the first half of the nineteenth century, the US diplomatic mind was isolationist in nature, following President James Monroe's model for diplomacy, known as the Monroe Doctrine. President Monroe, an isolationist himself, determined that the US–Europe economic competition should be based on a 'two-sphere' basis. The European countries, according to Monroe, were obligated to respect the Western Hemisphere as the United States' sphere of interest, and the US would reciprocate by refraining from interfering with European economic interest on their side of the Atlantic Ocean. In this context, 'The Eastern Question' of sharing the spoils of the dying Ottoman Empire was not of concern to the US as it was, notably, to the competing European powers of Britain, Russia and France. However, this isolationist policy was not favoured by many American missionaries and tradesmen active in the Ottoman lands. They wanted a more visible US presence in this part of the world.

It was with the growing appetite of the US for new markets that a new international engagement policy called the 'Open Door' replaced international isolationism. The new century brought the US to the realisation that she needed to obtain equal trading rights with the empires of the East, especially China. However, after the collapse of the Ottoman Empire, it became very visible that the former Ottoman territories also provided a degree of market value, especially after the most destructive war in history that shaped the twentieth century.

The conclusion of World War I opened up a new era of economic opportunism for the victors of the war and the US could not stand idly by and watch the European Powers dictate their political will and monopolise economic benefits. This period coincided with the tenure of Rear Admiral Mark Lambert Bristol as the US High Commissioner in the Ottoman Empire and later the Turkish Republic. Admiral Bristol can be credited as one of the most influential diplomats who helped shape US foreign policy in the Ottoman Empire, out of which the modern Middle East emerged. Admiral Bristol's observations and recommendations to the Department of State concerning the collapse of the Ottoman Empire and the emergence of the Republic of Turkey are of utmost significance for the historian, for they laid the very foundation of the strategic partnership between Turkey and the US, especially during the Cold War years. Despite the indisputable significance of the information contained within the reports Bristol sent to Washington, these reports have remained at the periphery of academic works. The main reason for this wilful omission was that Bristol's reports on sensitive issues went against the grain of international politics of the time and later dominant academic discourse. This book aims at presenting Bristol's changing views on a number of sensitive issues. The reader hopefully did not miss which of his views changed and which remained the same. The text discusses the evolution of Bristol's views, especially in his evaluation of the issue of the Greek and

Armenian minorities, and offers possible reasons for it. However, the reader can evaluate the reasons based on the wide context the book provides.

Admiral Mark Lambert Bristol was a fine example of a generation of American 'sailor-diplomats', stationed in different parts of the world. US Naval officers did not usually serve as long-term diplomats; their appointments were terminated when the specific international goals were completed.[1] In this sense, Bristol was exceptional as he served in a critical period and place in the world. His diplomatic service in Turkey lasted eight years, during which he witnessed remarkable events in the Middle East as the 600-year-old Ottoman Empire collapsed, and the many new states emerged.

This book aims at bringing together the reports he and his staff sent to Washington describing the developments on the ground, which were changing at lightning speed and with many unexpected twists and turns. The primary documents under examination here culminate in tens of thousands of pages and focus on many subjects that are critically significant in understanding the rise of the modern Middle East; however, I have selectively focused on certain themes mainly in and around the territories that became the Republic of Turkey. Researchers working on the Balkans and the Arab provinces of the Ottoman Empire can also find a significant collection of documents to enrich our understanding of those areas as well.

There are two groups of scholars who depict Admiral Mark Lambert Bristol in two differing lights on the issue of the Ottoman minorities in the post-World War I era. The first is the group formed mainly of Armenian scholars and those who sympathise with the Armenian plight during World War I. They paint the admiral as an anti-Armenian opportunist who would manipulate information to advance American economic interests at the expense of 'the truth'.[2] The second group regards him as a realist who championed American interests in a very volatile region. This group of scholars sees Bristol not as anti-Armenian or pro-Turk, but as someone who realised early on that an Armenian state cannot survive in this neighbourhood by antagonising the Turks and hence who carefully avoids giving the Armenians false hope.[3]

The massacres of Armenians during World War I are well documented and can readily be confirmed by historians. These events left an indelible and unjust mark on the Turkish/Muslim population in general, which paved the way for stereotyping and anti-Turkish racism in the West. The anti-Turkish feeling evident in the stereotyping 'the terrible Turk' was so widespread in the Christian world that public opinion in the US was against any Turkish regime having sovereignty over other Christian people. The anti-Turkish propaganda was so heightened that the Armenian and Greek lobbies felt no shame, according to Bristol, at manipulating the American people about the facts during the early years of the Turkish Republic. Accusations towards the new regime may have originated from the fact that until 1922, many people in the West associated the Kemalist/nationalist movement in Anatolia with the old Ottoman regime, which, they claimed, systematically massacred Christians. However, in many cases, these accusations emanating from the events after World War I were quite open to criticism, as Bristol believed, to form public opinion against the creation of a new Turkish state on a land that, as the Treaty of Sèvres stipulated, was so close to being recognised as Armenia or Pontus or even Kurdistan. With the rise of the Kemalists in Anatolia, supporters of the creation of these states were heartbroken.

Bristol was stationed in Constantinople during such a tumultuous period in history in which, as mentioned, the 'Turkish race' was deemed evil, and hence so was the emerging Turkish state. Bristol made a vital distinction between the old Ottoman regime and the new nationalist one early on. He was in agreement with others that the crumbling Ottoman regime was corrupt and should not be allowed to rule over other 'races'. However, the admiral directly challenged the perception that the Turks were evil, and other religious/ethnic groups in the empire were innocent victims. Therefore, Bristol became a controversial figure in the debates about the Armenian massacres/genocide. One should be very careful to note that Bristol reported events after World War I. However, since his position did not comply with the Western approach on the issue of the creation of an Armenian state, he was often misrepresented – even in the present scholarship – with wilful omissions of his stand on the minority-majority relations in Anatolia.

For example, Bristol's position against Armenian lobbying activities in the US during his tenure in the Middle East was not directed against the Armenian claims of 1915. He readily acknowledged the killings of the Armenians, and if the term had existed with its present connotations, he might arguably have called it 'genocide'. However, he also witnessed gross manipulations directed towards influencing American public opinion during the War of Independence in Turkey in 1919–22 and took a firm stand against them. He was a strong believer in the fact that victimhood did not always imply innocence. He insisted that the Armenians and, especially, the Greeks were as guilty as the Turks in the bloodshed in Anatolia during and after World War I. In other words, Bristol believed that certain segments in the non-Muslim population (read Armenians and Greeks) would quite possibly become killers as vicious as the Muslim population (Turks and Kurds) if they assembled sufficient military strength. He pointed out the 1919 Greek occupation of Western Anatolia as his proof. In that sense, he did not agree that the Turks were innately killers. He surely had an uphill battle to convince the American public, since the phrase 'the terrible Turk' was in such wide circulation in the West. Yet, he could not stand idly by while witnessing public manipulations and misrepresentations feeding the Western mind. This issue needs to be explored a little further to show why Bristol was unhappy with the false and exaggerated reports. Let us briefly look at one notable example.

Re-imagining 'the Terrible Turk'

Admiral Bristol was not the only American who relayed documents challenging the bloody events in Turkey as they appeared in the United States and Europe. Among the first-hand American sources, Mary Caroline Holmes's accounts, for example, are also noteworthy.[4] Miss Holmes was a member of the Near East Relief mission in Urfa and a reliable eyewitness to many atrocities in the city. Like Admiral Bristol, she tried to stay away from making one-sided statements just to discredit the Turks and the emerging Turkish state. In this context, a letter written by her to Admiral Bristol in response to some misinformation about the Turks in Urfa is notable. This letter, among the internal correspondence in the State Department's Division of Near Eastern Affairs, was labelled as 'remarkable'. The report indicates that Miss Holmes was the Director of Near East Relief work in Urfa, and her letter to Bristol 'gives rather a different picture of the Turks than that we have received from Yowell, Ward, and others. The difference is partly to be ascribed to the fact that Miss Holmes is a woman of tact, whereas our other reporters have been lacking in that quality.'[5]

Let me first inform the reader of the remarks made by Mark H. Ward[6] and Major Forrest D. Yowell.[7] These two relief workers were expelled from Turkey by the Kemalists in 1922 and gave interviews blasting the Turks and their treatment of the Christians in Anatolia. In these interviews, they accused the Turks of massacring one million Armenians, aiming at the extermination of the Christian minorities of Anatolia after 1919. Moreover, they claimed that the extermination of the Christians was continuing, especially in Urfa. Related sections from Miss Holmes's letter to Bristol protesting about the misinformation are as follows:

My Dear Admiral Bristol:
You will see by the date of this letter [29 May 1922, Bassoul's Hotel, Beirut] that I am at last out of Urfa. For more than two years, it has been quite impossible to send any communication to you owing to warring conditions exceedingly difficult for foreigners . . .

We were never restricted [by the Turks in Urfa] as to the scope of our work, never interfered with, and no monetary demands were made . . .

The mutasarrıf, Munir Bey, new mutasarrıf of Aintab, called one day to tell me about the repatriation of the Kurds from Van-Bitlis districts and, in rather a hesitating way, asked if any assistance in sending the 5000 [Kurds] he was responsible for would be along the line of activities of the Near East Relief. These Kurds I knew were deportees like the Armenians and suffered quite as much as they from starvation and disease . . . The next day, I sent a contribution of L.T.G. [?] 100 to Munir Bey, with a note in which I said I felt it wholly within the scope of our relief work to repatriate the Kurd . . .

The government in Urfa was one of the best in Turkey. During my residence there, I saw nothing which savored of oppression, with the exception of the taking of the property—real estate—of those Armenians who asked for vesecas [*vesika*, certification] to go to Aleppo. The vesecas were granted, but any real estate must be signed over to the government. Lately, they were not allowed to sell their property. Aside from this, the Armenians have nothing to complain of in Urfa . . .

All of the foregoing is but the prelude to a protest to you against the sweeping accusations of Mr. [Forrest D.] Yowell, late Director of the Near East Relief in Kharput as printed in the *London Times* of May 5th. Certain of his statements cannot be substantiated by the facts. He has jeopardized not only the N.E.R. activities in 'Kemalistan,' but missionary work as well.

Mr. Yowell stated that the relief workers along the route of the Greek deportees were not allowed to render any assistance to the dying nor to care for the orphans. In a conversation today with Mr. Mackenzie, who was Treasurer of the N.E.R. in Kharput, I learned that the Kharput authorities *did* [emphasis original] allow the N.E.R. to distribute bread to the deportees 'at times.' It is true that the deportees were sent on from Deirbekr through a mountainous region in cold and snow, and that many perished by the way in consequence. And so did more than 1000 Armenians who tried to go out from Marash when the French evacuated that city in the winter of 1920. They went with the French, a terrible storm of deep snow came on, and not less than 1000 fell by the wayside. Those who survived from Kharput and reached Deirbekr were all cared for by the N.E.R. at the request of the *Government* [emphasis original]. The adults were clothed, fed, and given medical attention, and orphans gathered into our N.E.R. Orphanage. Not only did the civil and military officials cooperate with Miss Wade, the Director, but when a gendarme guarding the deportees was proven to be immoral or extortionate upon request of Miss Wade, he was promptly replaced and often dismissed from the service . . .

It is so manifestly unfair and unjust to make *wholesale* [emphasis original] charges against a government with which our own government has at present no diplomatic relations, not to say unwise and within whose territory we have been living by courtesy and, so far as my experience goes, given every assistance when it was possible for the authorities to render it. As an old resident in Turkey, I protest with all my heart and soul against the wholesale accusations of Mr. Yowell, many of which cannot be verified, as I have indicated above . . .

I hold no brief for the Nationalists. Neither do I for the Greeks and Armenians. We Americans are here to relieve suffering and to care for homeless children. *Christian and Turk alike have committed atrocities, without doubt* [emphasis mine]. But we, the relief workers as I see it, are not the judges as to the placement of the guilt.[8]

The report by Ward and Yowell continues to be used as a trusted primary source even in the current debates; however, Miss Holmes's contradictory report is equally significant because it was prepared by a co-worker of Ward and Yowell. We know that the Turkish side protested against Ward and Yowell's account as 'fabrication'. Furthermore, the American archives recorded a document indicating that a Swedish newspaper, *Social Demokraten*, labelled the accusations against the Kemalists as 'lies' initiated by Britain to discredit the new regime.[9]

Mary Caroline Holmes's book *Between the Lines in Asia Minor* certainly cannot be labelled as pro-Turk; therefore, her testimony regarding false propaganda against the Turks had merit in the eyes of the State Department. We learn from this report that Ward and Yowell had had personal vendettas against the Turkish government since they were deported from Turkey. We also know that it was not only the Christians but also Muslim Kurds who were among the group of deportees from Diyarbakır. These statements in the US archives do not allow us to subscribe to the grossly generalised statement that the Turks, in the post-World War I and Kemalist period, systematically targeted and massacred Christians to purify Asia Minor. Nevertheless, the reader should be mindful that these reports do not claim nor prove that no Christian massacres took place. They did indeed. Yet they also confirm that Christians were not always on the receiving end and that, as stated by Miss Holmes, 'Christian and Turk alike have committed atrocities, without a doubt'. This was not an apology or a political statement; it was merely stating the fact that such reports and objections to painting the new Kemalist regime as anti-Christian do exist in reliable eyewitness accounts. And they do deserve due consideration, not unqualified dismissal.

As examined in Chapter 2, Bristol, despite his sympathy for the emerging Kemalist regime and its military leaders, cannot be labelled as pro-Turk and anti-Armenian. At times, he even entertained the idea of the creation of a state for Armenians in Anatolia. It is clear from his reports that he was unhappy with the invasion of Smyrna and its surroundings by the Greek army, and by the attitude of the Ottoman Greek population. He also did not approve, to say the least, of the British imperialist policies in the Middle East. Nevertheless, I believe that his opinion of the Greeks, in general, hardly qualifies him to be an enemy of Greece. He constantly warned the State Department that the invasion of Smyrna was bad judgement and would fuel the Turkish nationalist movement. The events which followed proved that he was correct.

Biographical information about Bristol reveals that he received an ordinary US Naval officer training without any crash course in diplomacy, yet he proved to be a very skilful diplomat for the US. The admiral probably came to the Middle East with common biases prevalent among the American public. It is certain that he was aware of the Armenian massacres of 1915.

However, we see from his reports that, as a result of the time he spent there, his was an orientalist view towards all 'Eastern races', regardless of their religious affiliations.

Chapter 3 traced the evolution of Bristol's approach towards the Ottoman Empire and later the Republic of Turkey. In this chapter, the reader can follow Bristol's distaste for the Ottoman government and curiosity towards the emerging one in Anatolia. However, the admiral interacted with both governments simultaneously. Both governments in Istanbul and Ankara were eager to win the favour of the US. In this chapter, we saw that Bristol predicted the success of the nationalists against the Greek forces. The tone of his reports to Washington reveals that he was happy to have correctly predicted the outcome, as he thought the Allied invasions of different parts of Anatolia and Constantinople were unwarranted and unfair. Consequently, the nationalist victory over the Greek forces made him first respect and then sympathise with the Kemalist government whose military background Bristol could relate to. He was impressed by the radical reform policies the Kemalist government initiated and implemented. However, he was also critical of the Kemalist government, especially on the issue of the extreme secularism that controlled even the Christian missionary educational activities such as the YMCA and the YWCA.

The reader, by now, will have noticed that the issue of religious minorities inevitably spilled over into all chapters. However, Chapter 4 dealt directly with Bristol's views on the Armenian mandate and the Greek invasion of Western Anatolia. I started out my examination of the US sources with a document vividly depicting the desperate outlook in Constantinople immediately after World War I. The imperial capital city was once the symbol of the wealth and the might of the empire. After reading the report of the deplorable conditions in the capital, the reader could visualise the conditions in other parts of the empire. The subsequent documents I presented here dealt mainly with the plight of people trying to live under these harsh post-war conditions. An overwhelming majority of the reports dwell on the Christians and the inter-communal tension.

World War I not only deeply affected the material foundation of the empire but, more importantly, it plagued the psyche of its citizens. The religious affiliation of the victors, namely the Allied Powers, created mistrust among the Muslim and Christian (Armenian and Greek Orthodox) population of the

Ottoman Empire. The CUP leaders in Constantinople were paranoid about the Armenians betraying the empire with Allied help. Interestingly, it was the Muslim Arabs who served the British interests and were more destructive for the well-being of the empire than the Armenians or the Greek Orthodox population. This paranoia is understandable and certainly had its merits, yet none of the atrocities against the civilian population initiated by the government forces or under government protection should be justified. The US archives are filled with documents detailing the anguish and misery of non-Muslims reportedly caused by the Muslim population directly organised or allowed by the government. These reports vary from the highly questionable accusations of those who were disappointed to see the Turks' victory against the Allies during the Turkish War of Independence to those who objectively reported what they saw on the ground. Reports by the Christian population in Anatolia and their contacts in the United States give clear indications that many local Armenians and Greeks held understandable grudges against the Turks and even, to an extent, against the Western Powers for the fact that they failed to create Armenian and Greek governments in Anatolia. The bias is noticeable in these kinds of reports. However, there are sizeable collections of reports that fall into a middle category, and determining their reliability could prove to be a great challenge even for the trained historian. Needless to say, the period was one of confusion and conflicting political ambitions among which the truth could readily be lost, and, certainly, motivations for political manipulation did exist.

Against this background, I presented a collection of documents, certainly in a very small minority, contradicting many of the reports portraying the Turks as uncivilised and vicious sub-humans. These documents lift the image of the Turks to the level of humans who made terrible wartime mistakes. Some of them even depict their own misery. At present, the scholarship is so polarised that even mentioning the terrible conditions endured by the Turks/Muslims is regarded as political bias and certainly taken as disrespect for the suffering of the other side.

However, since reports which do not fully fall in line with the Christian claims do exist, how do we read them? Should we ignore them entirely for the sake of amplifying the atrocities certainly committed by the Turkish/Muslim side? Partisan scholarship on both sides tends to accept the documents that support their own political agenda and dismiss any others that fail to fully comply with their political orientation. Just as Admiral Mark Bristol responded to the accusation of him being a pro-Turk in the 1920s, many academic works – even in the twenty-first century – dealing with this controversial subject are highly politicised and polarised. Unfortunately, even today, if one does not subscribe to any view in its entirety, one is always accused of being an agent of the other side. In pointing out reports in the US archives that raise questions about the stereotyping of the Turk as a savage who wished to exterminate the Christian 'race' in Anatolia, I do not have any hidden agenda aiming to diminish the tragedy experienced by the non-Muslims in Turkey. I just want to provide the reader with information that is not readily available to those who wish to tackle the issue from the centre.

It is possible that documents presented by both sides portray a degree of reality. These seemingly contradictory snapshots prove one thing: that is, it is deceptive to draw a big picture based on majority or minority documents. In the case of the Greeks and Armenians as minorities in the post-World War I period, one should be careful not to make overgeneralisations, for information in archives is not unanimous.

Beyond the minority issues, Bristol provides us with a wealth of primary accounts collected from his network of informants. Thanks to these reports sent to Washington, we have an alternative view of the collapse of the Ottoman Empire and the rise of the modern Middle East. I hope this book will inspire the younger generation of scholars in the direction of exploring the American archives further for Middle Eastern Studies. I also hope that new studies will show due respect to Bristol's reports in understanding the Middle East during the tumultuous years of the immediate aftermath of World War I.

Notes

1. Charles Oscar Paullin, *Diplomatic Negotiations of American Naval Officers 1778–1883* (Baltimore: Johns Hopkins Press, 1912), p. 9.
2. Marjorie Housepian Dobkin, *Smyrna 1922* (London: Faber and Faber, 1972); Levon Marashlian, 'Finishing the Genocide: Cleansing Turkey of Armenian Survivors, 1920–1923', in Richard Hovannisian (ed.), *Remembrance and Denial: The Case of Armenian Genocide* (Detroit: Wayne State University Press, 1999), pp. 113–47; Peter Balakian, *Burning Tigris: The Armenian Genocide and America's Response* (New York: HarperCollins, 2003); Robert

Shenk, *America's Black Sea Fleet: The U.S. Navy Amidst War and Revolution, 1919–1923* (Annapolis: Naval Institute Press, 2017).

3. Roger R. Trask, *The United States Response to Turkish Nationalism and Reform 1914–1939* (Minneapolis: University of Minnesota Press, 1971), p. 246; John DeNovo, *American Interests and Policies in the Middle East, 1900–1939* (Minneapolis: University of Minnesota Press, 1963), pp. 50–3; Peter M. Buzanski, 'Admiral Mark L. Bristol and Turkish-American Relations, 1919–1922', PhD dissertation, University of California, Berkeley, 1960; Thomas A. Bryson, 'Admiral Mark L. Bristol, an Open-Door Diplomat in Turkey', *International Journal of Middle East Studies*, 5.4 (1974): 450–67.

4. The principal of the American orphanage for Armenian children in Urfa and a member of the American Near East Relief mission. She is the author of *Between the Lines in Asia Minor*, in which she refers to a remarkable incident in the city: 'It would have been a town devoid of every human instinct which would not have been moved with pity for the three hundred Armenian women refugees who approached Urfa stark naked, having been robbed of their clothing some days before. These were all cared for in the town, and many lived the four years following in Moslem homes. Some of them were legally married to Moslems, others served as domestics in their houses unmolested and unafraid.' See Mary Caroline Holmes, *Between the Lines in Asia Minor* (New York and Edinburgh: Fleming H. Revell Company, 1923), p. 31.

5. 867.4016/768. The author of the State Department's letter is unknown, but it was addressed to an M. Phillips.

6. Mark H. Ward was a medical doctor who was sent to Turkey as a medical missionary for the Near East Relief in 1915. From 1918 he was stationed at the Harput unit, where he organised relief work, as the Medical Director and temporarily as acting Director.

7. Mark Ward sent a letter to Secretary of State Charles E. Hughes reporting on the condition of the Christians in Anatolia; 867.4016/575, 5 May 1922. A careful historian might take note that Ward was reporting that he and Yowell give many numbers based on hearsay. They also listen to the accounts of local Christians who were desperate to capture the attention of the Western Powers. This does not disqualify the report as false; however, it does bring the credibility issue to the fore. Both Ward and Yowell were very public in their accusation of the Turks; see the *New York Times*, 6 May 1922, p. 2; the London *Times*, 5 May 1922; Mark H. Ward, *The Deportations in Asia Minor, 1921–1922* (London: Anglo-Hellenic League, 1922).

8. 867.4016/768. For more information on the Ward and Yowell report and Bristol's position against it, see Benny Morris and Dror Ze'evi, *The Thirty-Year Genocide: Turkey's Destruction of its Christian Minorities 1894–1924* (Cambridge, MA, and London: Harvard University Press, 2019), p. 427. The authors successfully list references supporting the Ward and Yowell report; however, no reference was made to Miss Holmes's contradictory account.

9. 867.4016/580 is a report dealing with this issue, sent from Stockholm on 6 July 1922, from the US Minister H. Johnson to the Secretary of State. From this report we know that the Swedish newspaper disputed these claims. The diplomat claims that such blunt denial of massacres was 'inspired' by Kemal Bey, the Turkish Minister (diplomat) in Sweden. The report includes a portion of the article blaming the British for these lies: 'The reports of Turkish massacres of Christians in Asia Minor are lies, probably originating from the British in order to strengthen anti-Turkish propaganda.' This paper refers to the 'campaign of hate started in England against Turkey in order to make a peaceful agreement impossible and to permit a further offensive against Turkey'.

BIBLIOGRAPHY

Archival Sources (detailed information is provided in the Introduction)

US Sources

'The Bristol Papers' in the Library of Congress Manuscript Division
Foreign Relations of the United States (FRUS)
General Records of the American Commission to Negotiate Peace 1918–1931
'The King-Crane Commission Digital Collection' at the Oberlin College Archives
Records of the Department of State Relating to Internal Affairs of Turkey 1910–1929
Records of the Department of State Relating to Political Relations between the
    United States and Turkey, 1910–1929

Turkish/Ottoman Sources

ARIT (American Research Instiute in Turkey) Archives
Bilkent University Archives
Cumhurbaşkanlığı Cumhuriyet Arşivi (Former Başbakanlık Cumhuriyet Arşivi)
Cumhurbaşkanlığı Osmanlı Arşivi (Former Başbakanlık Osmanlı Arşivi)
Istanbul Atatürk Library, Manuscript Collection
Milli Kütüphane Archives in Ankara
Turkish Foreign Ministry Archives
Turkish Grand National Assembly Archives

Other Primary and Secondary Sources

Akgün, Seçil Karal, 'Louis Edgar Browne and the Leaders of 1919 Sivas Congress', in George S. Harris and Nur Bilge Criss (eds), *Studies in Atatürk's Turkey: The American Dimension* (Leiden and Boston: Brill, 2009), pp. 15–55.

Akgün, Seçil, 'The Turkish Image in the Reports of American Missionaries', *The Turkish Studies Association Bulletin*, 13 (September 1989): 97.

Allen, Annie T., in *Digital Library for International Research*, <http://www.dlir.org/archive/orc-exhibit/items/show/collection/12/id/16655> (last accessed 28 September 2020).

'Anatolia Deportee Here; Dr. Ruth Parmlee, Ousted by Kemalists, Says They Are All Corrupt', *New York Times*, 17 June 1922, p. 5.

Bachman, Robert, 'The American Navy and the Turks', *Outlook*, 132 (September–December 1922): 288–9.

Bacque-Grammont, Jean-Louis, and Hasseine Mammeri, 'Sur le pèlerinage et quelques proclamations', *Turcica*, 14 (1982): 226–47.

Balakian, Peter, *Burning Tigris: The Armenian Genocide and America's Response* (New York: HarperCollins, 2003).

Bali, Rıfat, 'Amerikan Büyükelçisi Charles H. Sherrill'in Raporu: Atatürk'ün Dine Bakışı', *Toplumsal Tarih*, 153 (September 2006): 14–19.

Bali, Rıfat (ed.), *New Documents on Atatürk: Atatürk as Viewed through the Eyes of American Diplomats* (Istanbul: ISIS, 2007).

Bali, Rıfat, *The Saga of a Friendship: Asa Kent Jennings and the American Friends of Turkey* (Istanbul: Libra, 2010).

Beers, Henry P., 'United States Naval Detachment in Turkish Waters, 1919–24', *Military Affairs*, 7.4 (Winter 1943): 209–20.

Bidwell, Robin (ed.), *British Documents on Foreign Affairs: Reports and Papers from the Foreign Office Confidential Print. Part II, From the First to the Second World War. Series B, Turkey, Iran, and the Middle East, 1918–1939*, 1997.

Bradford, James C., *Admirals of the New Steel Navy: Makers of the American Naval Tradition, 1880–1930* (Annapolis: Naval Institute Press, 1990).

Braisted, William R., 'Mark Lambert Bristol: Naval Diplomat Extraordinary of the Battleship Age', in James C. Bradford (ed.), *Admirals of the New Steel Navy: Makers of the American Naval Tradition 1880–1930* (Annapolis: Naval Institute Press, 1990), pp. 331–73.

Bryson, Thomas A., 'Admiral Mark L. Bristol, an Open-Door Diplomat in Turkey', *International Journal of Middle East Studies*, 5.4 (1974): 450–67.

Buzanski, Peter Michael, 'Admiral Mark L. Bristol and Turkish-American Relations, 1919–1922', PhD dissertation, University of California, Berkeley, 1960.

Buzanski, Peter M., 'The Interallied Investigation of the Greek Invasion of Smyrna, 1919', *The Historian*, 25.3 (1963): 325–43.

Cardashian, Vahan, 'American Committee Opposed to the Lausanne Treaty', in *The Lausanne Treaty: Turkey and Armenia* (New York, 1926).

Central Intelligence Agency, 'Letter to Mr. Allen W. Dulles from Robert H. Eldridge', 15 September 1960, *Central Intelligence Agency Library*, <https://www.cia.gov/library/readingroom/document/cia-rdp80b01676r003600050014-5> (last accessed 28 September 2020).

Cole, Bernard D., *Gunboats and Marines: The United States Navy in China, 1925–1928* (Newark: University of Delaware Press, 1983).

Daniel, Robert L., *American Philanthropy in the Near East, 1820–1960* (Athens, OH: Ohio University Press, 1970).

DeNovo, John, *American Interests and Policies in the Middle East, 1900–1939* (Minneapolis: University of Minnesota Press, 1963).

Dobkin, Marjorie Housepian, *Smyrna 1922* (London: Faber and Faber, 1972).

Dunn, Robert, *World Alive: A Personal Story* (New York: Crown Publisher, 1956).

Editorial, 'Rear Admiral Mark L. Bristol: The President of American Peace Society', *World Affairs*, 101.2 (June 1938): 66.

Ekrem, Selma, *Unveiled: The Autobiography of a Turkish Girl* (New York, 1942).

Foreign Office (Great Britain), *Documents on British Foreign Policy, 1919–1939* (London: Her Majesty's Stationery Office, 1972).

FRUS, <https://history.state.gov/historicaldocuments> (last accessed 28 September 2020).

Gidney, James B., review of Joseph L. Grabill, *Protestant Diplomacy and the Near East: Missionary Influence on American Policy, 1810–1927*, in *The American Historical Review*, 77.3 (June 1972): 831–2.

Gordon, Leland J., 'Turkish-American Treaty Relations', *The American Political Science Review*, 22.3 (August 1928): 711–21.

Grabill, Joseph L., *Protestant Diplomacy and the Near East: Missionary Influence on American Policy, 1810–1927* (Minneapolis: University of Minnesota Press, 1971).

Grew, Joseph C., *Turbulent Era: A Diplomatic Record of Forty Years, 1904–1945*, vol. 1 (Cambridge, MA: The Riverside Press, 1952).

Heck, Lewis, 'Rear Admiral Mark L. Bristol', *World Affairs*, 102.3 (September 1939): 158–9.

Holmes, Mary Caroline, *Between the Lines in Asia Minor* (New York and Edinburgh: Fleming H. Revell Company, 1923).

Hoover Institution, Stanford University, *Edgar Browne's Private Papers*, <http://pdf. oac.cdlib.org/pdf/hoover/browne.pdf> (last accessed 28 September 2020).

Horton, George, *The Blight of Asia: An Account of the Systematic Extermination of Christian Population by Mohammedans and of the Culpability of Certain Great Powers; with the True Story of the Burning of Smyrna* (Indianapolis: Bobbs-Merrill Company, 1926).

Hovannisian, Richard, *The Republic of Armenia: From Versailles to London*, vol. 2 (Los Angeles and London: University of California Press, 1982).

King, Henry Churchill, 'Henry Churchill King Papers', RG 2/6/1 box 20, <http:// www2.oberlin.edu/archive/oresources/letter_indices/HCK/index.html> (last accessed 28 September 2020).

Koloğlu, Orhan, 'Avrupaya Karşı Osmanlıyı Müdafaa Eden Bir Avrupalı Blak Bey', <http://earsiv.sehir.edu.tr:8080/xmlui/bitstream/handle/11498/13988/ 001582250010.pdf?sequence=1> (last accessed 28 September 2020).

Koloğlu, Orhan, *Osmanlı Basınının Doğuşu ve Blak Bey Ailesi – Bir Fransız Ailesinin Bâbıâli Hizmetinde Yüz Yılı: 1821–1822* (Istanbul: Mütef?errika, 1998).

Köse, İsmail, *Türk Amerikan İlişkilerinin Şekillenmesinde Amiral Mark L. Bristol'un Rolü, 1919–1927* (Ankara: Türk Tarih Kurumu, 2016).

Lippe, John M. Vander, 'The "Other" Treaty of Lausanne: The American Public and Official Debate on Turkish American Relations', *The Turkish Yearbook of International Relations (Milletlerarası Münasebetler Türk Yıllığı)*, 23 (1993): 31–62.

Lowry, Heath, 'American Observers in Anatolia ca. 1920: The Bristol Papers', in Justin McCarthy et al., *Armenians in the Ottoman Empire and Modern Turkey (1912–1926)* (Istanbul: Bosphorus University, 1984), pp. 42–58.

Lowry, Heath, *Clarence K. Streit's The Unknown Turks* (Istanbul: Bahçeşehir University Press, 2011).

Lowry, Heath, 'I. Uluslararası Atatürk Sempozyumu, Ankara April 2, 1920–August 16, 1921', *Halide Edib Hanım in Ankara* (Ankara: Atatürk Araştırma Merkezi, 1994), p. 703.

Lowry, Heath, 'Richard G. Hovannisian on Lieutenant Robert Steed Dunn', *The Journal of Ottoman Studies*, 5 (1986): 209–52.

Marashlian, Levon, 'The Armenian Question from Sevres to Lausanne: Economics and Morality in American and British Policies, 1920–1923', PhD dissertation, UCLA, 1992.

Marashlian, Levon, 'Finishing the Genocide: Cleansing Turkey of Armenian Survivors, 1920–1923', in Richard Hovannisian (ed.), *Remembrance and Denial:*

The Case of Armenian Genocide (Detroit: Wayne State University Press, 1999), pp. 113–47.

Mert, Timuçin, *Atatürk'ün Yanındaki Mehdi* (Istanbul: Karakutu, 2006).

Morgenthau, Henry, *All in a Life-Time* (New York: Doubleday and Page, 1922).

Morgenthau, Henry, 'The Butchery of Christians in Asia Minor', *The Literary Digest*, 23 September 1922, pp. 34–5.

Morgenthau, Henry, III, 'The Rest of the Story', in Henry Morgenthau III and Peter Balakian, *Ambassador Morgenthau's Story* (Detroit: Wayne State University Press, 2003), pp. 281–317.

Morris, Benny, and Dror Ze'evi, *The Thirty-Year Genocide: Turkey's Destruction of its Christian Minorities 1894–1924* (Cambridge, MA, and London: Harvard University Press, 2019).

National Congress of Turkey, *The Turco-Armenian Question: The Turkish Point of View* (Constantinople: Société anonyme de papeterie et d'imprimerie, 1919).

Near East Relief, *Salt Reseach*, <https://archives.saltresearch.org/handle/123456789/43> (last accessed 28 September 2020).

Özoğlu, Hakan, *From Caliphate to Secular State: Power Struggle in the Early Turkish Republic* (Santa Barbara: Praeger, 2011).

Özoğlu, Hakan, 'İngiltere'nin İstanbul'daki Yüksek Komiser Vekili Nevile Henderson'un Raporu: Halife Abdülmecid'le Görüşme', *Toplumsal Tarih*, 225 (September 2012): 78–80.

Özoğlu, Hakan, 'Mustafa Kemal'Atatürk'ün Amerika'ya Mektubu', *Toplumsal Tarih*, 150 (June 2006): 59–61.

Özoğlu, Hakan, 'Sultan Vahdettin'in ABD Başkanı Coolidge'e Gönderdiği Bir Mektup', *Toplumsal Tarih*, 142 (October 2005): 100–3.

Parkin, Robert S., *Blood on the Sea: American Destroyers Lost in World War II* (New York: Da Capo Press, 2001).

Paullin, Charles Oscar, *Diplomatic Negotiations of American Naval Officers 1778–1883* (Baltimore: Johns Hopkins Press, 1912).

Reynolds, Clark G., *Famous American Admirals* (Annapolis: First Naval Institute Press, 2002).

'Robert Dunn Papers', <http://ead.dartmouth.edu/html/stem42.html> (last accessed 28 September 2020).

Said, Edward, *Orientalism: Western Conceptions of the Orient* (New Delhi: Penguin, 2006).

Shenk, Robert, *America's Black Sea Fleet: The U.S. Navy Amidst War and Revolution, 1919–1923* (Annapolis: Naval Institute Press, 2017).

Shenk, Robert, 'Ethnic Cleansing, American Women, and the Admiral: Deep in Anatolia during the Turkish Nationalist Revolution', in George N. Shirinian (ed.), *Genocide in the Ottoman Empire: Armenians, Assyrians, and Greeks, 1913–1923* (New York and Oxford: Berghahn, 2017), pp. 187–213.

Sherrill, Charles Hitchcock, *Bir Amerikan Büyükelçisinin Gözünden Gazi Mustafa Kemal* (Istanbul: Karakaya, 2017).

Sherrill, Charles Hitchcock, *Bir Elçiden Gazi Mustafa Kemal*, trans. Alp Ilgaz (Istanbul: Tercüman Yayınları, 1973).

Sherrill, Charles Hitchcock, *Gazi Mustafa Kemal Hz. Nezdinde Bir Yıl Elçilik*, trans. Ahmet Ekrem (Istanbul: Muallim Ahmet Halit Kitaphanesi, 1934).

Sherrill, Charles Hitchcock, *Mustafa Kemal'in Bana Anlattıkları* (Istanbul: Örgün, 2007).

Sherrill, Charles Hitchock, *A Year's Embassy to Mustafa Kemal* (New York and London: C. Scribner's Sons, 1934).

Trask, Roger R., 'The "Terrible Turk" and Turkish-American Relations in the Inter-war Period', *The Historian*, 33 (1970): 40–53.

Trask, Roger R., *The United States Response to Turkish Nationalism and Reform 1914–1939* (Minneapolis: University of Minnesota Press, 1971).

Ülker, Necmi, 'Mustafa Kemal Paşa'nın Evliliği', in Latif Daşdemir, *Az Bilinen Yönleriyle Atatürk* (İzmir: Ege University, 2004), p. 28.

US Congress, *Hearings. The United States Congress House. Committee on Appropriations: Naval Appropriation Bill, 1922, Sixty-Six Congress, Third Session* (Washington, DC: Government Printing Office, 1921).

US Congress, *Near East Relief: Report of the Near East Relief for the Year Ending December 31, 1923* (Washington, DC: Government Printing Office, 1924).

US Department of State, *Papers Relating to the Foreign Relations of the United States, 1923* (Washington, DC: US Government Printing Office, 1923).

US Department of State, *Papers Relating to the Foreign Relations of the United States, The Paris Peace Conference, 1919*, <http://digicoll.library.wisc.edu/cgi-bin/FRUS/FRUS-idx?type=turn&id=FRUS.FRUS1919Parisv09&entity=FRUS.FRUS1919Parisv09.p0054&q1=inter-alliedcommissionofinquiryonthegreed> (last accessed 28 September 2020).

US Navy, *United States Naval Institute Proceedings*, 45.7 (July 1919): 1816.

US Senate, 'Message from the President of the United States, communicating, in compliance with a resolution of the Senate, copies of correspondence in relation to the commerce and navigation carried on in the Turkish dominions and Pachalick of Egypt. February 11, 1839', in *25th Congress, 3rd Session. Public*

Documents Printed by Order of the Senate of the United States, vol. 3 (Washington, DC: Blair and Rivers, 1939).

Vekaleti, Hariciye, *Türkiye ile Amerika hükumet-i müttehidesi beynindeki münasebâtın tanzimi zımmında Hariciye Vekili Doktor Tevfik Rüştü Bey Efendi hazretleriyle Amerika mümessil-i siyasisi Amiral Mark L. Bristol arasında teati olunan notalar* (Ankara: Hariciye Vekaleti, 1927).

Ward, Mark H., *The Deportations in Asia Minor, 1921–1922* (London: Anglo-Hellenic League, 1922).

Yaylalıer, Dinç, 'American Perceptions of Turkey, 1919–1927', PhD dissertation, University of Utah, 1996.

Yetkiner, Cemal, 'After Merchants before Ambassadors: Protestant Missionaries and Early American Experience in the Ottoman Empire, 1820–1860', in Nur Bilge Criss, Selçuk Esenbel, Tony Greenwood and Louis Mazzari (eds), *American Turkish Encounters: Politics and Culture, 1830–1989* (Newcastle upon Tyne: Cambridge Scholars, 2011), pp. 8–34.

Yılmaz, Şuhnaz, *Turkish-American Relations, 1800–1952: Between the Stars, Stripes and the Crescent* (New York: Routledge, 2015).

INDEX

Abdülmecid (last Caliph), 171–2, 185
  Neville Henderson's interview with,
    166
abolition of
  the Sultanate, 2, 12, 14, 88, 151,
    164, 168, 184
  the Caliphate, 14, 165–76, 184
  *tekke*s, 96
  fez, 97
Adams, John (US President), 4
Adıvar, Halide Edip, 69, 100
Allen, Annie T., 30, 33, 42, 53, 69
American Board of Commissioners for
    Foreign Missions (ABCFM) 27,
    41, 53, 55, 165, 185
American Committee for Armenian
    and Syrian Relief (ACASR) 28
American Hospital *see* Bristol Hospital
Armenian mandate, 11, 60, 98, 108, 197
Asiatic Fleet, 47–8

Barton, James L., 28, 30, 39, 42
Blacque Bey, 71, 101

Bristol, Helen Beverly Moore Thomas,
    8, 17, 48, 50–1
Bristol Hospital, 9–10, 34–5, 48, 54, 57
Browne, Edgar
  visit of Ankara, 67–8
  private papers, 100
Buddhism, 27, 182
business offers
  of nationalist to the US, 73

Cardashian, Vahan
  anti-Turkish statements, 106
  lobbying at Lausanne, 82, 102
  State Department's view of, 83
Churchill, Winston, 1
Clemenceau, Georges, 123, 125, 148
Committee of Union and Progress
    (CUP), 28, 121, 144, 172, 198
competition
  among Allied High Commissioners,
    22–5
Congregationalist Church of New
    England, 27

Constantinople Chapter of the
    American Red Cross, 24
Constantinople Women's College, 30
Coolidge, Calvin, 45, 166–7, 186
Council of Four, 122, 148
Crane, Charles, 67–8
    Bristol's letter to, 137
creation of Armenia, 109–16,
    120
Curzon, Lord Earl, 55, 130–1
    at Lausanne, 63

Darlington, Bishop J. H., 33
    Armenian Cilicia, 158
Dodge, Cleveland H.
    creation of ACASR, 28
Dulles, Allen W., 44, 83, 102
    director of CIA, 53, 55
    support of Bristol, 33
Dunn, Robert S., 9, 26–7, 52, 126,
    137, 149–50

Ekrem, Selma, 53
    experiences in the US, 32
enlightened dictatorship, 87
evkaf, 174

Foreign Relations of the United States
    (FRUS), 8, 14
Fowle, Luther R., 54
    on the living conditions of
    Constantinople, 152–3

Gates, Caleb Frank, 30
Geddes, Auckland
    removal of Bristol, 44, 55
    request for a US military action, 78

genocide, 14, 144
    Bristol's view of Armenian, 110,
    145, 192
George, Lloyd, 131, 133–4, 148
    discussion of Smyrna invasion, 123
Gerard, James W.
    lobbying at Lausanne, 82
Greek occupation of Smyrna, 10, 13,
    64, 74, 106, 122–4, 126
    Bristol's views of, 125, 133–6,
    139–40, 145
    President Wilson's support of, 123
Greeks bands
    in Samsun, 156–7
Grew, Joseph, 9, 47, 63, 84, 90, 93
    appointment to Turkey as
    ambassador, 86
    at Lausanne, 82
    on Armenian home, 83

Harbord Commission, 68
    report of, 137
Hay, John
    on the Open-Door Policy, 36
Heck, Lewis J., 19, 23–4, 58, 108,
    148, 152
    report on Turk–Greek relations in
    Smyrna, 124–5
    situation in Constantinople, 153
Holmes, Mary Caroline
    atrocities committed by all sides,
    193–6
Hoover, Herbert, 19
    praise of Bristol, 46
Horton, George, 149
    accusations of Bristol, 39
    fire of Smyrna, 134, 138

Hovannisian, Richard, 27, 52
Hughes, Charles E., 42, 44, 75,
   80, 200
   praise of Bristol, 45–6
   response to British pressure, 78
hyperinflation in Constantinople,
   153–5

Indian Muslims, 169
   donation of, 175–6
Inter-Allied Commission of Inquiry, 9,
   13, 122, 124–5, 136
   report, 76, 116, 137, 139, 148

Jackson, Andrew, (US President), 4
Jaquith, Harold C.
   fundraising in the US, 40–1
Jews, 27, 35, 76, 162

Karabekir, Kazım, 173
Kemalistan, 194
Khatissian, Alexandre
   Armenians in the Caucasus, 111–13
King, Henry Churchill, 9
King, William H., 86, 90, 115
   conversation with Bristol, 32, 92
King-Crane Commission, 9, 67–8, 137
Knapp, Harry Shepard, 71, 147
   views on Armenian character, 118
Kurdistan, 192
   oil fields of, 61–2
Kurds, 5, 193
   atrocities committed by, 41
   refugees, 194, 196

Latife (Mustafa Kemal's wife)
   divorce of, 177, 187

Lausanne, 12, 79, 113, 120, 141, 143
   Conference, 3, 11, 25, 45, 63, 98,
      142, 150
   Treaty of, 8, 47, 82, 88, 91, 115, 171
Law on Maintenance of Order, 96
Lovejoy, Esther
   view of Greek refugees, 135

Mazarakis, Alexander, 132, 137
   objection to Inter Allied
      Commission's report, 127
Ministry of Religious Affairs, 174
Monseigneur Meletius IV
   on the future of Ottoman Greeks,
      141–2, 150
Morgenthau, Henry, 9, 28–9, 36
   Morgenthau III (grandson of), 35

National Advisory Committee on
   Aeronautics, 17
Near East Relief, 10, 21, 27–8, 30,
   39–41, 69, 100, 109, 144, 160–2,
   193–4, 200
   establishment of, 50
NER see Near East Relief
New York Times, 9, 24, 28
North Atlantic Fleet, 17
Nutuk, 183–4

Offley David, 4
Open Door, 6, 34, 36–7, 53, 70, 80,
   97, 99, 190, 169
orientalism, 119

Pan-Islamic Congress, 171–2, 176
Paris Peace Conference, 11, 13, 59–60,
   125

Patrick, Mary Mills, 30
Peet, William W. 30, 42
    Christian exodus, 41
Pontus, 139, 192
population exchange, 142–3, 161
Porter, David, 4, 15
Progressive Republican Party, 95, 173
    closure, 87

Rauf Bey (Orbay), 26, 67, 166,
        172–3, 175
    protest of Greek atrocities, 73–4
Ravndal, Gabriel Bie, 24, 58
    background, 99
    political situation in Anatolia, 64
Red Crescent, 160
Red Cross, 21, 24
Refet Paşa (Bele), 67, 76, 165, 170
    comments on Mustafa Kemal, 173
    secret meeting against Ankara,
        171–2
refugees, 77, 114, 116, 140–3
    Armenian, 200
    camps, 161
    Greek, 76, 135, 138
    Turkish, 150, 159–60
Rhind, Charles, 4
Robert College, 18, 30, 73
Russian arms deal, 157

Sefa Bey
    Sultan's private property for the US
        investment, 72
Senior United States Naval Officer
    Present, Turkey, 12, 19–20,
        24, 58
Shaikh Said, 96

Shaw, Gardiner Howland, 25
    on the Ankara regime, 89–92, 94
Sheik Senoussi, 168–71, 176
Sheikh al Islam Mustafa Sabri Efendi,
    125
Sherrill, Charles, H.
    interview with Mustafa Kemal on
        religion, 178–81
Sims, Admiral William S., 19, 37,
        53, 143
Skinner, Robert, 9
smallpox, 161
Spanish Embassy, 18
Streit, Clarence K.
    views of nationalists, 70
Sultan Abdul Hamid, 53, 171
Sultan Vahdettin, 65, 164–7
    British contact of, 61–2
    escape of, 65, 79
    letter to US president, 186
Swedish Legation, 18–9

terrible Turk, 2, 32, 192–3
Treaty of Sevres, 83, 136, 152, 186
Turkish Medical Fraternity, 35
Turkish–American Treaty of
    Commerce and Amity, 3, 98
typhus, 161

United States Shipping Board in the
    Near East, 19, 24

Venizelos, Eleftherios, 38–9, 132, 137,
    143, 148
    Greek occupation of Smyrna, 123
Vickrey, Charles, 42
    killing of Muslims, 40

Ward, Mark H., 193, 195–6, 200–1
Webb, Richard
    Bristol's protest of Britain, 61
Williams, Paul
    conversations with Halide Edip, 69

Wilson, Woodrow, 19, 30, 36, 68, 122, 148

YMCA, 88, 197
Yowell, Forrest D., 193–6, 200–1
YWCA, 88, 197

Printed and bound by CPI Group (UK) Ltd, Croydon, CR0 4YY

13/01/2025

01819159-0007